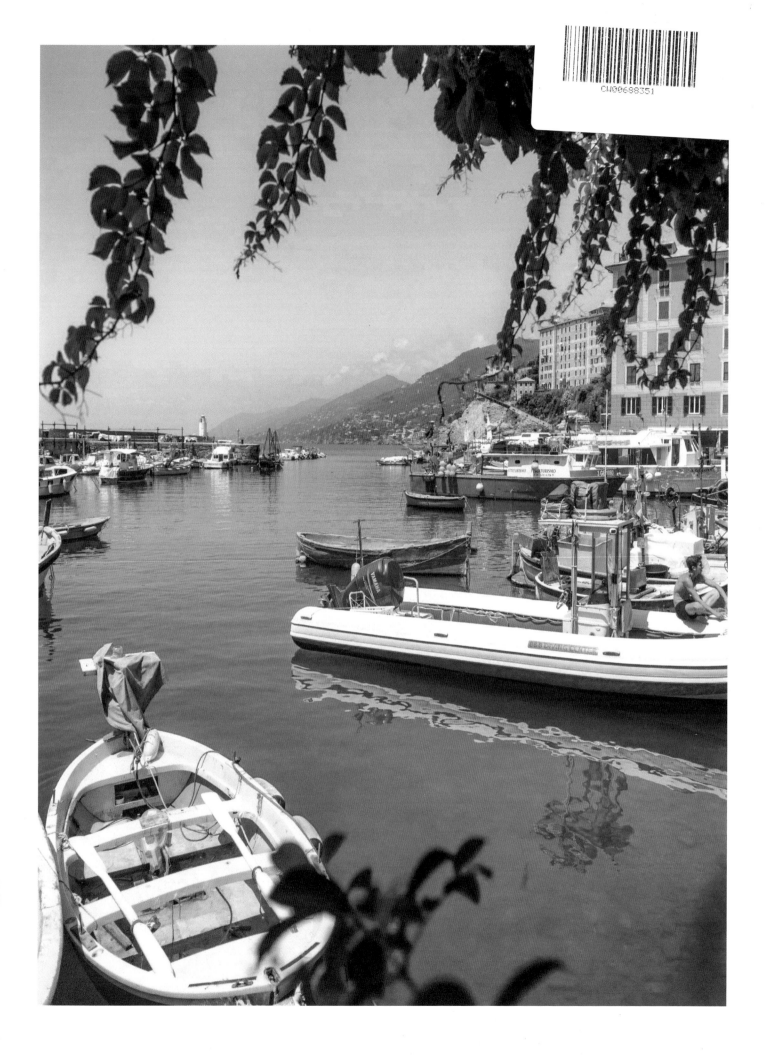

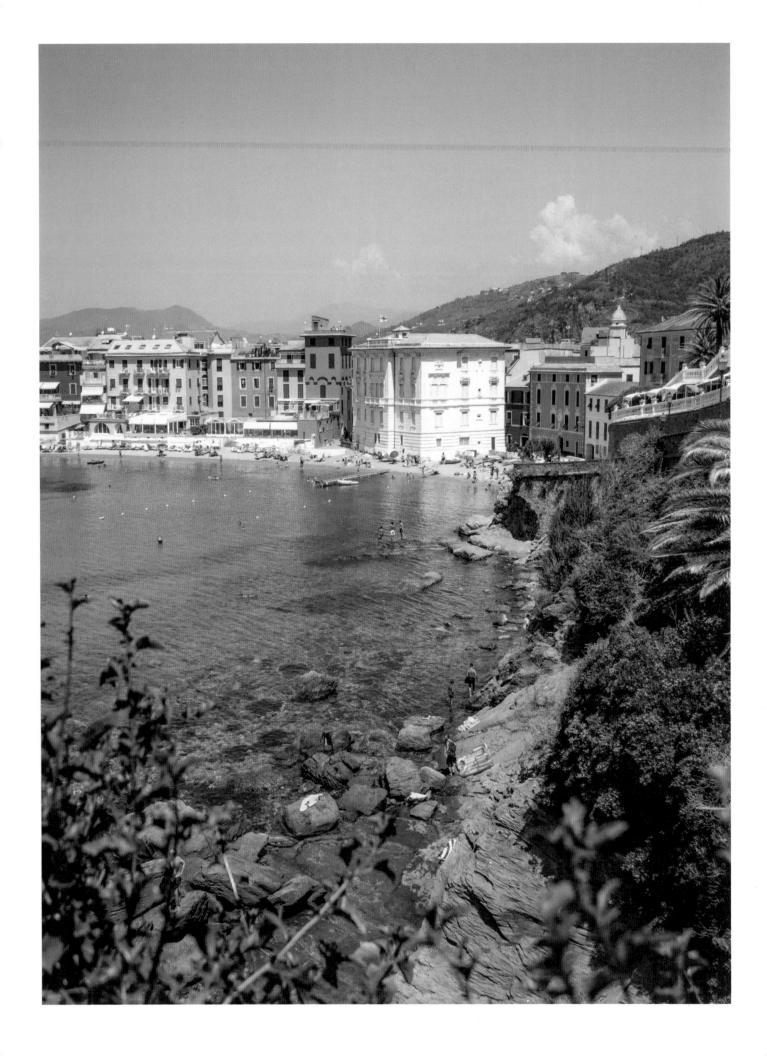

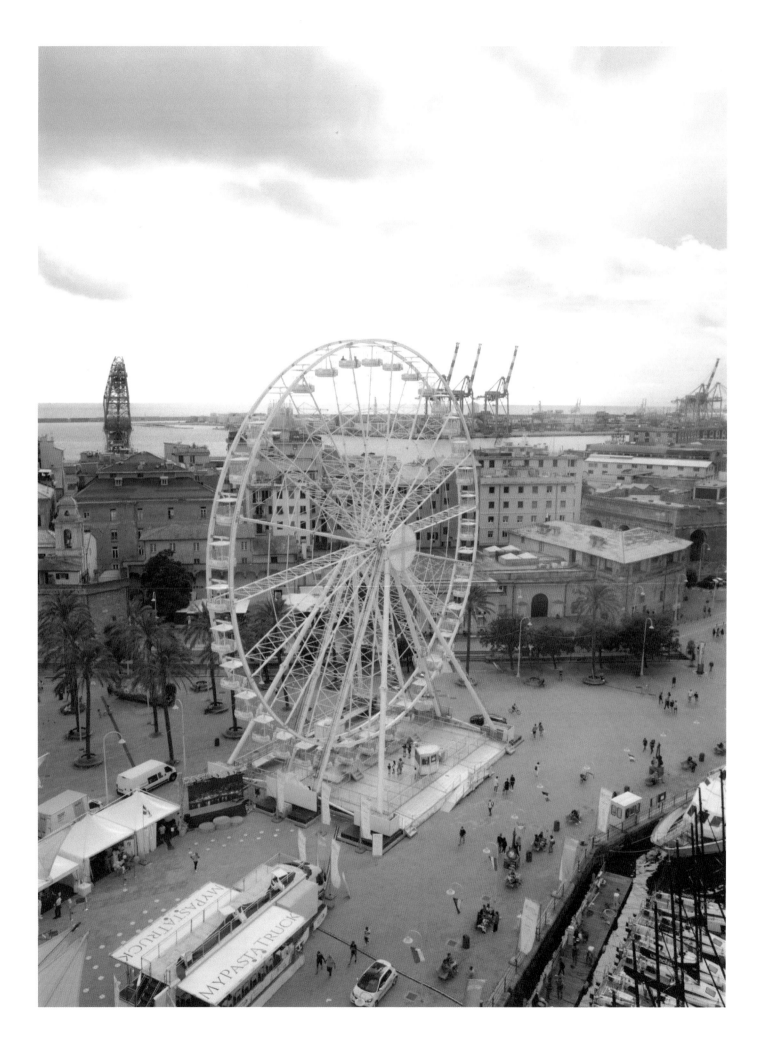

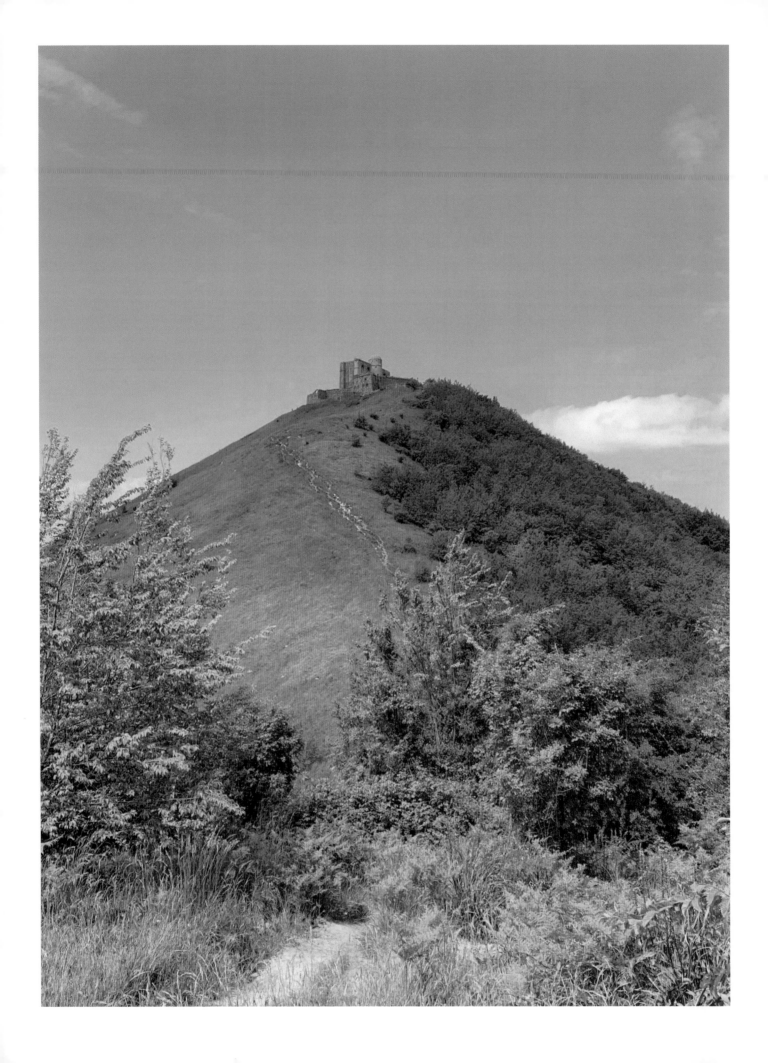

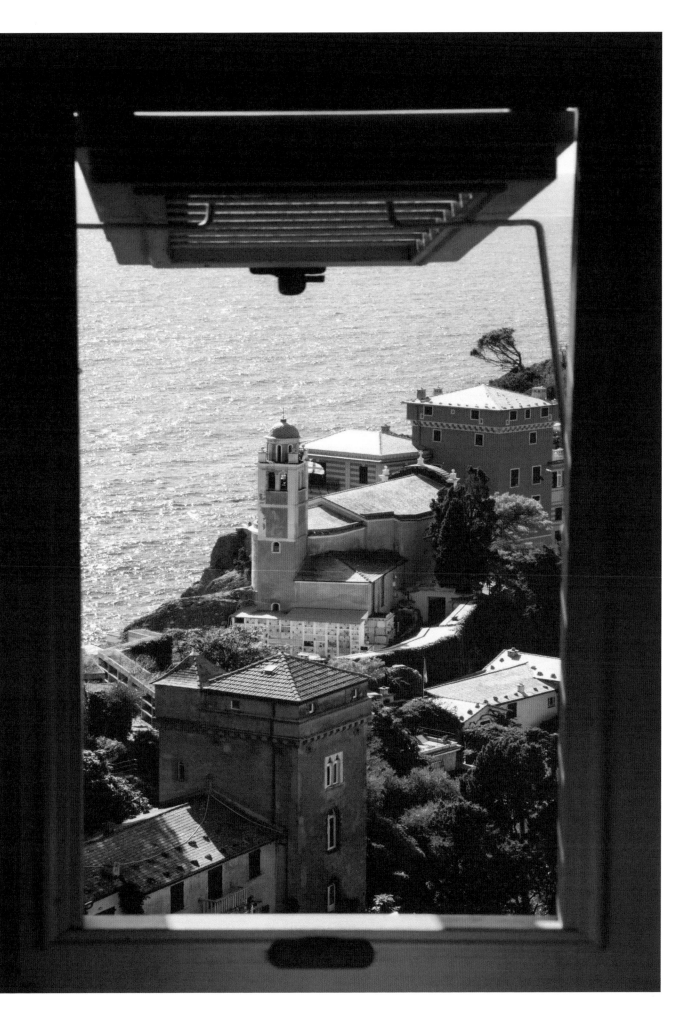

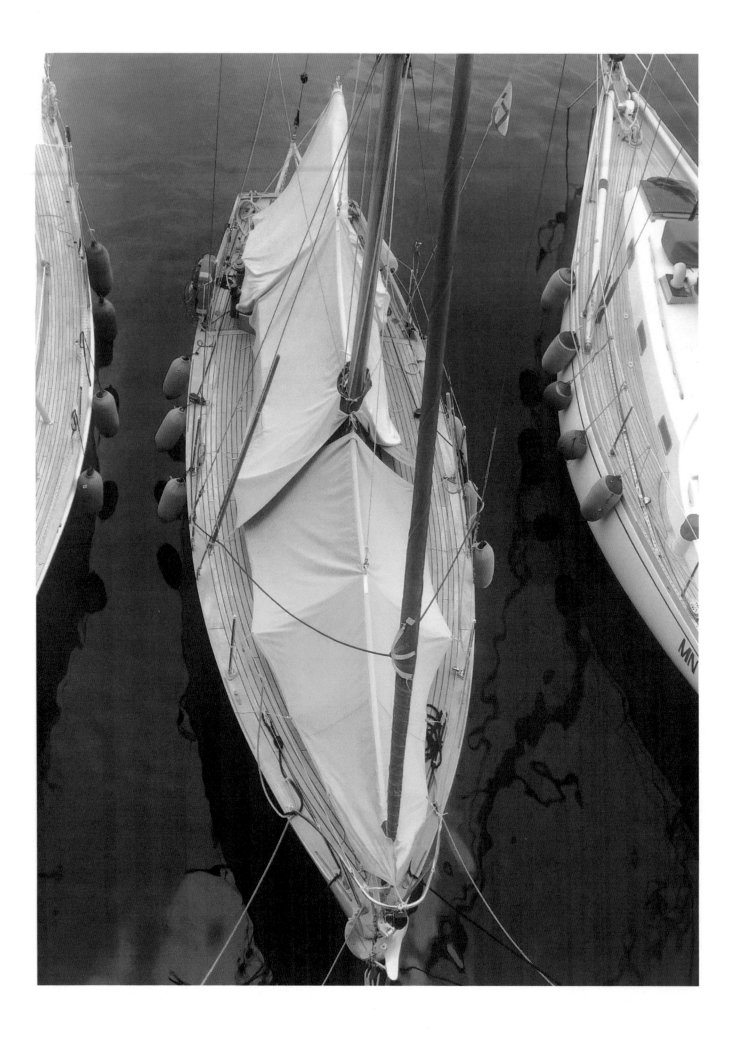

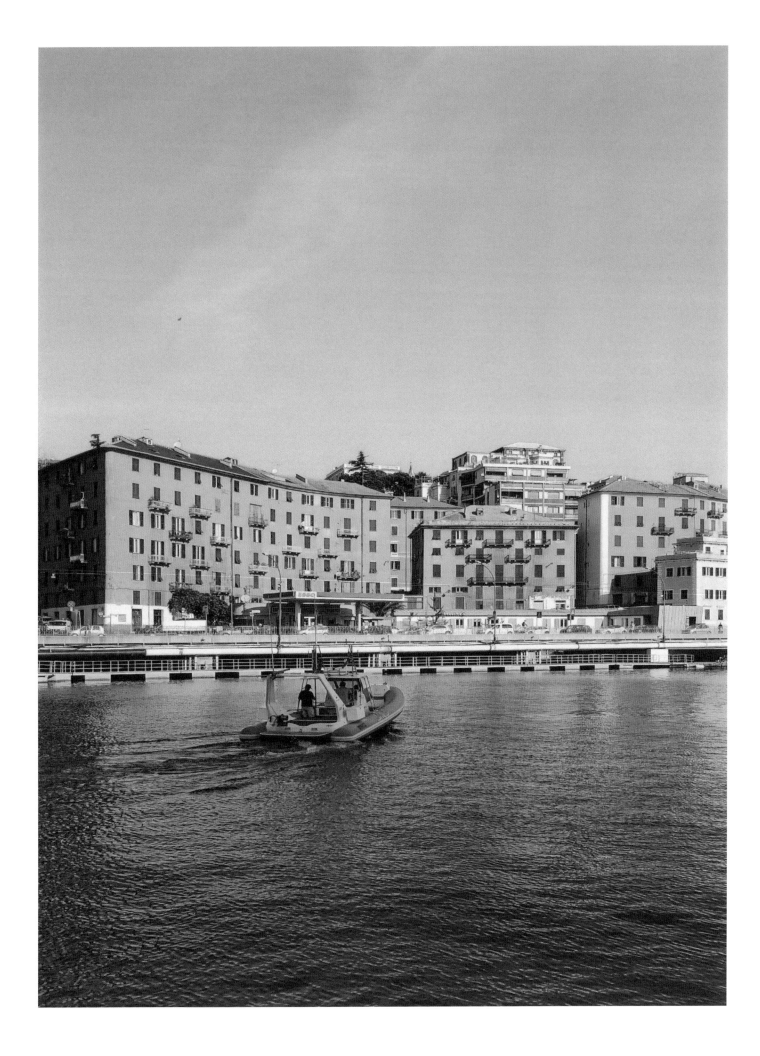

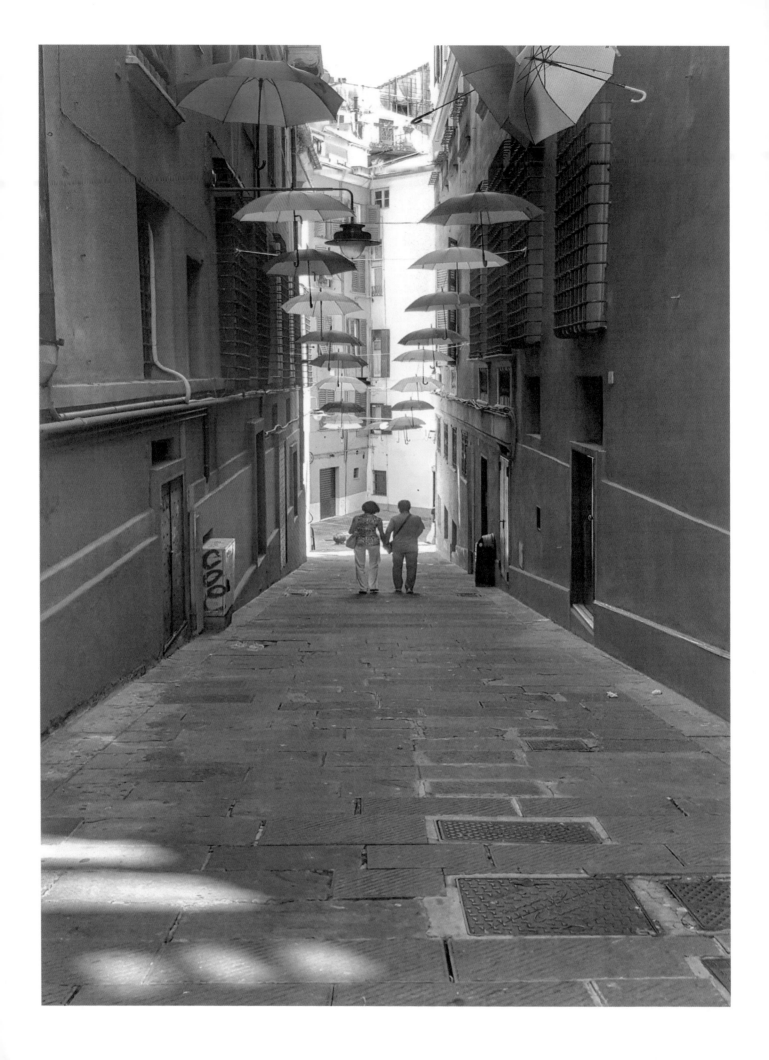

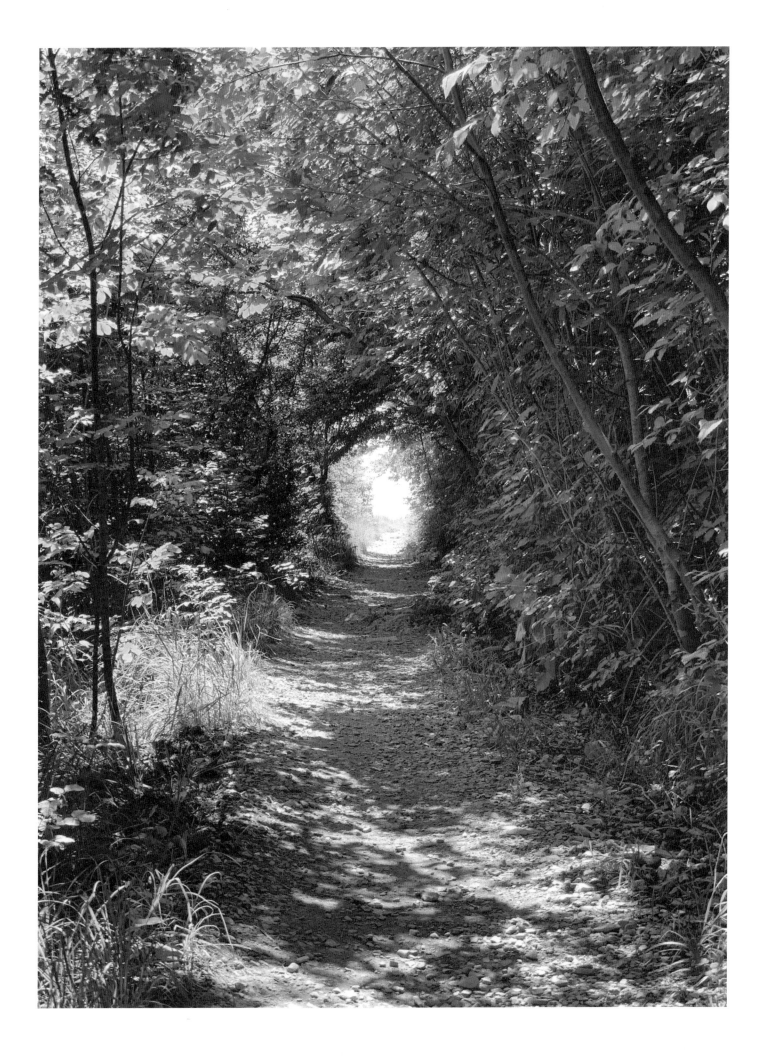

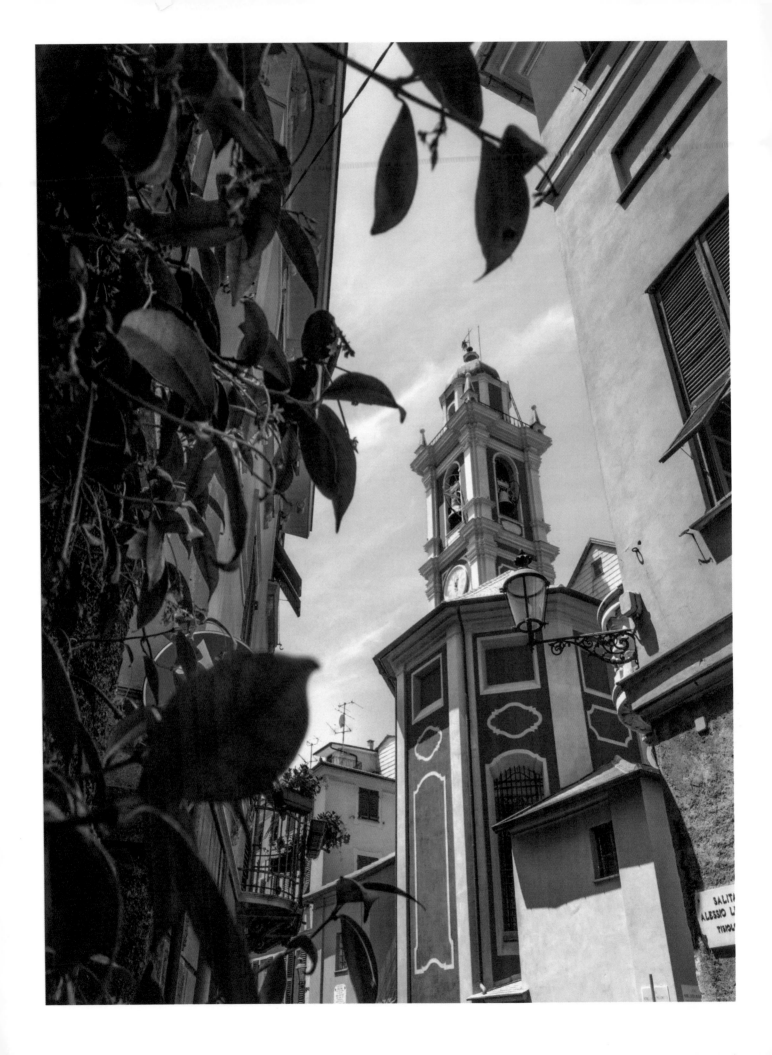

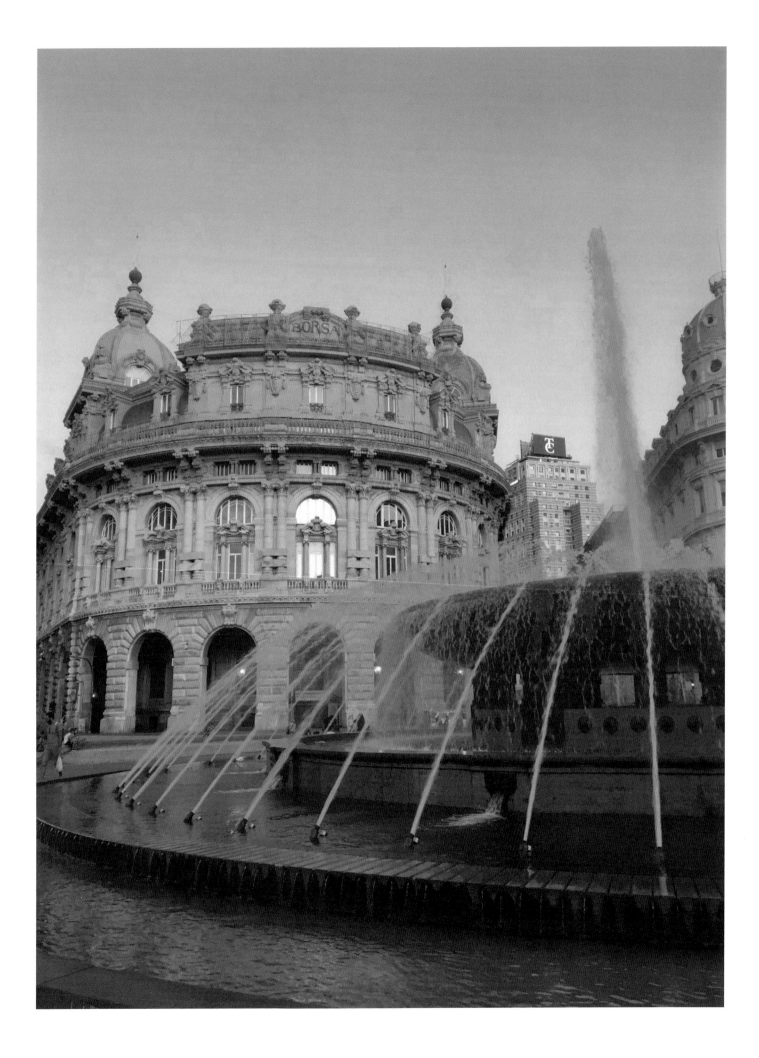

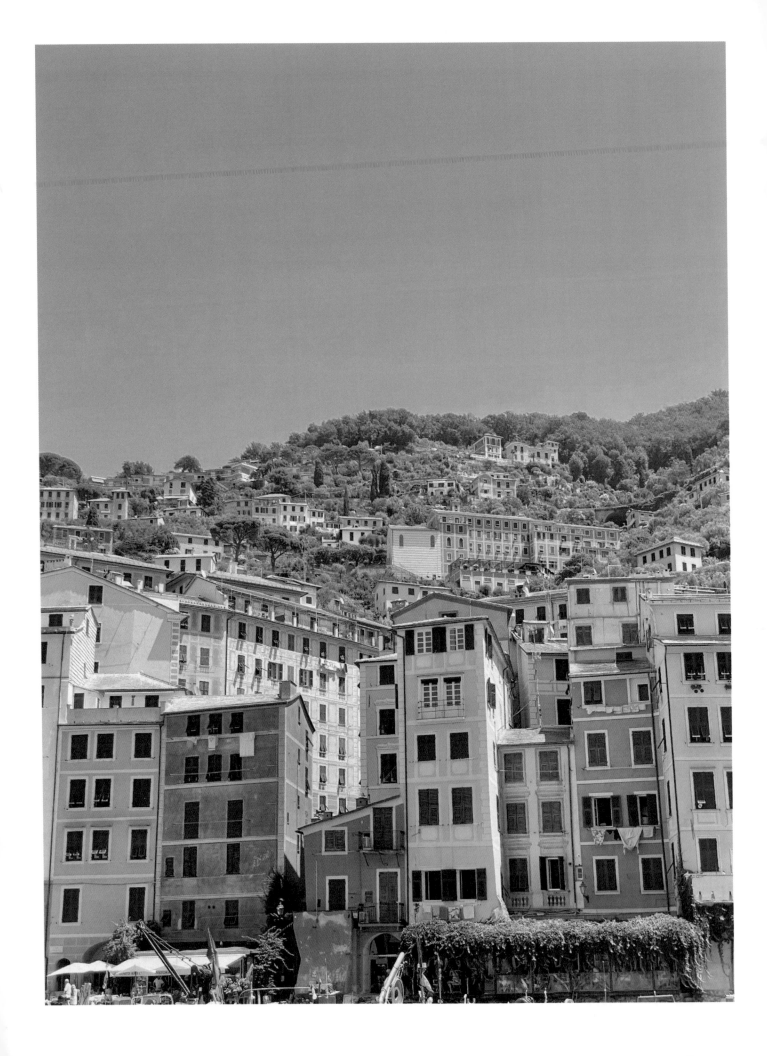

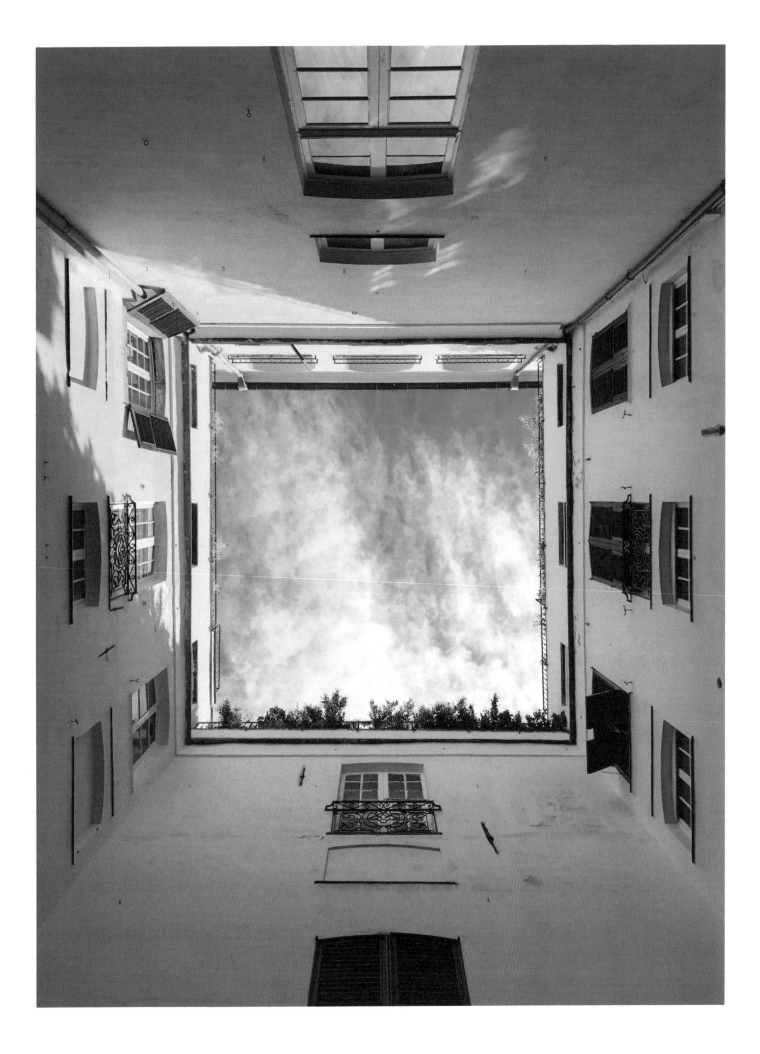

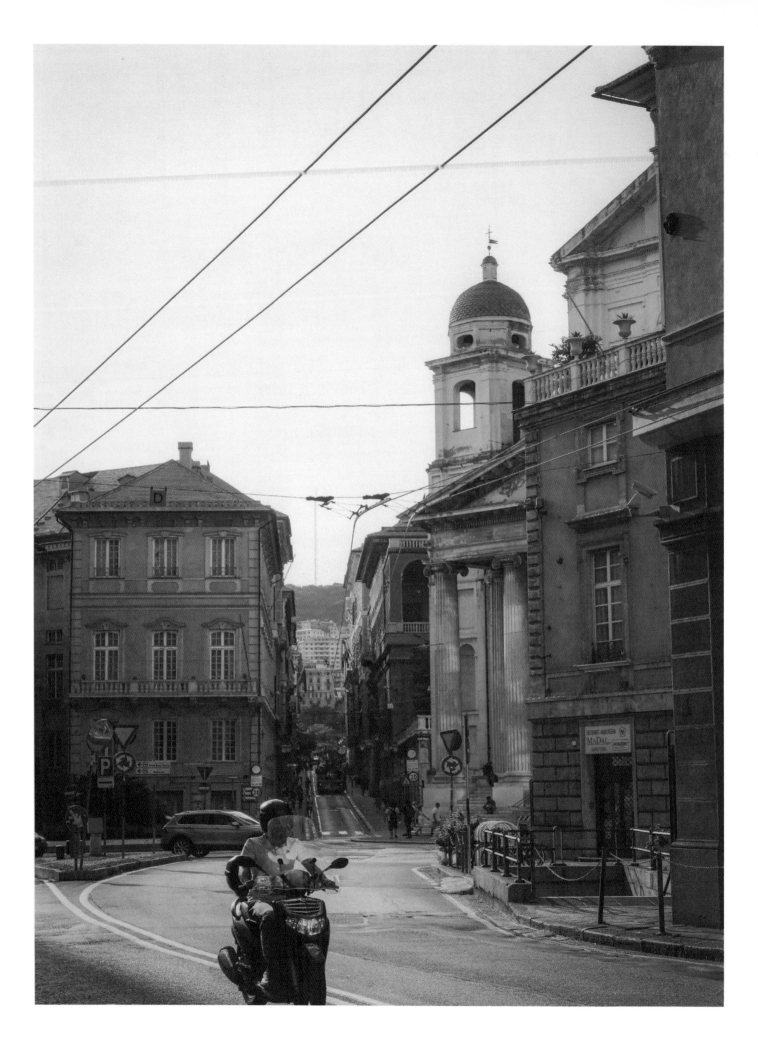

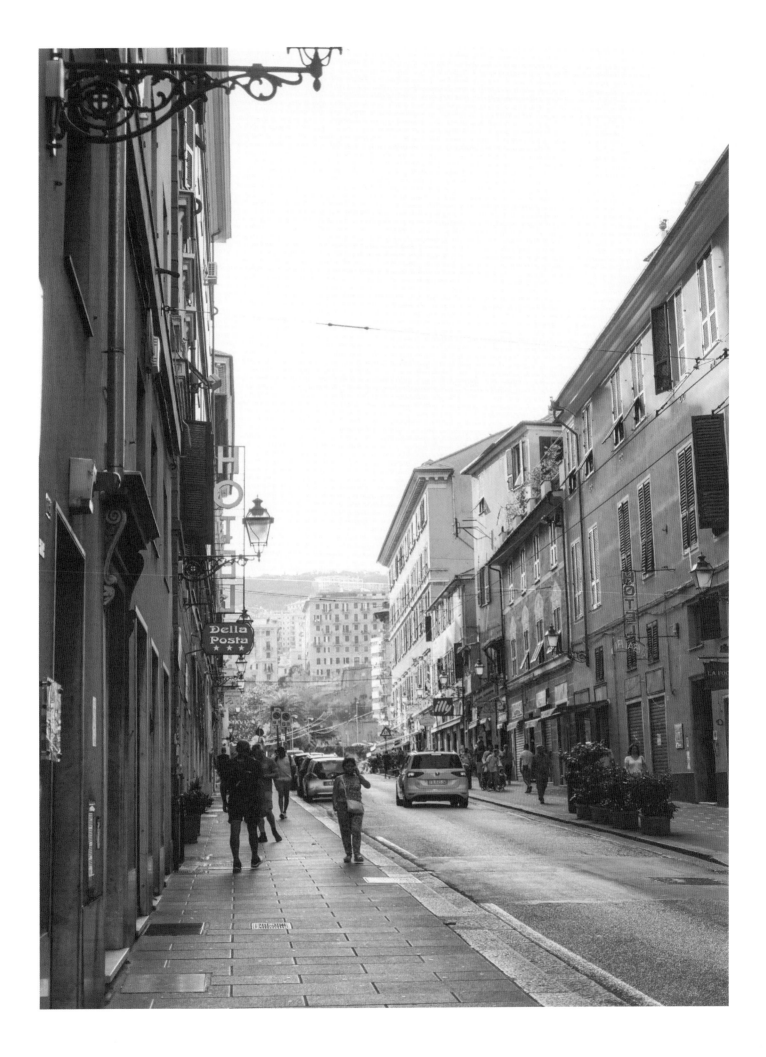

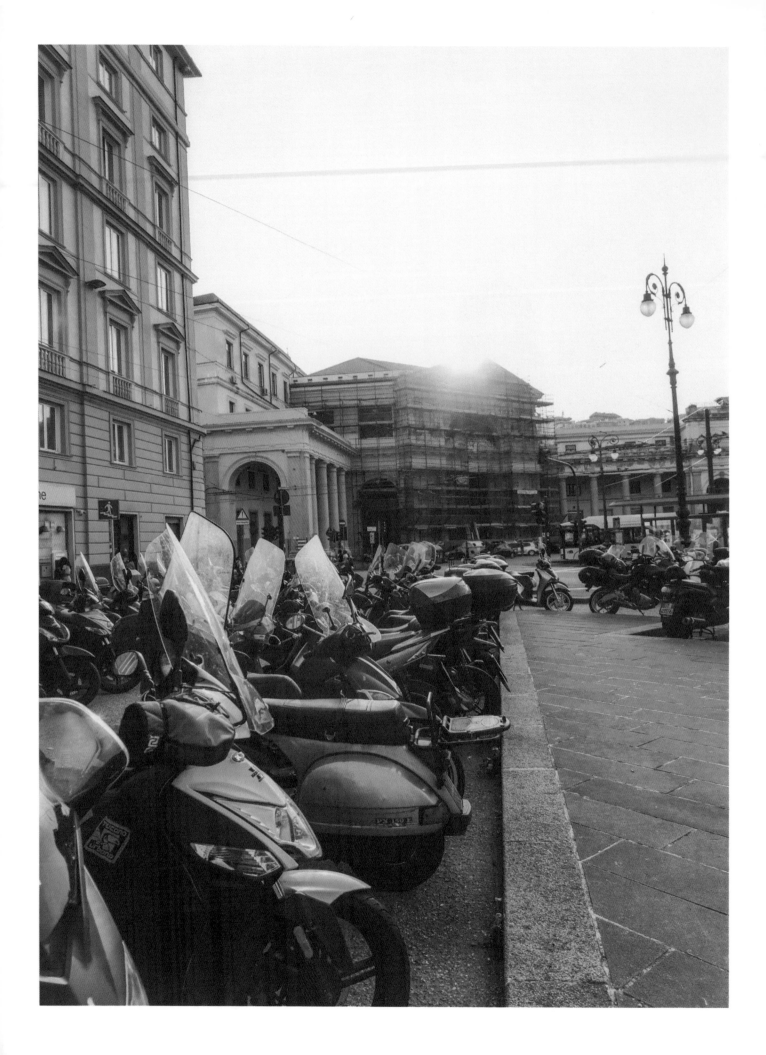

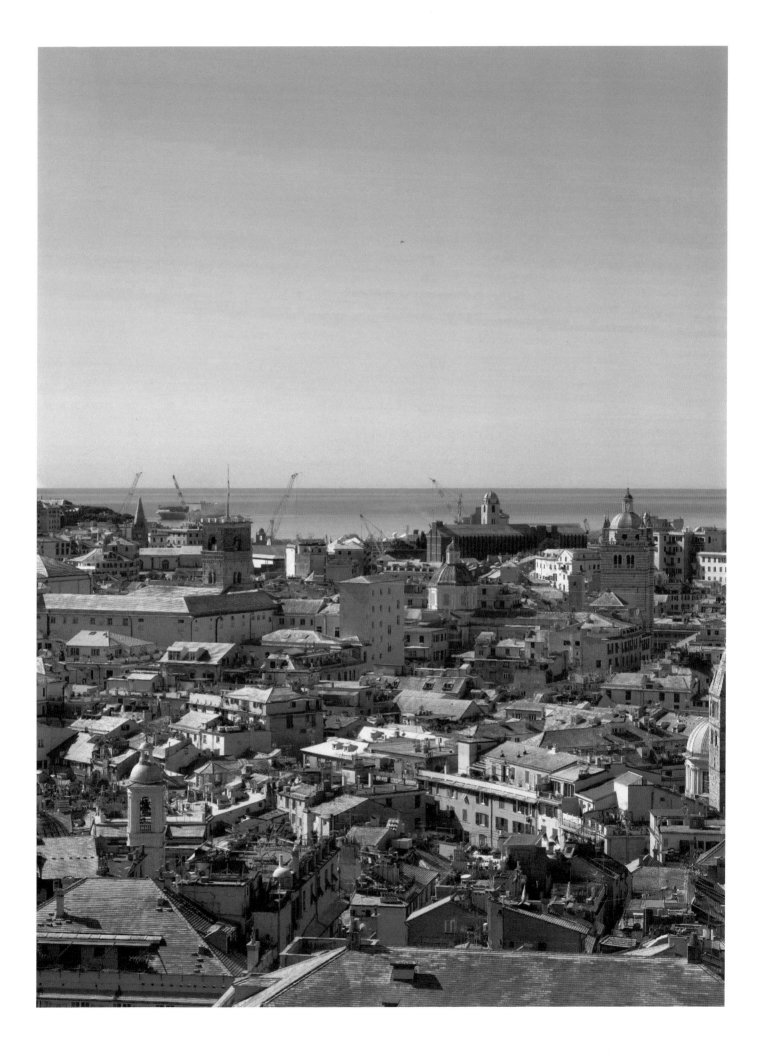

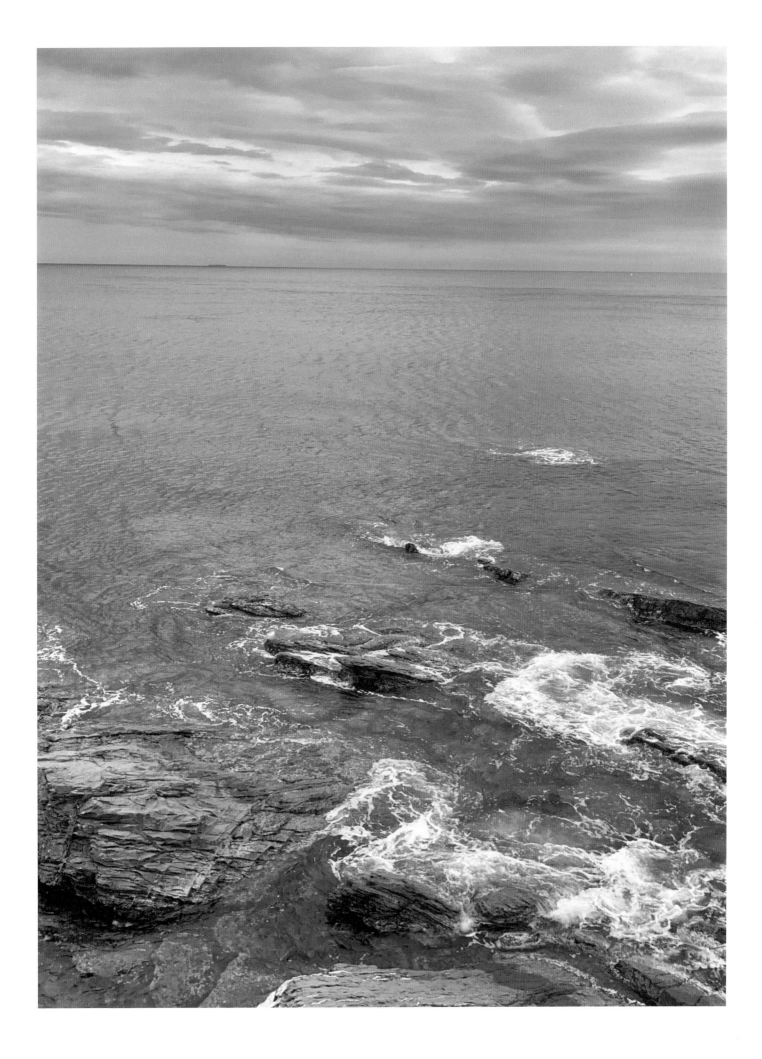

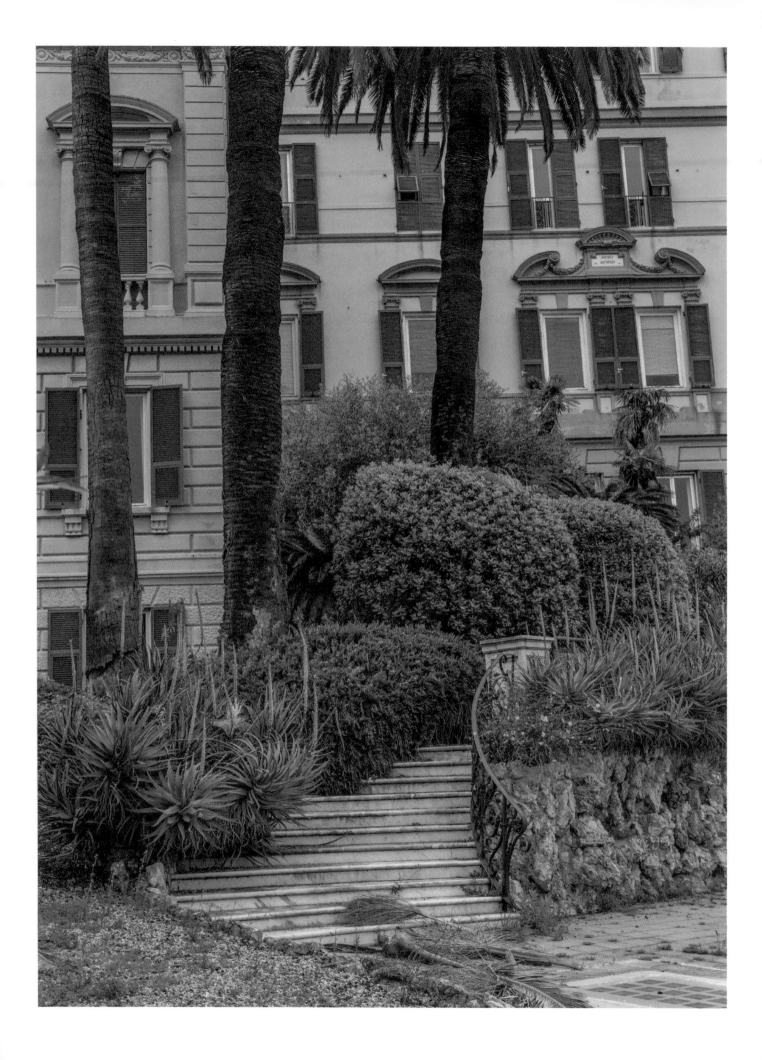

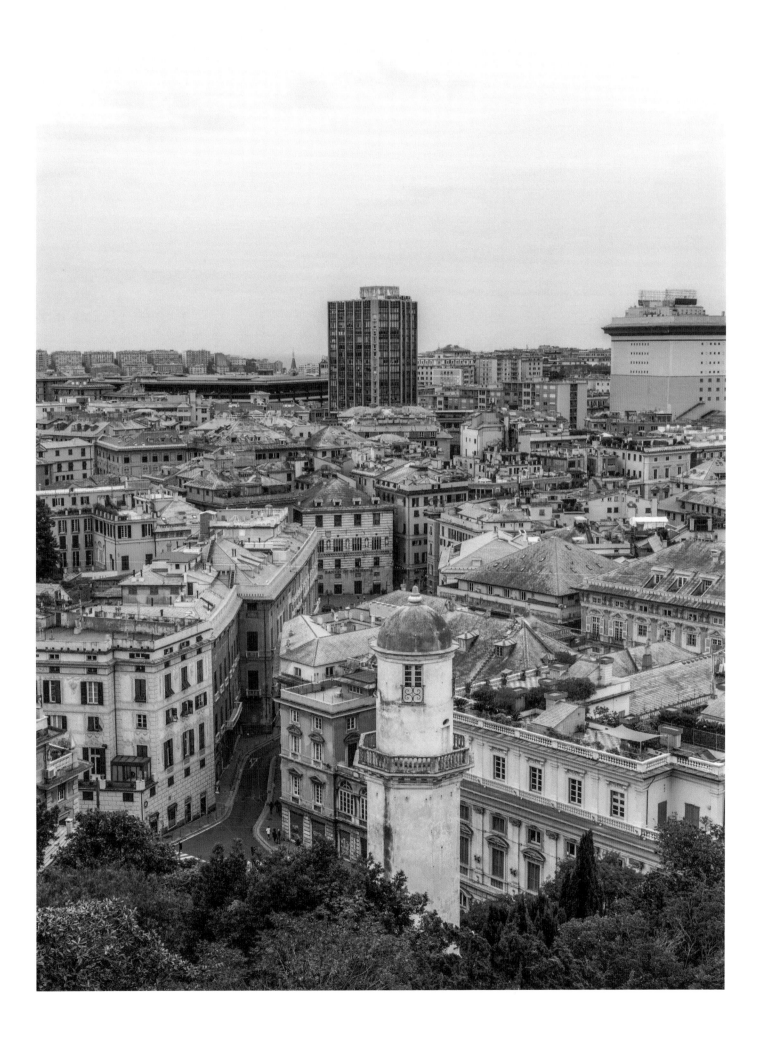

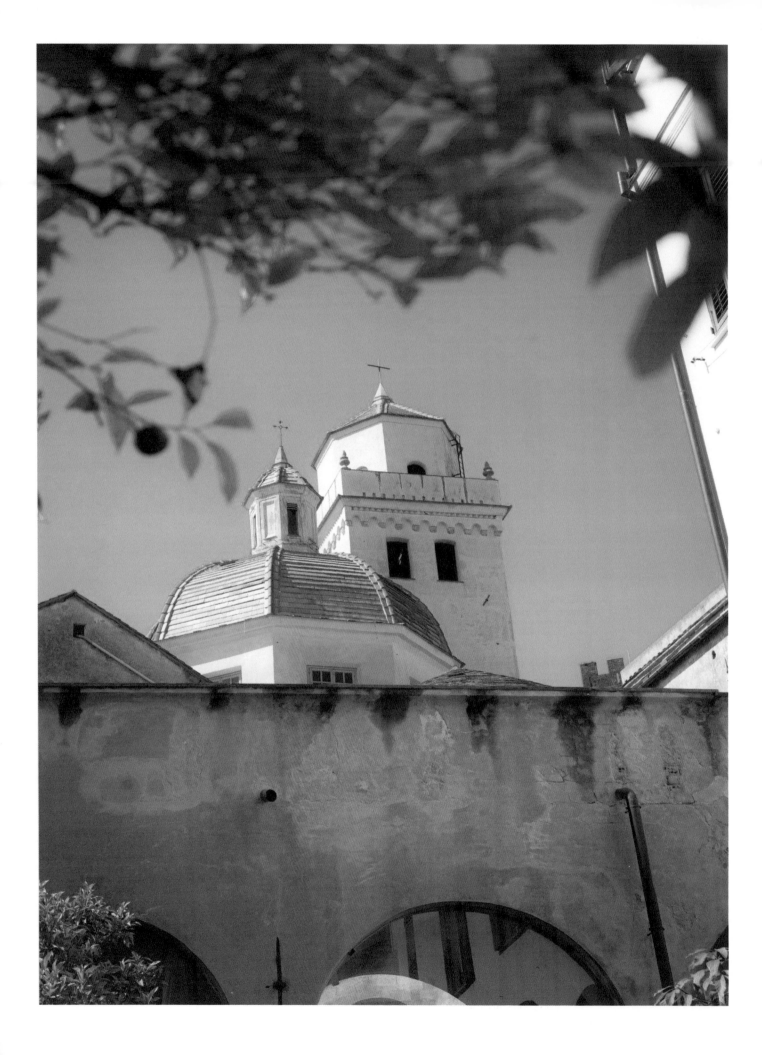

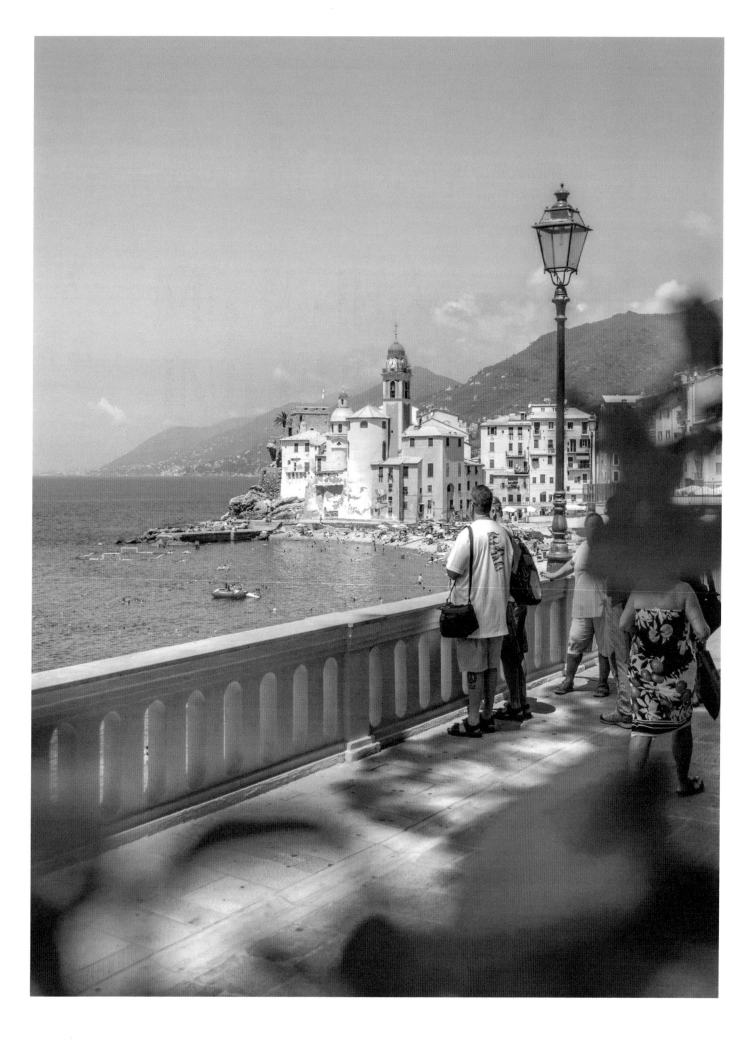

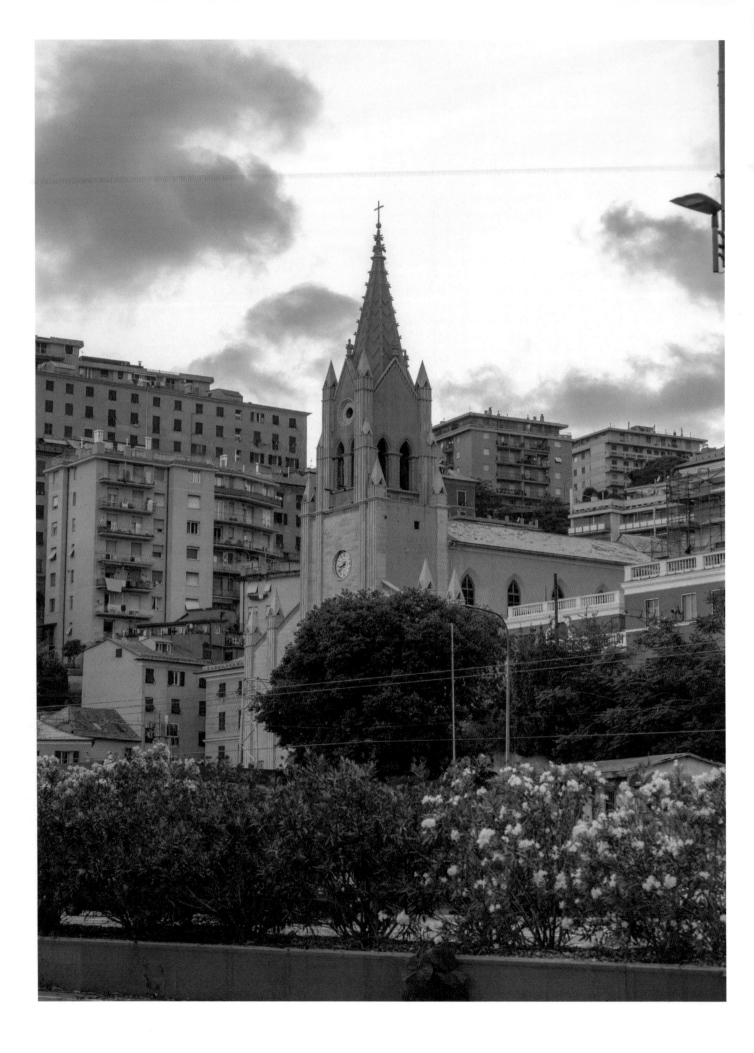

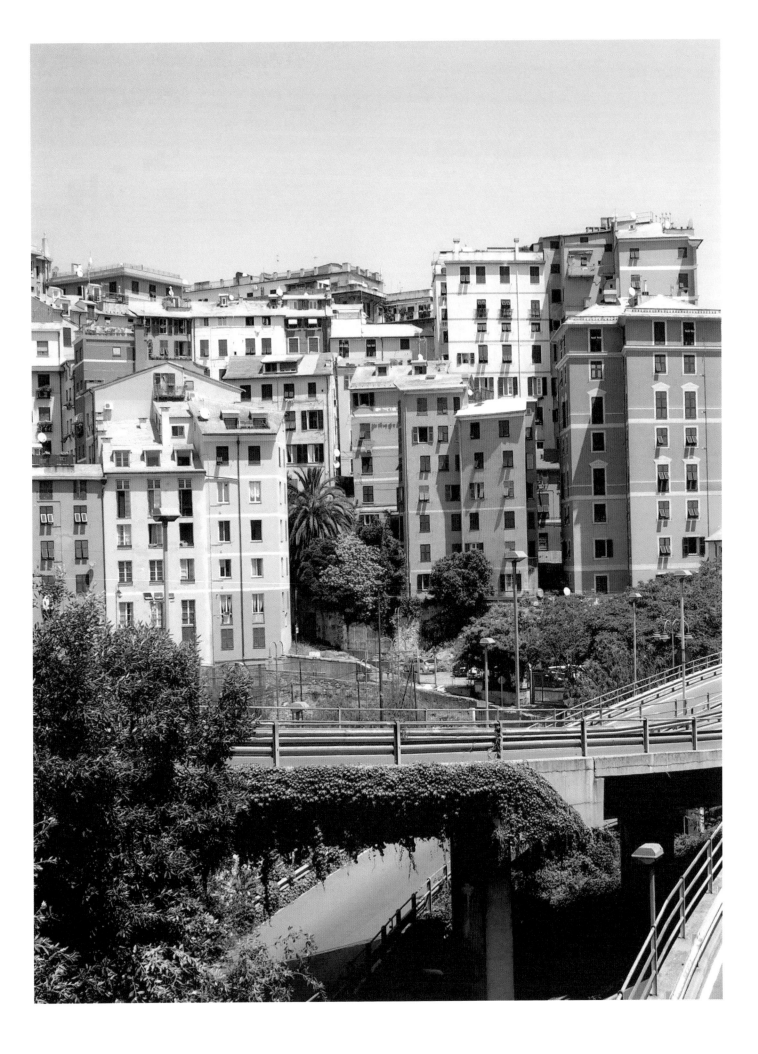

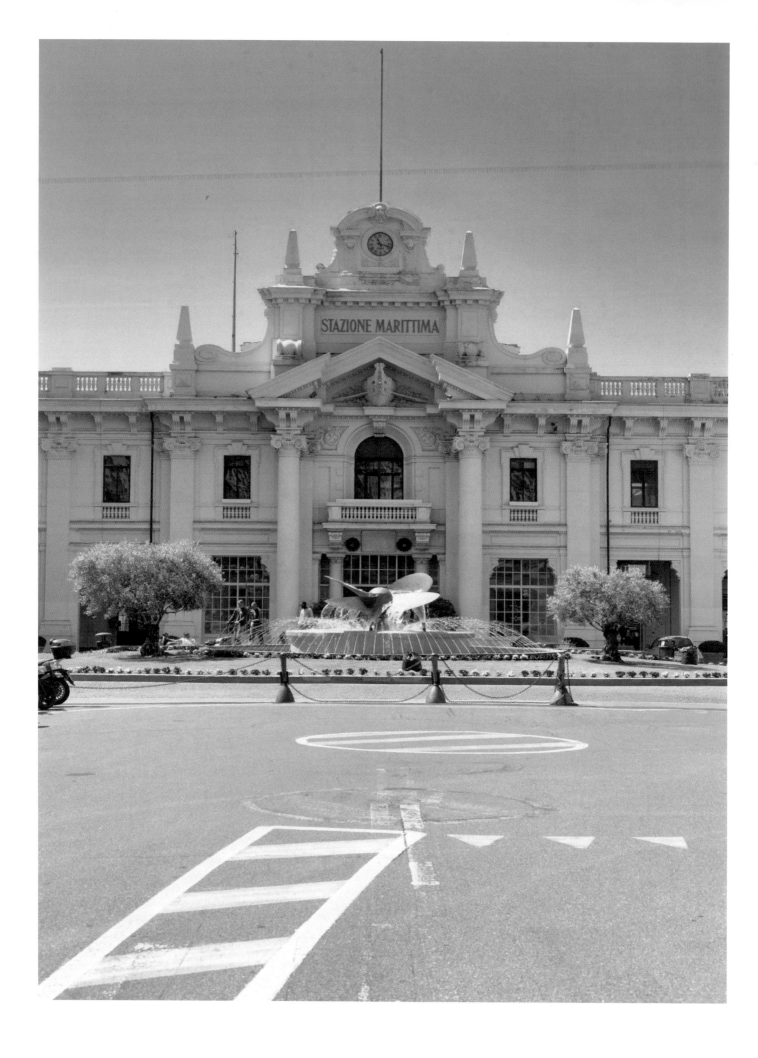

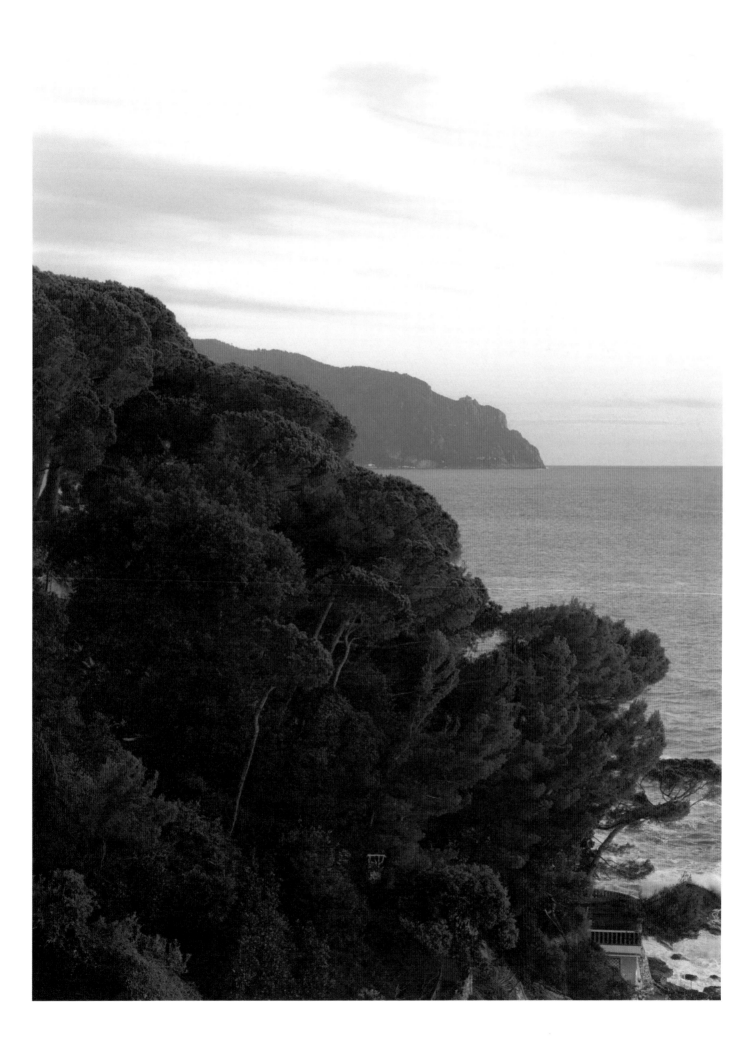

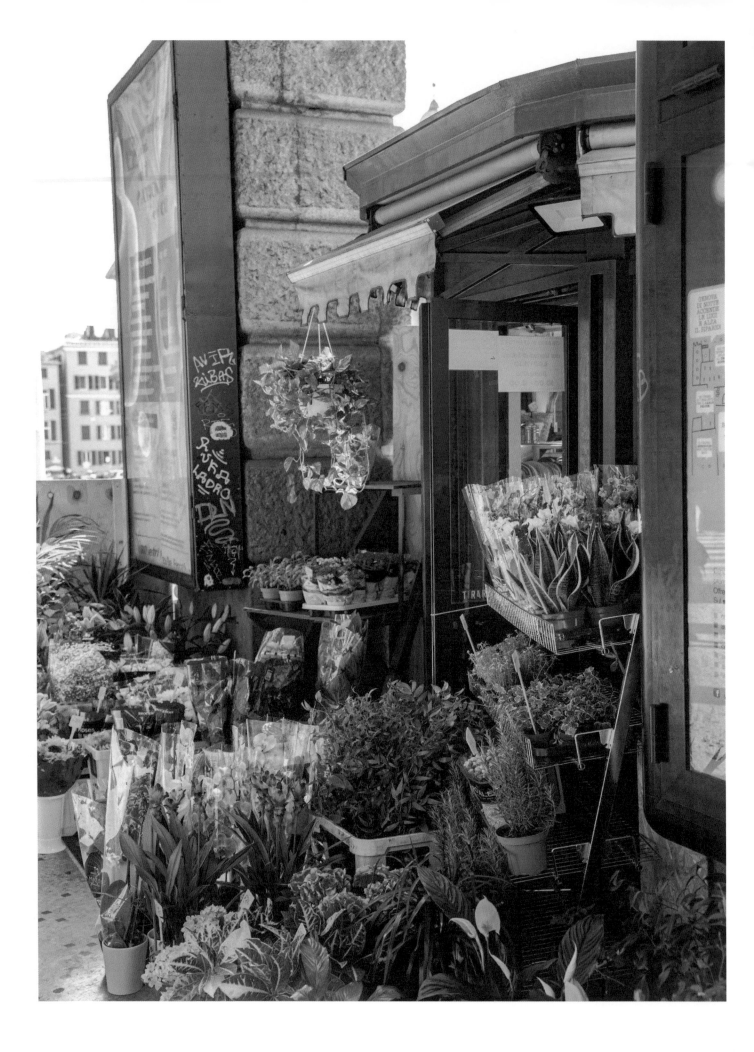

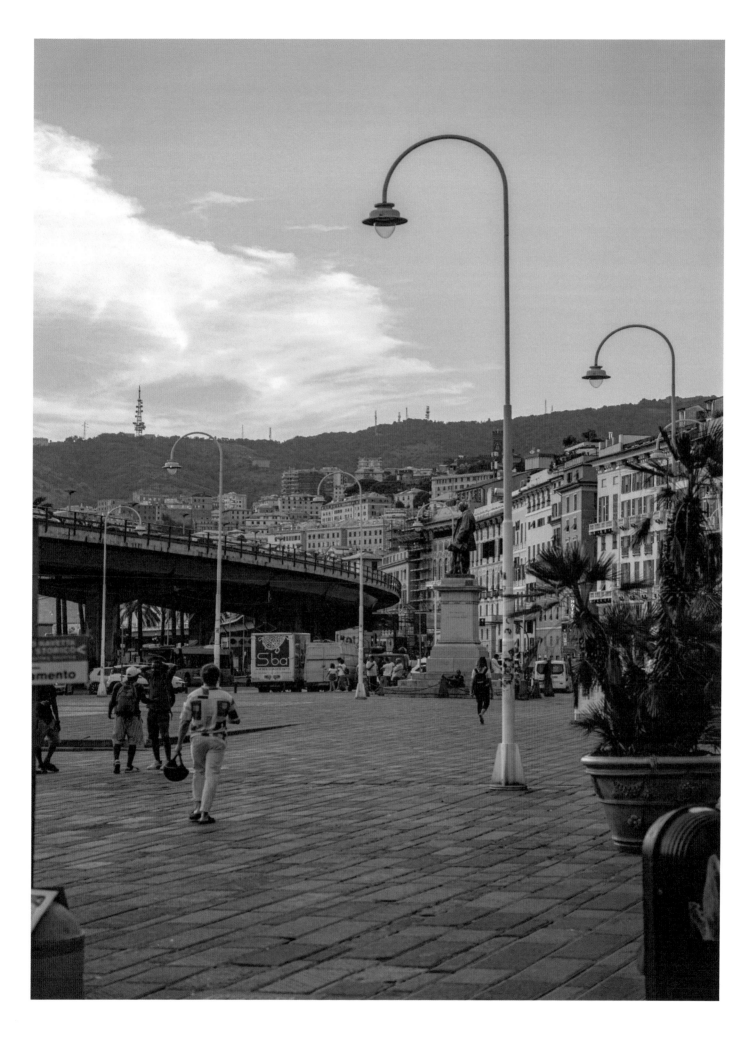

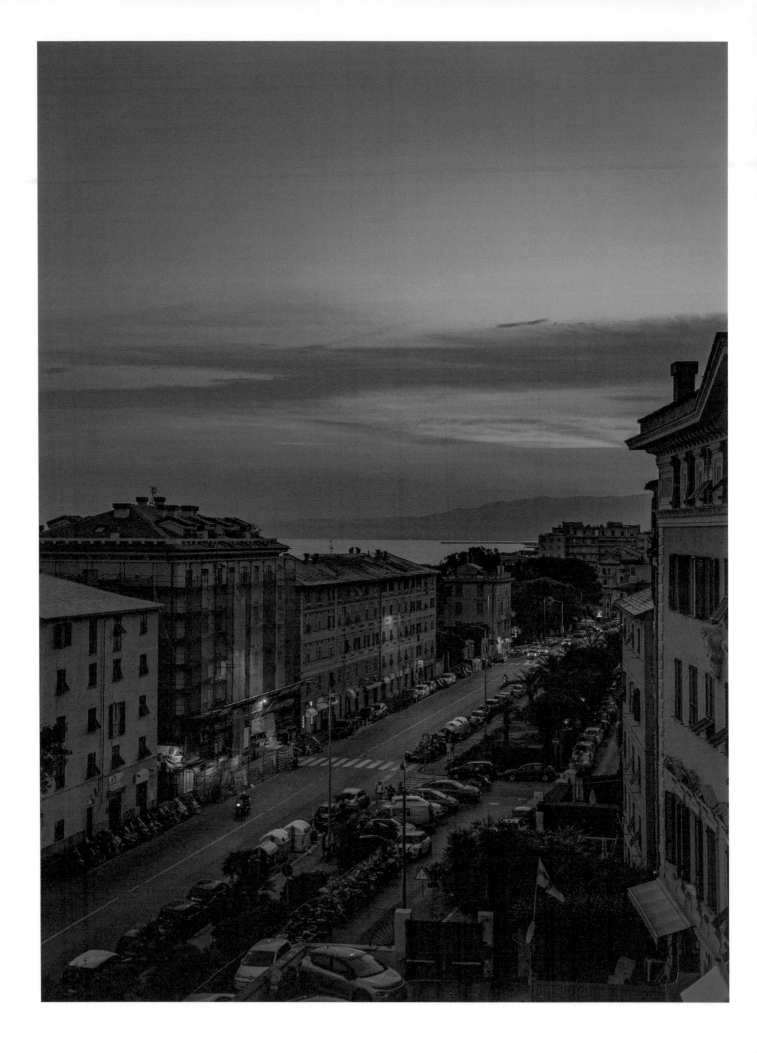

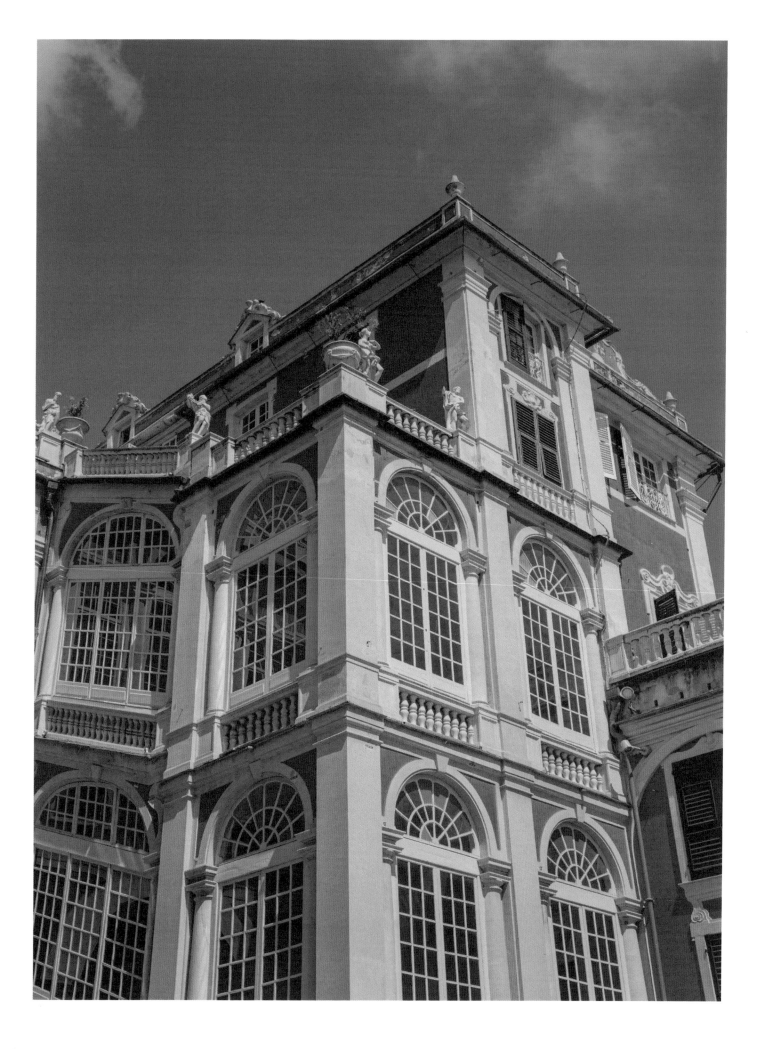

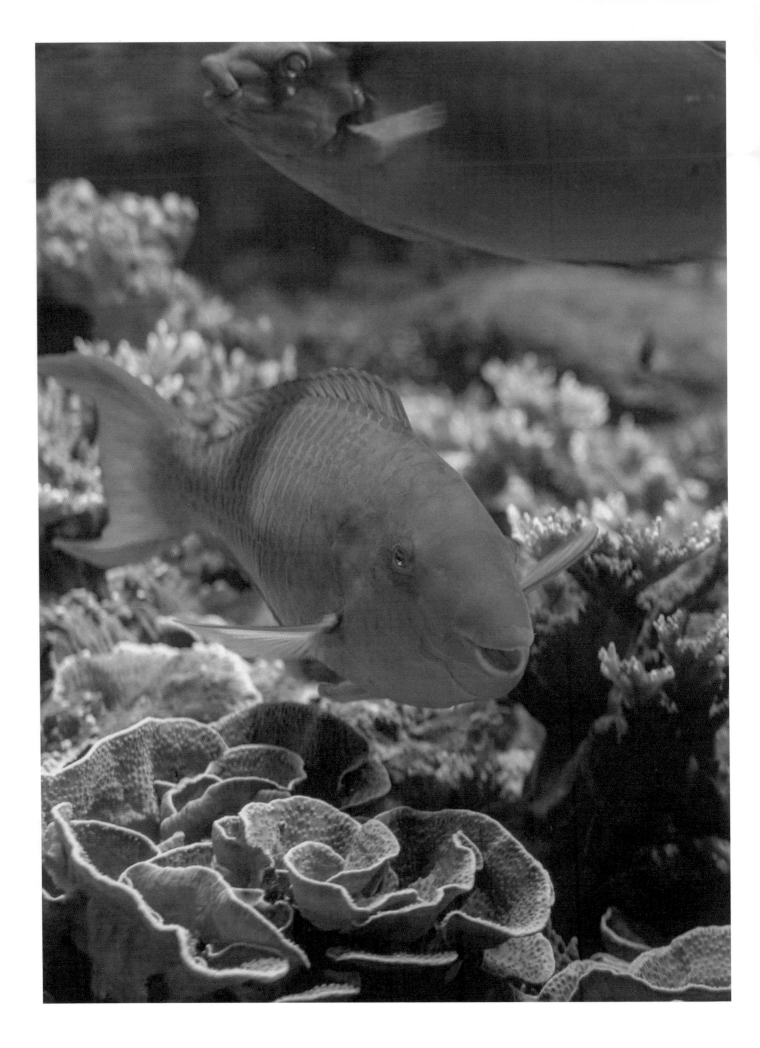

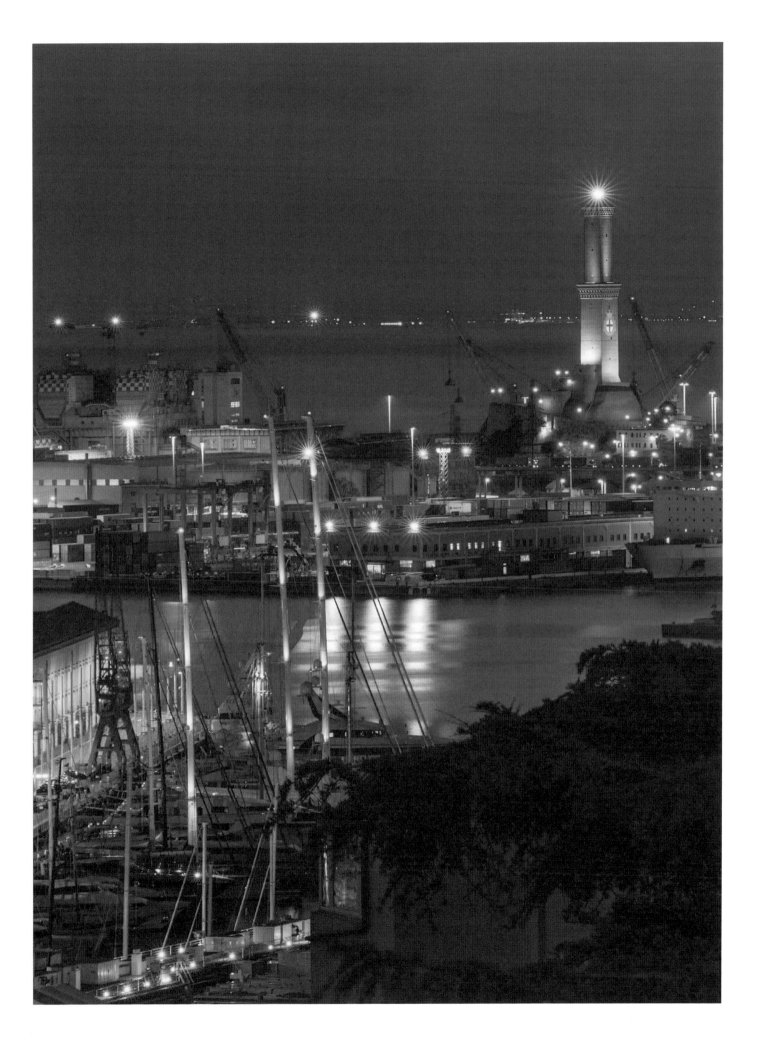

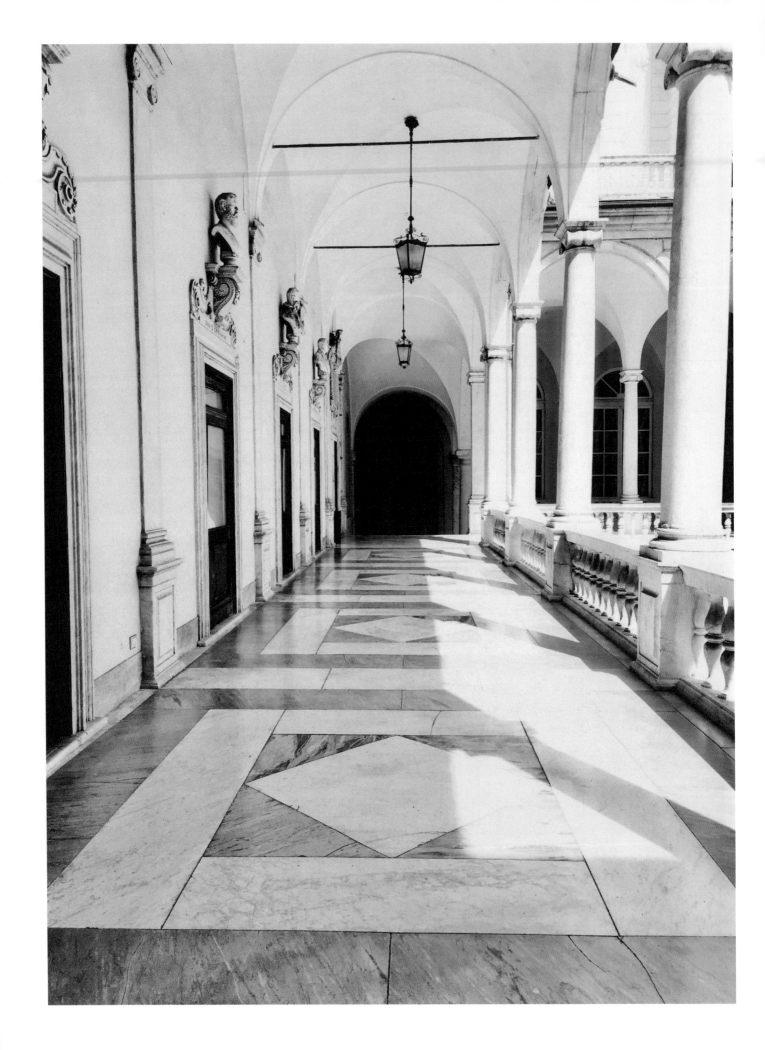

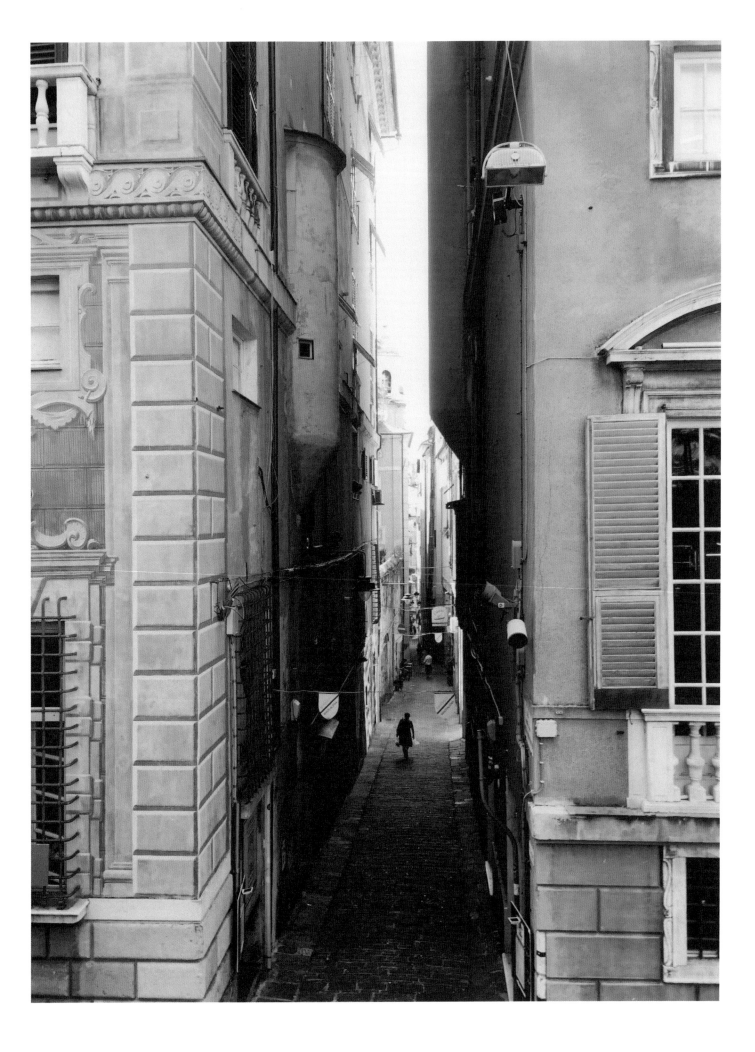

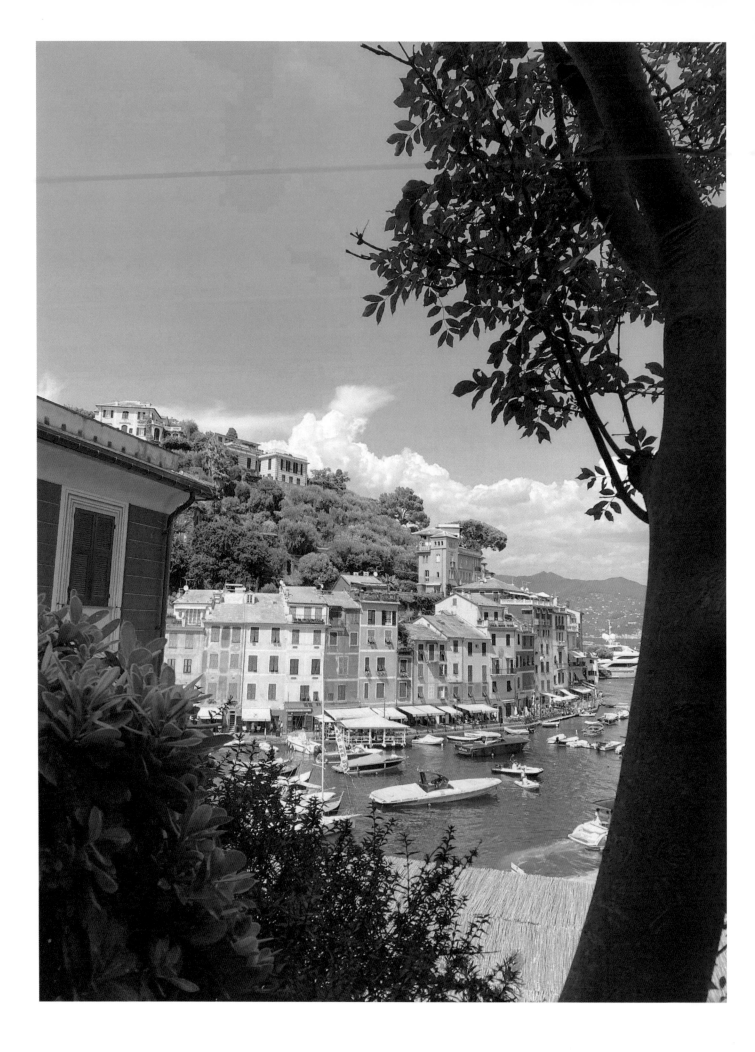

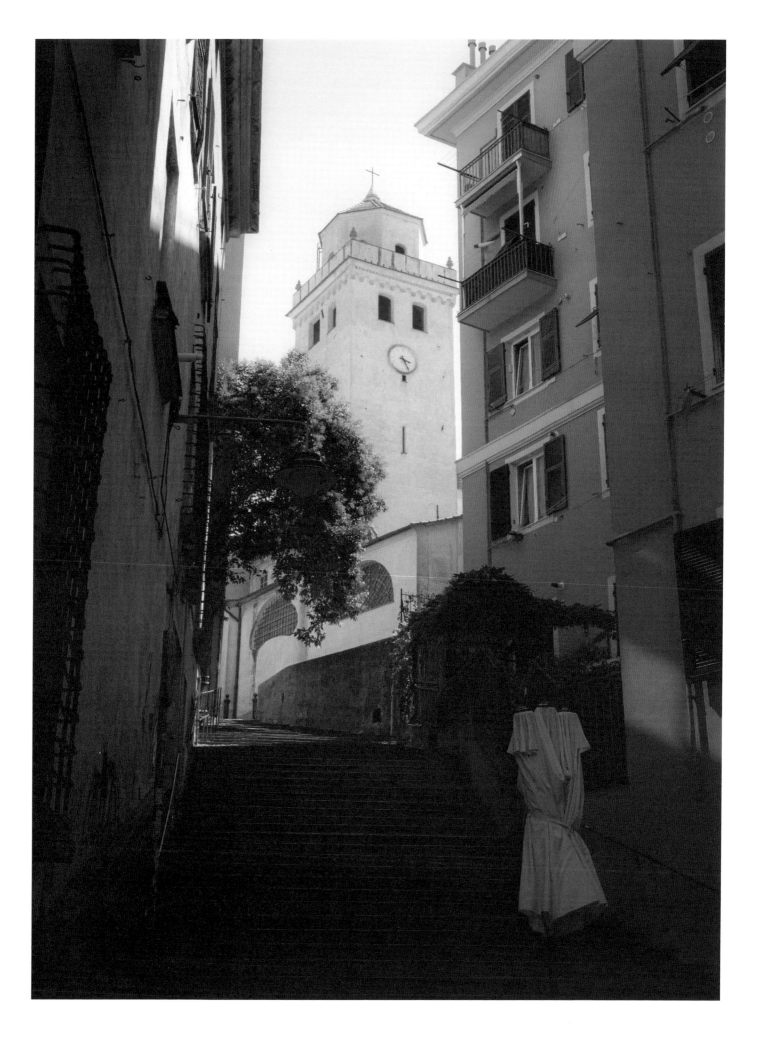

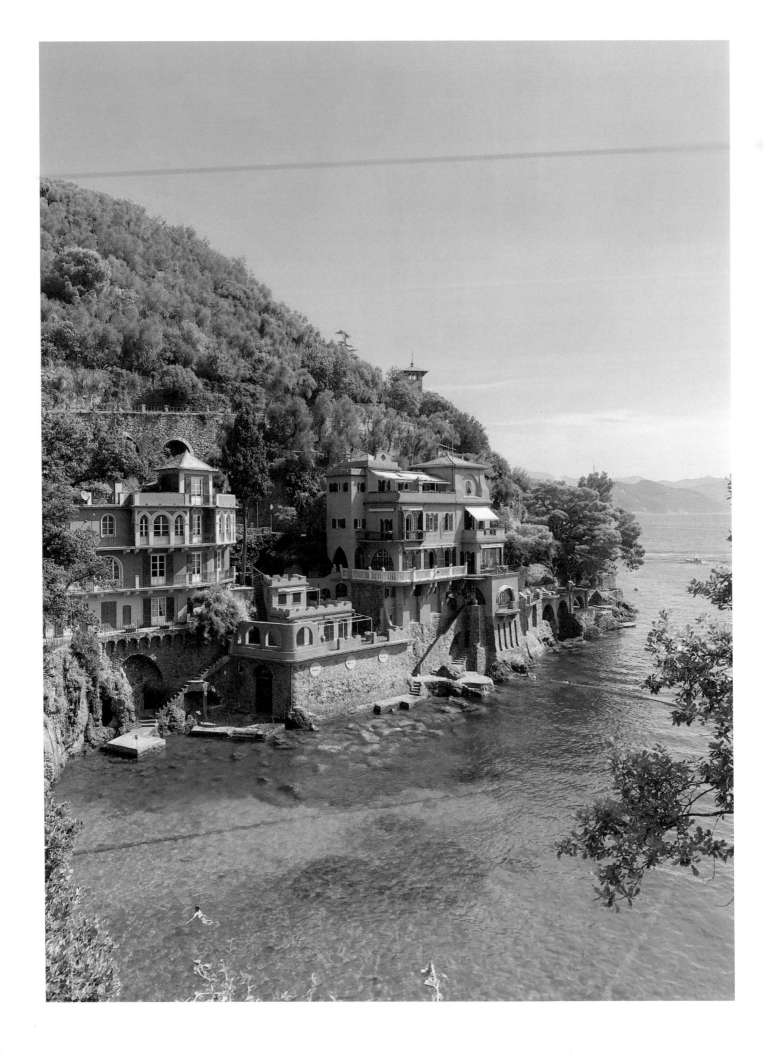

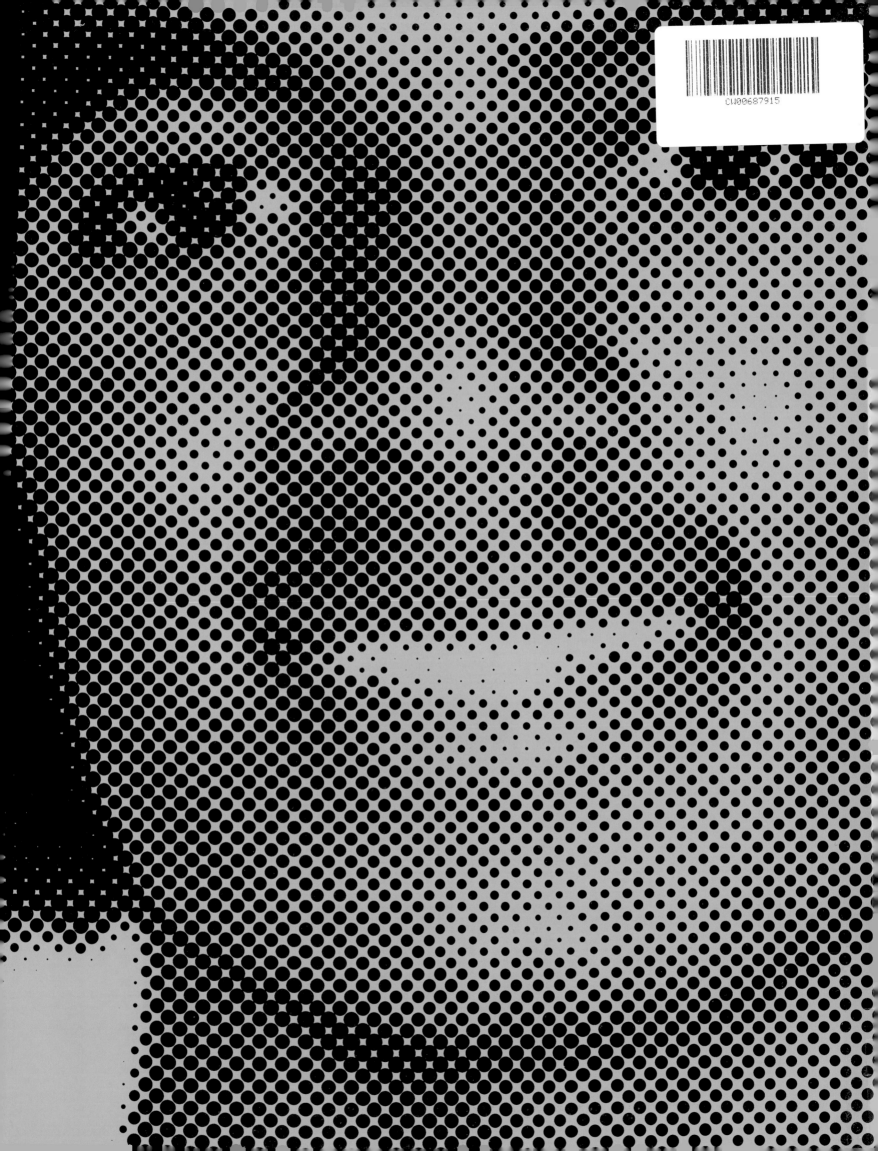

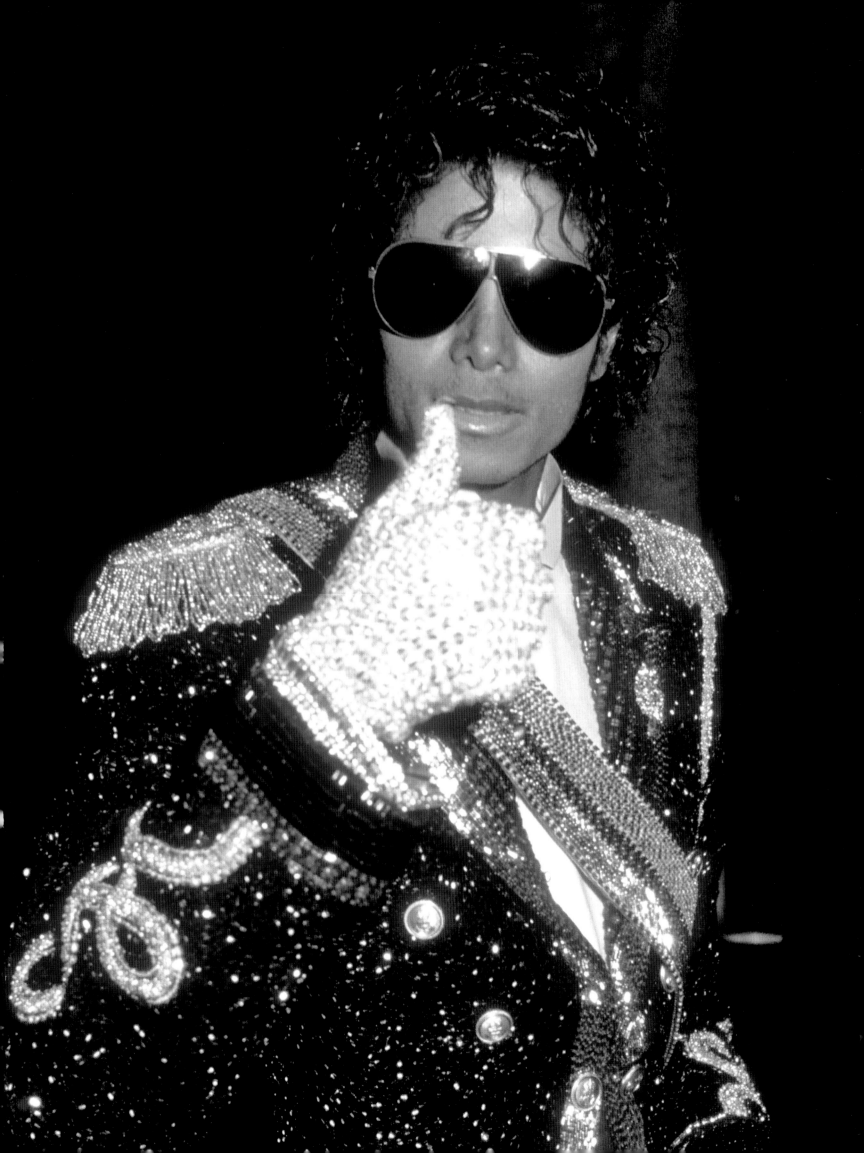

COVER and P.1 February 28, 1984: Beverly Hills, California
L'Ermitage Hotel
26th Annual Grammy Awards after party
Michael Jackson gives photographer Ron Galella a thumbs
up after shaking his hand. Jackson was in good spirits af-
ter his record-breaking eight Grammy wins: Record of the
Year ("Beat It"), Album of the Year (*Thriller*), Best Male
Pop Vocal Performance ("Thriller"), Best Male Rock
Vocal Performance ("Beat It"), Best Male R&B Vocal
Performance ("Billie Jean"), Best Rhythm and Blues Song
("Billie Jean"), Best Recording for Children (*E.T. The Extra-
Terrestrial*), and Producer of the Year (Non-Classical).

# Man in the Mirror
# MICHAEL JACKSON
## by Ron Galella

Introduction by Brooke Shields
Essay by Susan Blond

(pH) powerHouse Books Brooklyn, NY

# INTRODUCTION  Brooke Shields

In February 1984, Michael called me about a week before the Grammys to ask if I'd go with him. Although it wasn't much time, a week was actually longer than he'd usually give me to get ready for one of our outings. He told me he really wanted me to be with him, and that Emmanuel Lewis would probably also be with us. That was also not unusual because the three of us often did things as a team: the odd—but to us perfectly normal—version of the Three Musketeers. We were all quite famous and had been working basically our entire lives. Emmanuel was much younger and we called him "Rubba" because he had this adorable little face with chubby cheeks, and he could make funny faces and move like he was made of rubber. We would all laugh so much our sides would hurt. I think Michael and I simply appreciated the freedom we felt when we were together. We could laugh, act silly, and not have to be the professional adults we were normally expected to be.

I think Michael wanted me with him at this particular Grammys because of how groundbreaking *Thriller* was, and how huge it was for his career. I believe he felt safe with me around, and he knew I never wanted anything from him and that I would take care of him. Events like the Grammys can be daunting for anybody, especially somebody nominated for over seven awards. He knew I was familiar with the spectacle that accompanies such events and that I would not get star-struck or lose sight of him in any way.

I'm not sure if he thought he was going to win as many awards as he did. When I said congratulations on the numerous nominations, he just kept saying, "It's crazy isn't it?!" I joked with him that he probably would have gotten even more nominations if he had put me in the video instead of the girl he chose. He just got this mischievous smile on his face that I had seen so many times before and said, "Oh Brooke!"

Michael seemed to take all of it in stride. That evening he just kept getting up to accept another honor. He had such humility and grace, and although he was almost maniacally ambitious and a perfectionist, he never gloated about his success. He would just look ahead and try to find ways in which he could be even better. He wanted to be the best at everything, including being a friend. Nothing was ever about ego. It was about his heart and how that motivated him. Even getting eight awards seemed to just make him more humble.

Anyway, he asked and, as usual, I said I'd be glad to join him and help in any way I could. I promised we would have fun no matter what. On Grammy night I found a fancy Mary McFadden dress in my closet that I had been given as a gift, I did my own hair and makeup, and waited for the bell to ring. The car arrived and we were on our way. Michael had a way of making you want to care for him. Hopefully that is what I did that Grammy night.

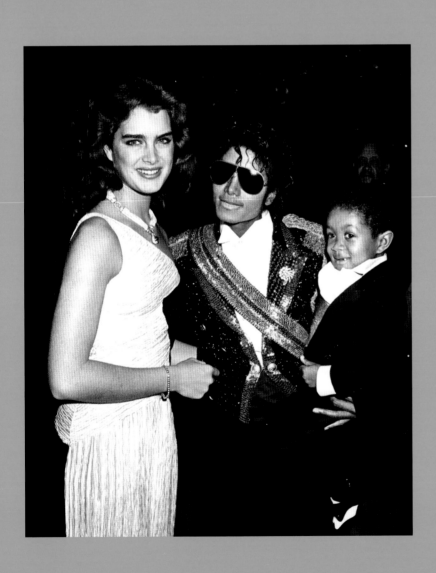

# REFLECTIONS  Susan Blond

I've worked with thousands of talented artists in my life, but Michael was the most talented of all. He was the greatest entertainer, singer, dancer, and songwriter ever. He was a star from the moment he was born.

Michael and I hit it off from the first time we met at a press conference Ron Alexenburg and Jim Tyrrell had at the Rainbow Room after the Jacksons were signed to Epic Records. We at Epic knew the Jacksons could have hit *albums*, not just hit singles as they had previously. Michael wanted more magazine covers than the Osmonds and we wanted to help.

During those early years Michael, Randy, and I hung out together. When I was in L.A. I took them to the Polo Lounge at the Beverly Hills Hotel, but no one was there so we didn't get a good feeling of the place. Before the CBS (who owned Epic) Grammy party, we went to the National Academy of Recording Arts and Sciences party. Michael was my date. He was so handsome then and so much fun to be with. I introduced Michael to Tatum O'Neal at On the Rox in Hollywood. Her father Ryan flirted with me a little, so Tatum sat on Michael's lap (she was still a kid, although she had won an Academy Award). I was there when Michael got his star at Grauman's Chinese Theatre—there were so many fans, there was a mini-riot. One time we went to Washington, D.C. together, to the Air and Space Museum. Michael hated the IMAX movie *Flying*, because it was photographed above the clouds and he thought it was improper to show where G-d was. He told me I was out of line when I told him to shave the little wisps of hair he had on his face—his religion forbade that. I remember him telling me in the hallway of the hotel in D.C. that my body reminded him of Diana Ross. We had a party for *Goin' Places* at Studio 54 in New York; the invite was a plane ticket.

Michael and I went to see *The Wiz* on Broadway with Stephanie Mills. He signed hundreds of autographs and I said, "Why don't you just sign 'MJ' like Andy Warhol does?" and Michael said, "Oh, I could never do that, these are my fans, *they made me!*" We went to Regine's with Stephanie and Andy Warhol. I asked Michael to dance and he replied, "Oh no—that's work." He also asked Andy why he didn't have kids. When he did the movie of *The Wiz* in

Astoria, Queens with Diana Ross, I got to be with Michael as they transformed him into the scarecrow. His makeup took hours to apply. We had another Studio 54 party, where Bethann Hardison found gorgeous models to dress as scarecrows.

*Off the Wall* was the record that launched Michael into superstardom—although we had to fight like crazy to get his first cover of *Rolling Stone*. The *Off The Wall* tour was the best I've ever seen, even better than the *Thriller* tour. Most white fans didn't see it—by *Thriller* that changed. I went to the studio in L.A. to see the "Billie Jean" video, and Michael was happy that I liked it. He said I was "so New York" so it was important to him that I liked it. During those days, the publicity departments at CBS (where I was Vice President) worked with MTV. The network refused to play "Beat It" because there was some silence at the beginning of the video, and they still considered it "black" and not for their audience. I thought I convinced them to add it until (then CBS Records President) Walter Yetnikoff's book came out a few years ago, where he says he actually threatened to remove all of our artist's videos if they didn't play Michael.

*Thriller* became the biggest record of all time. We got him on the cover of *Time* and *Newsweek*. The *Thriller* tour opened in Oklahoma City; when it came to Madison Square Garden, it was the hottest ticket ever. Steve Rubell (owner of Studio 54 and fresh out of jail at the time) led Michael, Calvin Klein, and I through the bowels of the Helmsley Palace Hotel. Michael posed for pictures with the kitchen staff as we went through to our waiting car to get to the Garden. When we came outside, Steve went in the street and acted like he represented the king—the press had named Michael the "King of Pop." Michael had caught fire the night before, during a Pepsi commercial, so he was fragile, but the show was phenomenal. Then it was off to our party at the Museum of Natural History—I came up with the the idea to use a white glove as the invitation. Outside the museum he waved to thousands of fans; inside he accepted his 35 million sold award and danced. It was a great night.

# THE MAN IN THE MIRROR  Ron Galella

*Ah! Sweet mystery of life*; this seems to be the foundation to superstardom, celebrity, and the making of legends. People yearn to know more about those in the public eye, and mystery and intrigue lead them on and on. What makes a *legend*? Fame, beauty, talent—and dying young, their talent cut short, their beauty buried in graves too soon. Some great legends of the past include Rudolph Valentino, Judy Garland, John F. Kennedy, Martin Luther King, Jr., James Dean, and Andy Warhol, but I believe the greatest of all legends was Marilyn Monroe who was surpassed only by Elvis Presley. *Legends* are forever—*celebrities* now, with few exceptions, are fleeting. Michael Jackson possesses all the necessary elements to become a legend, but the question remains, *how will history rate the man in the mirror's legacy?*

The masses, people and fans, are the barometer of a celebrity's popularity, and attendance numbers, whether at a rock concert or at the funeral of a pope, are good measuring tools. For the most popular, even after death the cult lives on. Elvis fans still make the pilgrimage to Graceland. Lady Di and John F. Kennedy's graves are revered as sanctuaries. Michael did not want to be forgotten after death, and he won't be, but he may not be remembered only for his art.

Michael Jackson gave us 40 years of great music and dance. Michael holds eight Guinness World Records, including highest annual earnings for a pop star, and most successful concert series of all time. In 1982 he reached his peak with *Thriller,* which sold 27 million copies in the U.S. and 109 million copies worldwide—making it the best selling album of all time. He would never again see this kind of success. In the minds of many, as a solo performer only Elvis rivaled his cultural impact and popularity, and not coincidentally, both had the ability to synthesize traditionally black and white styles of music. However, the most intriguing similarity between these legends is the mystery surrounding their deaths: was it accidental, was it murder, or was it suicide? We are forever seeking these answers, but with the most enduring legends answers cannot be found.

In life, Michael knew how to use intrigue and spectacle to promote himself; his famous stunts included crotch grabbing and moonwalking. He would cover his face with masks, and wear dark sunglasses and long, curly wigs. He was soft-spoken like Jackie O and Warhol. Dubbed "The Gloved One," wearing a white glove on his right hand became his trademark along with his fedora. But, did he wear the rhinestone glove to hide his vitiligo as his dermatologist Arnold Klein claims? In both life and death Jackson was extraordinarily mysterious and seemingly eccentric to the hundreds of millions of fans who would never know him personally.

Elvis was a more romantic and sexy superstar, but Michael surpassed him with his superior dancing, truly earning the title of "King of Pop." As Elvis did before him, Michael wore costumes onstage. Often they were of a military-style design, and he regularly wore short trousers to reveal his white socks and show off his footwork—a trick Michael picked up from Fred Astaire. His dancing reflected the male and female gestures he learned from *West Side Story, Saturday Night Fever,* and the choreography of Bob Fosse, Judy Garland, Marcel Marceau, and Diana Ross. Michael and Diana Ross had a lot in common. They both started their careers at Berry Gordy's Detroit mansion, both were from large families, and both skyrocketed to fame with Motown Records. Both were cast in *The Wiz,* a children's dream world. Although Michael's music and dance were professional and mature, in his personal life he was an innocent boy. Ross once said of Michael, "He spends a lot of time, too much time, by himself. . .Michael has a lot of people around him, but he's very afraid." Michael remained a child at heart, playing with electronic toys and pets. He spent hours in darkened rooms watching cartoons.

As a boy, many people criticized Michael's appearance, including his father, Joe. This made Michael self-conscious and shy, and lowered his self-esteem as well as his point-of-view regarding his own ethnicity. He began changing the way he looked as soon as he could afford surgical operations. I believe he wanted to look like his sister Janet: tiny nose, thinner lips, new chin and cheekbones—Michael sculpted his face as a work of art. He was the man in the mirror, looking at his reflection and forever changing it.

Michael's former wife, Lisa Marie Presley, reported that he had said about Elvis, "I am afraid that I am going to end up like him, the way he did." Michael's supposed drug addiction allegedly began when he was filming a commercial for Pepsi, in Los

Angeles, in 1984. His hair caught fire and his scalp was burned. Painkillers given to him during his recovery are said to have led to more and more. It was reported that he often suffered from insomnia because he was so hyped up from dancing and singing. He began taking drugs to fall asleep. These addictions seemed to grow out of control along with the weight of his depression and stress after accusations of sexual molestation were leveled against him. The trials and settlement cost him a lot of money. Because he was a big spender he was in debt and lost control of Neverland to the bank. To pull him out of debt, his business advisors arranged a 50-concert tour beginning in London. This was supposed to be his comeback, but he collapsed during his second rehearsal. In the end, it seemed that Michael's death was not only predictable, but it was inevitable. The only uplifting things he had were his children Prince Michael I, Paris, and Prince Michael II.

In over 50 years as a photojournalist, I had some highlights when photographing Michael. The first big take in which I photographed him was on August 26, 1977 at the star-studded gala for the Sixth Annual Robert F. Kennedy Pro-Celebrity Tennis Tournament at the Rainbow Room. I managed to photograph Michael with Muhammad Ali, Ted Kennedy, Shirley MacLaine, and alone. Jackie was there, of course, and she would later publish Michael's book *Moonwalk*.

The second time I met and photographed Michael was March 10, 1978 at the First Annual Rock & Roll Sports Classic at the University of California in Irvine. It was a swimming competition and I photographed Michael all wet in swim trunks, with his young sister Janet helping to dry him off.

A big night for both Michael and myself was on February 28, 1984 after Michael received an unprecedented eight Grammy awards at the Shrine Auditorium. I followed him to his hotel, L'Ermitage, in Beverly Hills. He was with Brooke Shields who was his date and close friend. He also had his friend Emmanuel Lewis with him, and I photographed all three together, and got shots of them with Brooke's mother, Teri. As I had known Brooke since she was 12, she introduced me to Michael, and as I shook his hand he said, "Oh, I've heard of you." This paid off later when photographing him on May 8, 1984, when he went to see *Cats* at the Winter Garden Theatre with Sean Lennon. It was impossible to take pictures as they entered, because Michael's limo had pulled up onto the sidewalk, right next to the stage door, and they were surrounded by security. The same situation repeated when he left, but he saw me as he entered the limo and he flashed his bare hand at me and his many fans. I got the shot, and it ran as a double-page in *US Magazine*.

On February 3, 1992, after Michael signed his third sponsorship deal with Pepsi at a press conference at Radio City Music Hall, he left in his limo to rush to his flight back to L.A. He saw me and opened the window to say hi, and I took the back cover photo for this book.

Along with his many other celebrity friends, through the years, Michael was extremely close with Elizabeth Taylor. They probably bonded over the fact that they were both child stars. Michael even escorted Taylor down the aisle at her 1991 marriage to Larry Fortensky, at Neverland. When she heard of Michael's death she could not stop crying, yet as the *New York Post* reported, she was not invited to the funeral by the Jackson family, and at his memorial at the Staples Center, she was not given a seat with them. I believe she was snubbed deliberately because his family felt Michael was closer to her than to his own parents.

Michael had a big ego, and he believed he could do no wrong, nor could he ever admit defeat, or come to terms with his fading stardom and riches. Bob Jones, who worked with Michael as his PR Agent, summed it up in his book, *Michael Jackson: The Man Behind the Mask*, "I saw a mad genius in Michael Jackson. Someone who loved and cared only for himself. I saw a master of self-promotion and a self-destructive multi-millionaire spending millions trying to buy friendship and favors whether it was [from] little boys, Princess Diana, or Elizabeth Taylor."

Who do we have to blame for Michael Jackson's death? I believe all human beings are responsible for their own survival. Michael had already experienced the ecstasy of his first 40 years, ascending to the peak of his great talent, and it must have been an agonizing journey towards his tragic death. The man in the mirror is now finally at peace.

# I WANTED MORE THAN ANYTHING ELSE TO BE A TYPICAL LITTLE BOY.

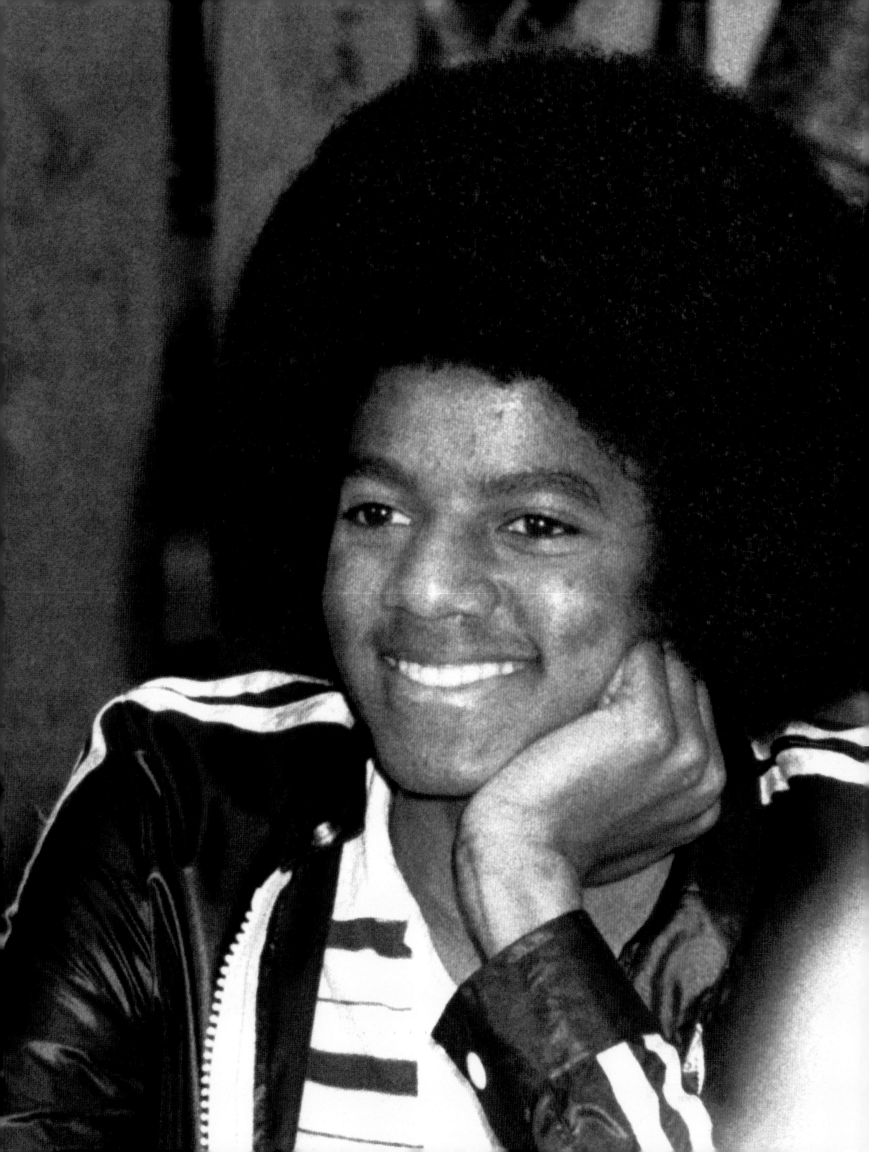

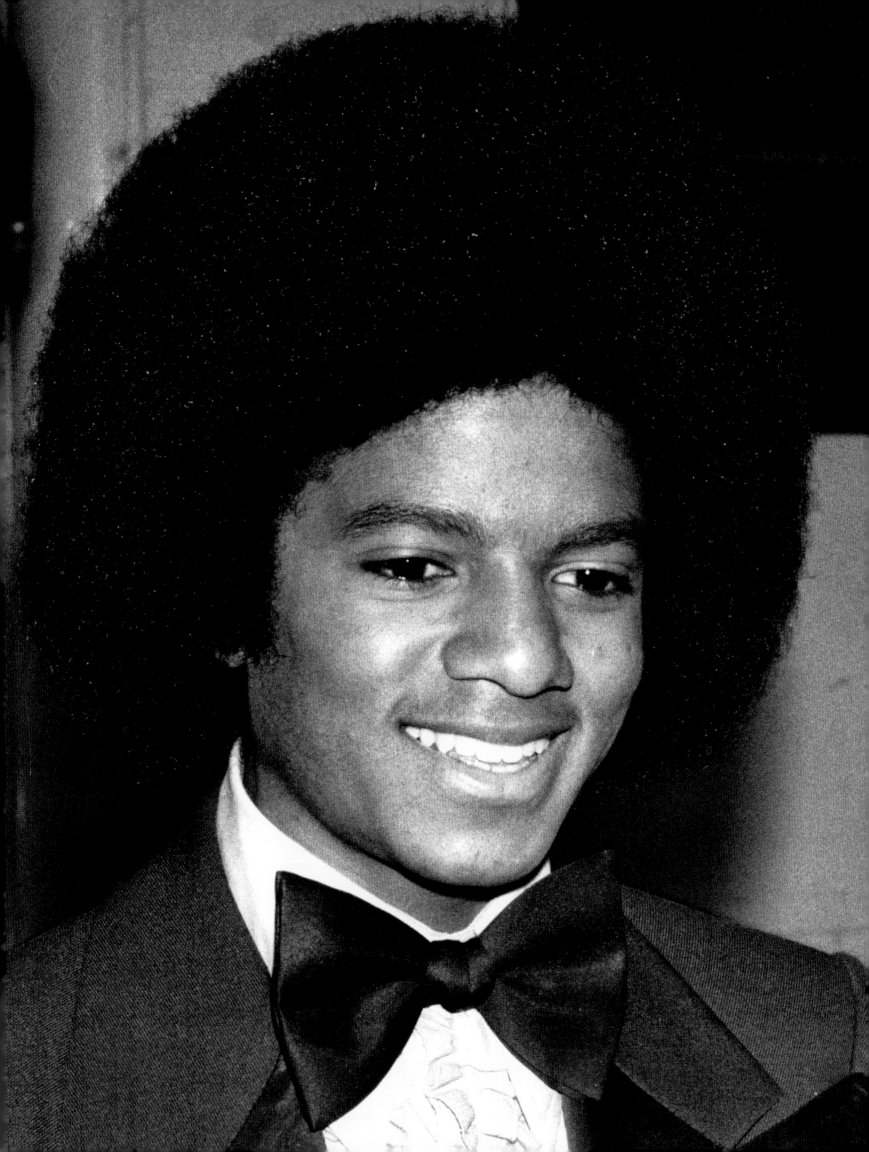

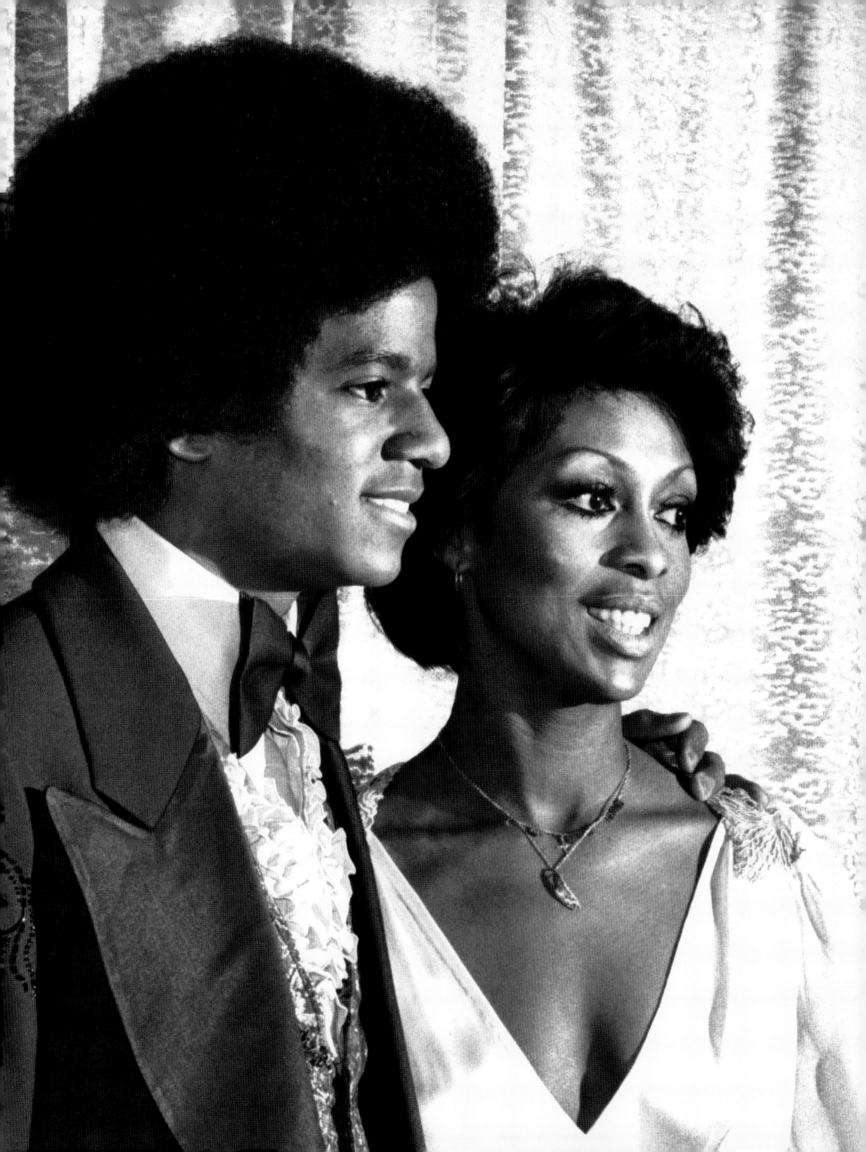

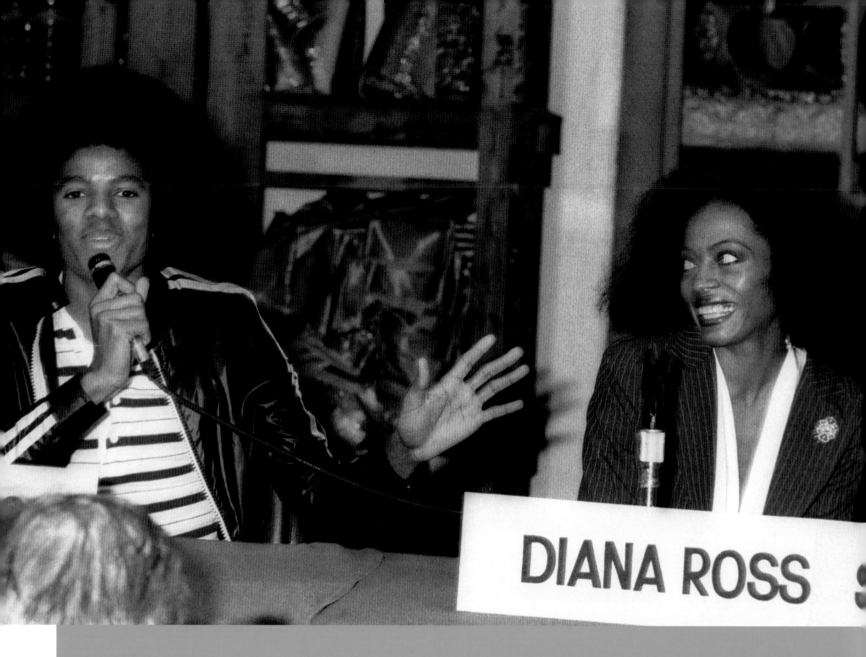

I'VE BEEN IN THE ENTERTAINMENT INDUSTRY SINCE I WAS SIX YEARS OLD. . . .BUT I WOULD NOT CHANGE MY CAREER.

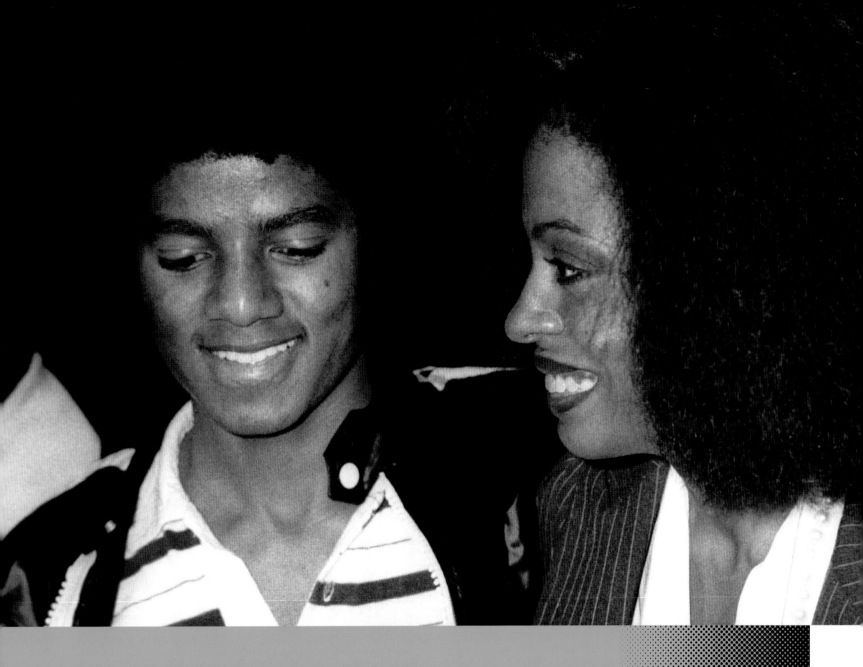

HE COULD BE MY SON.
Diana Ross

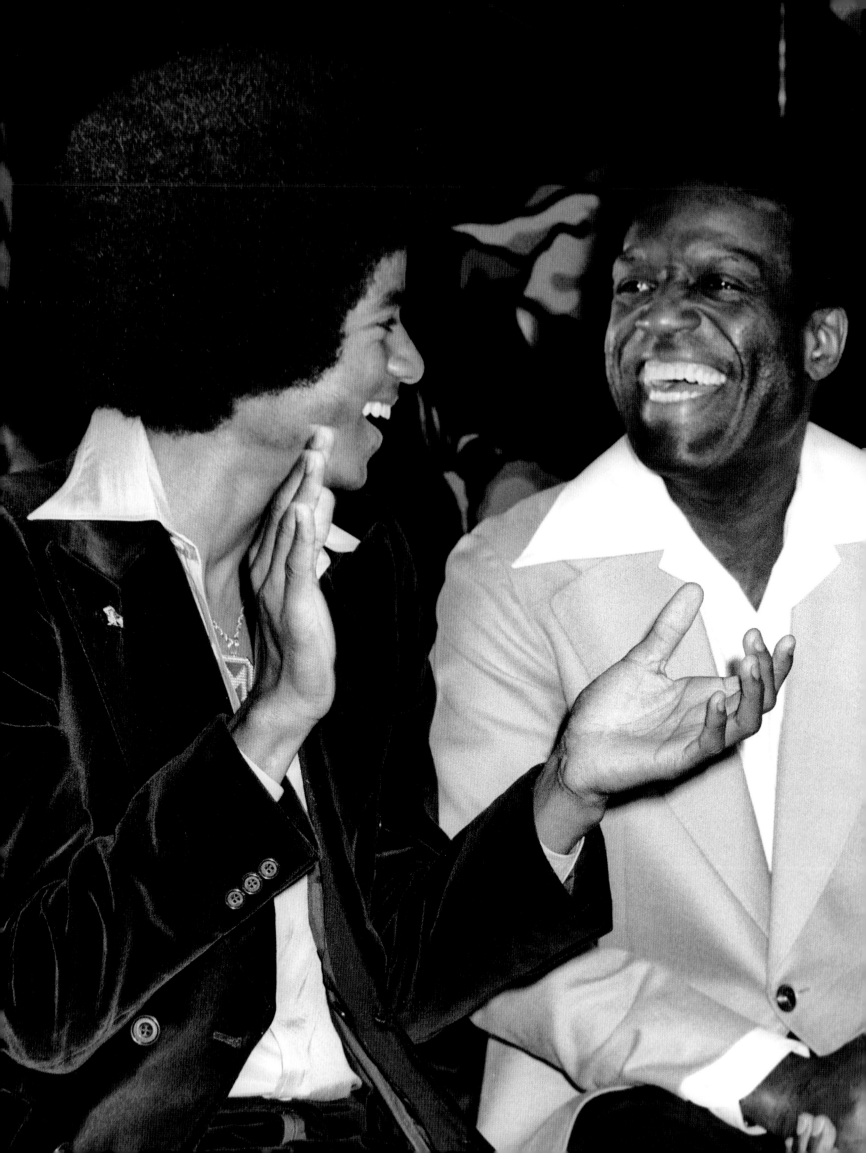

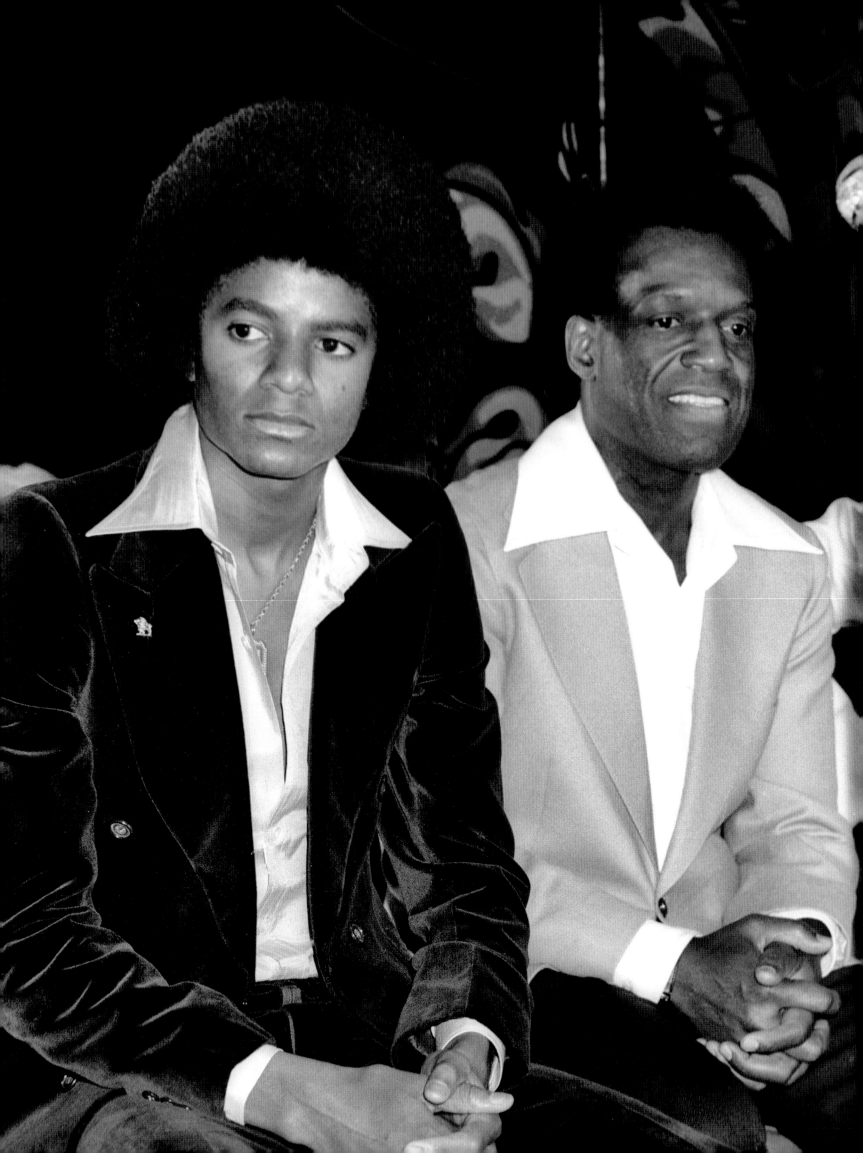

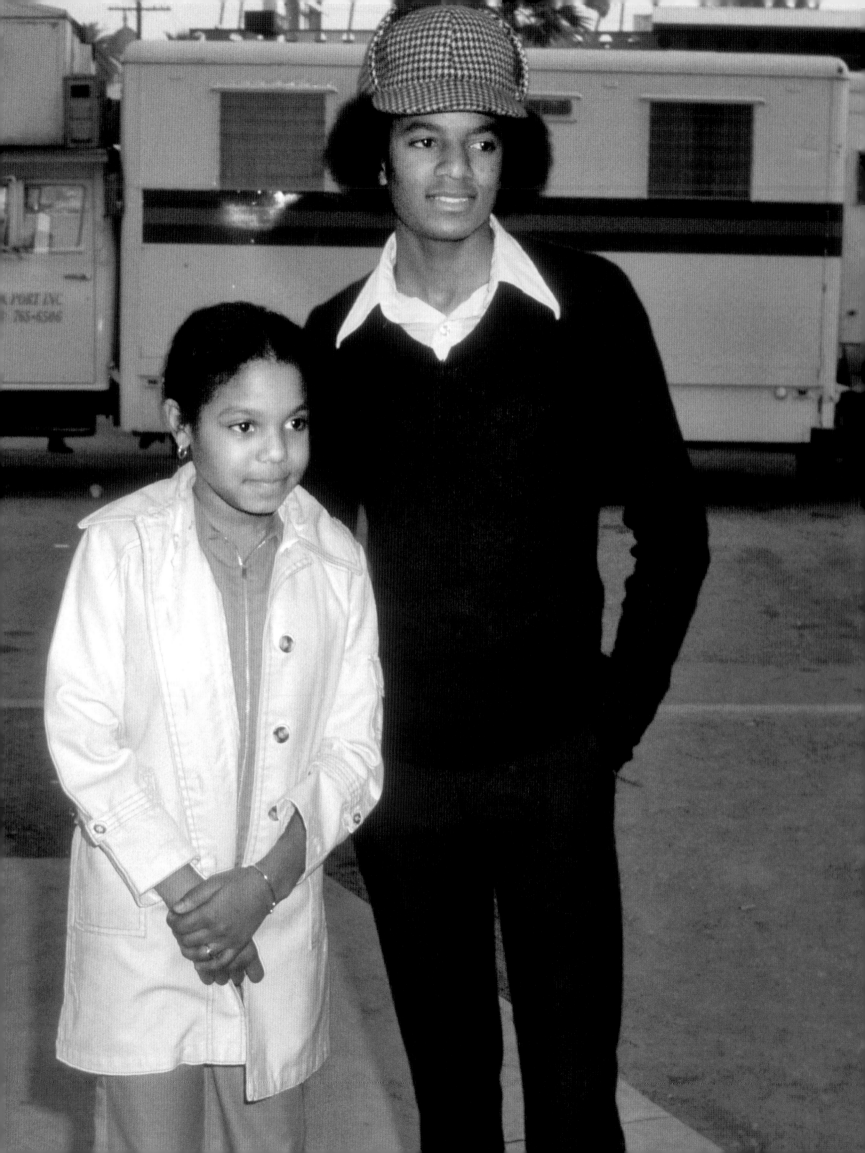

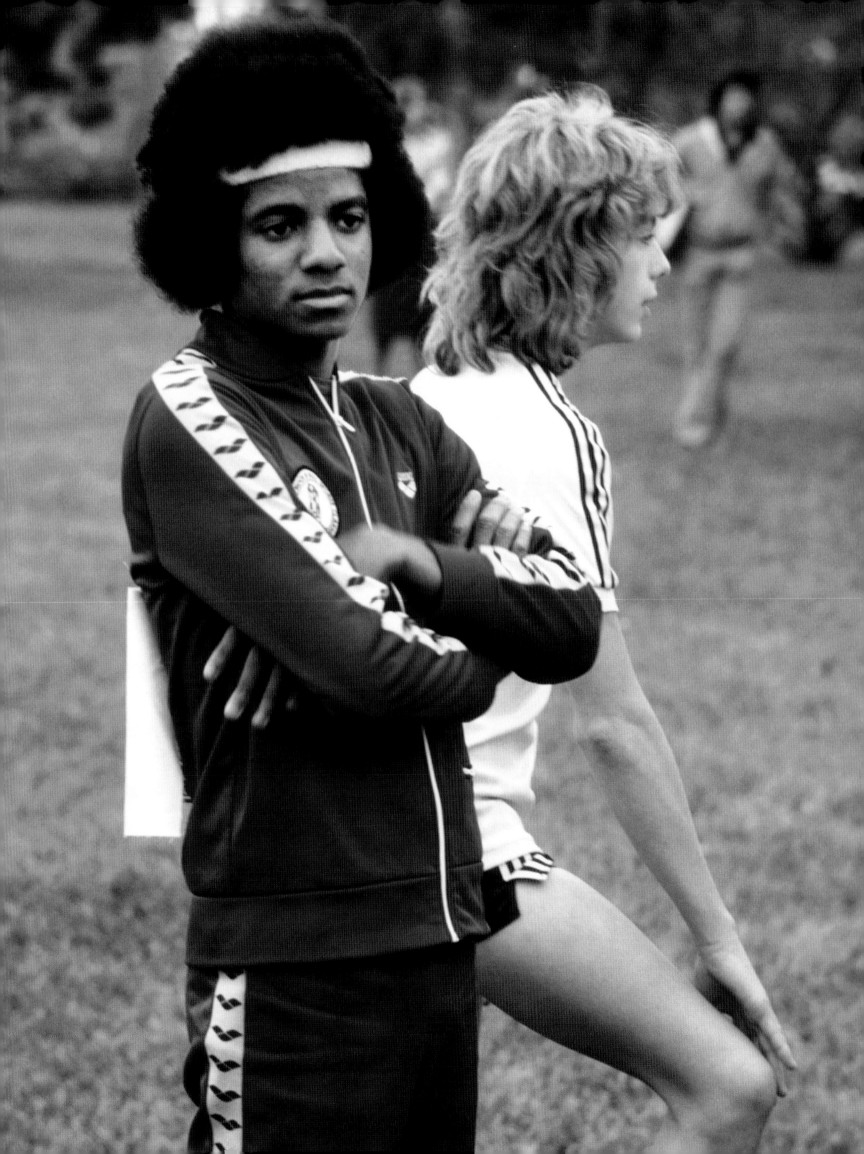

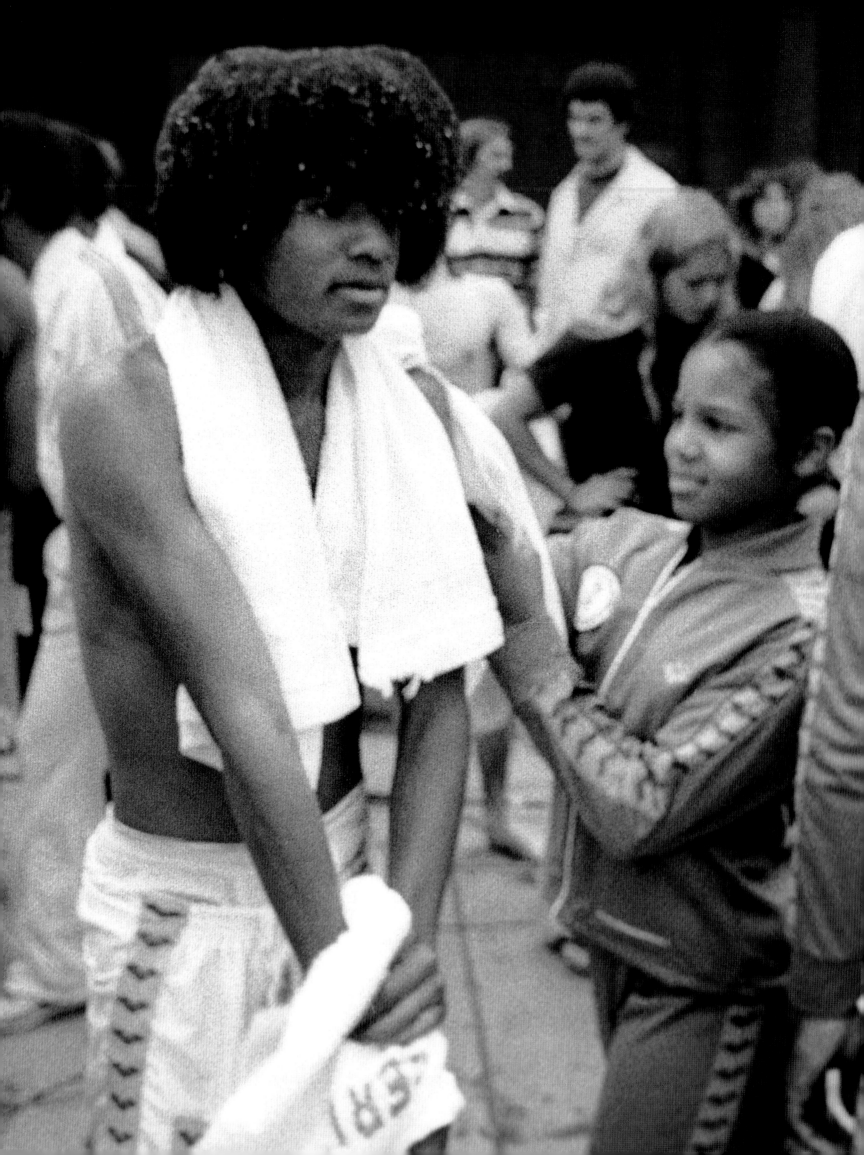

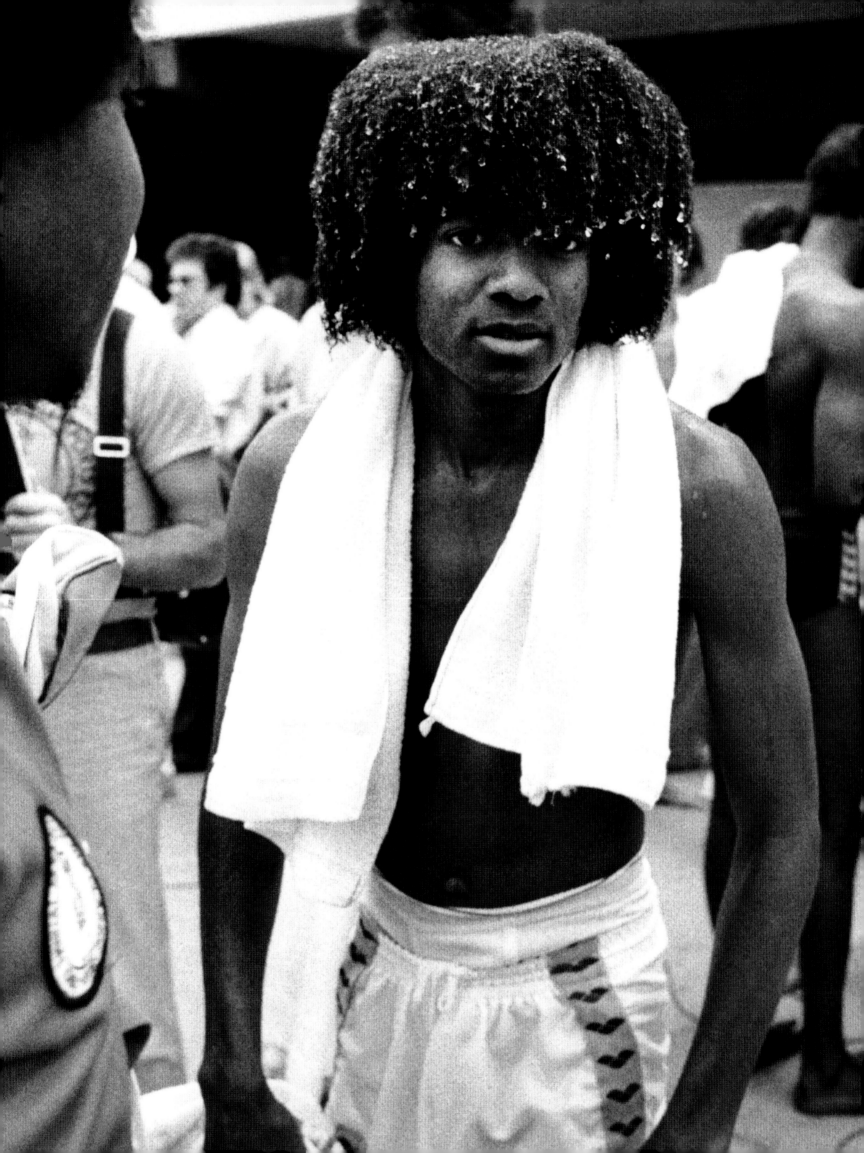

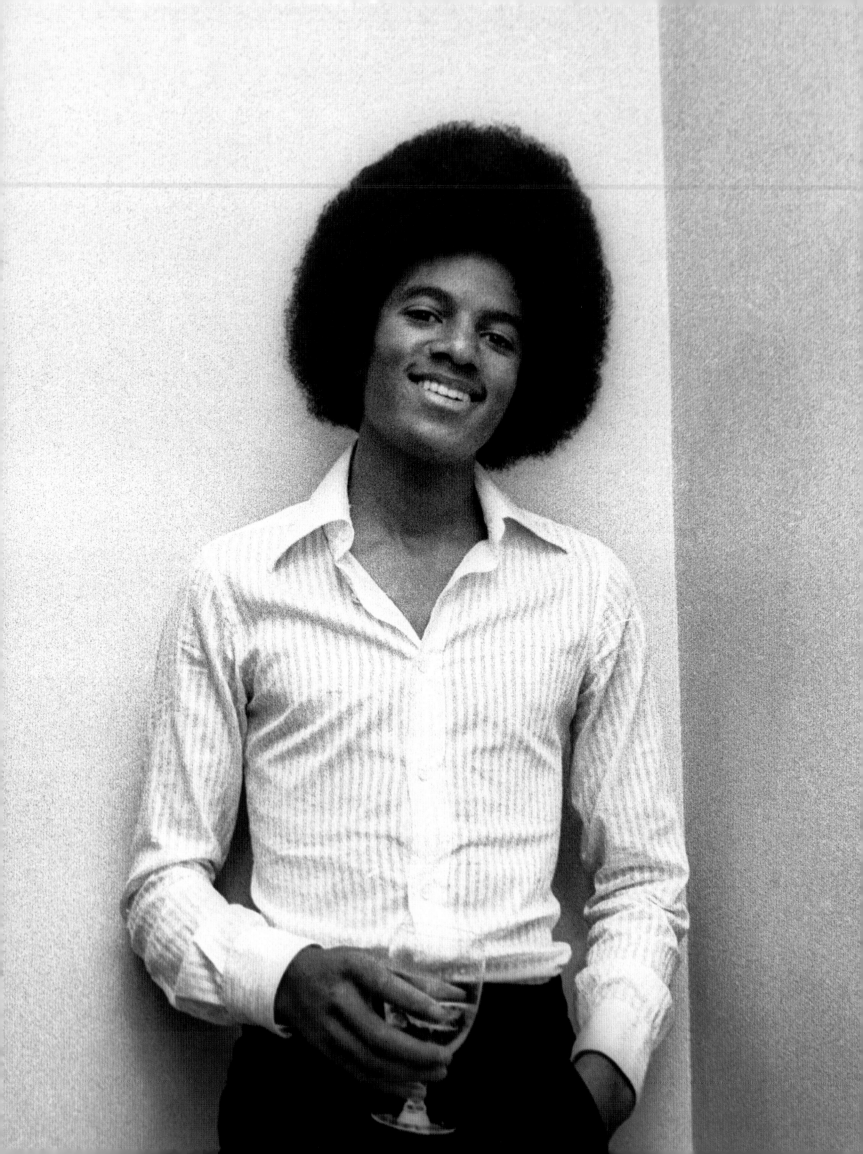

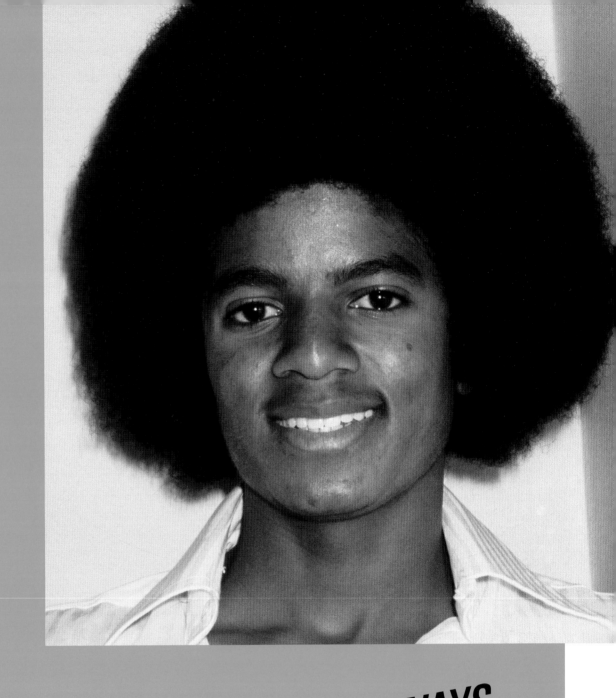

WHEN I WAS LITTLE, IT WAS ALWAYS WORK, WORK, WORK. . . .IF IT WASN'T A CONCERT IT WAS THE RECORDING STUDIO, IF IT WASN'T THAT, IT WAS TV SHOWS OR PICTURE SESSIONS. THERE WAS ALWAYS SOMETHING TO DO.

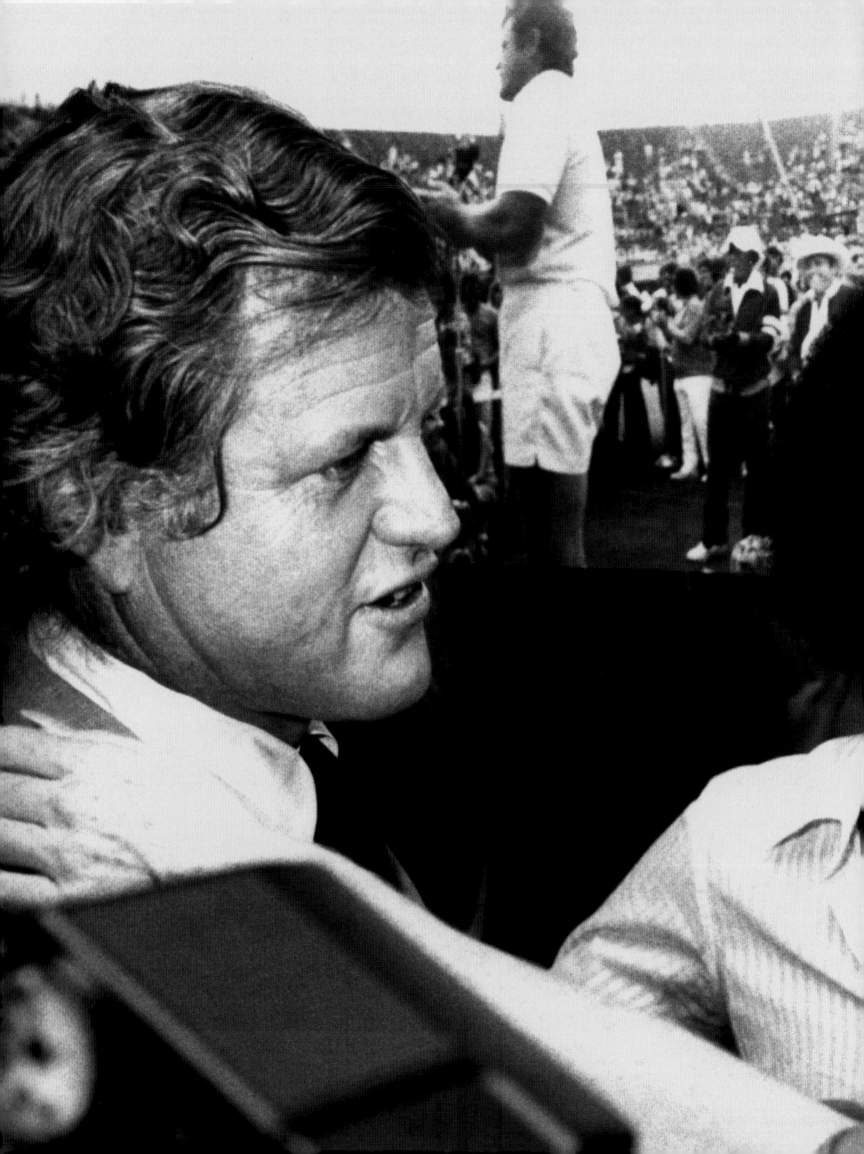

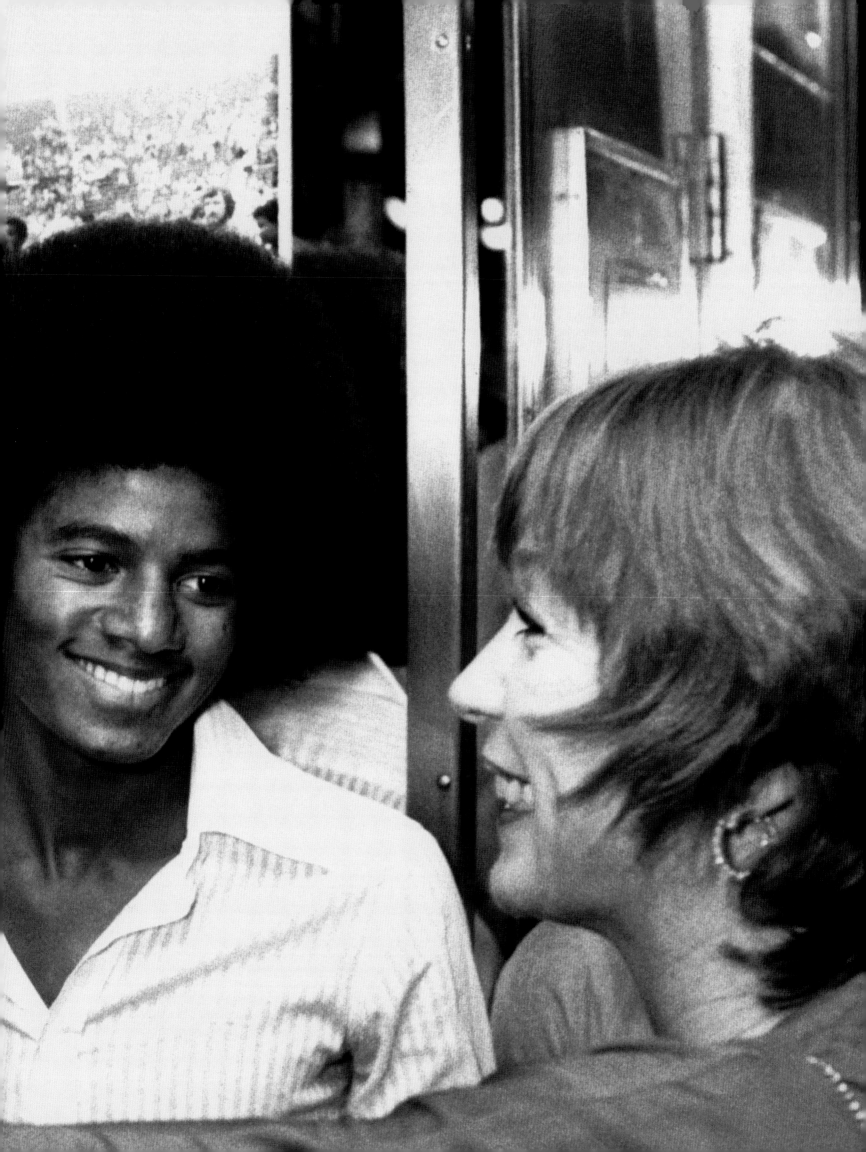

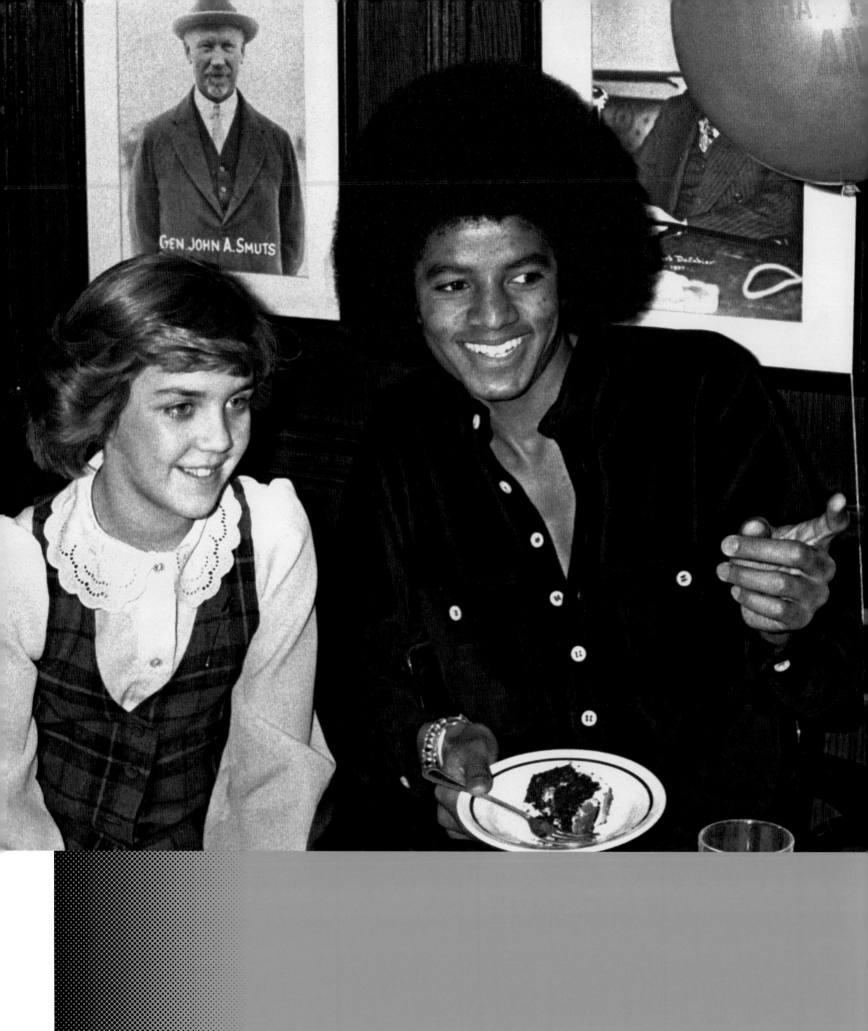

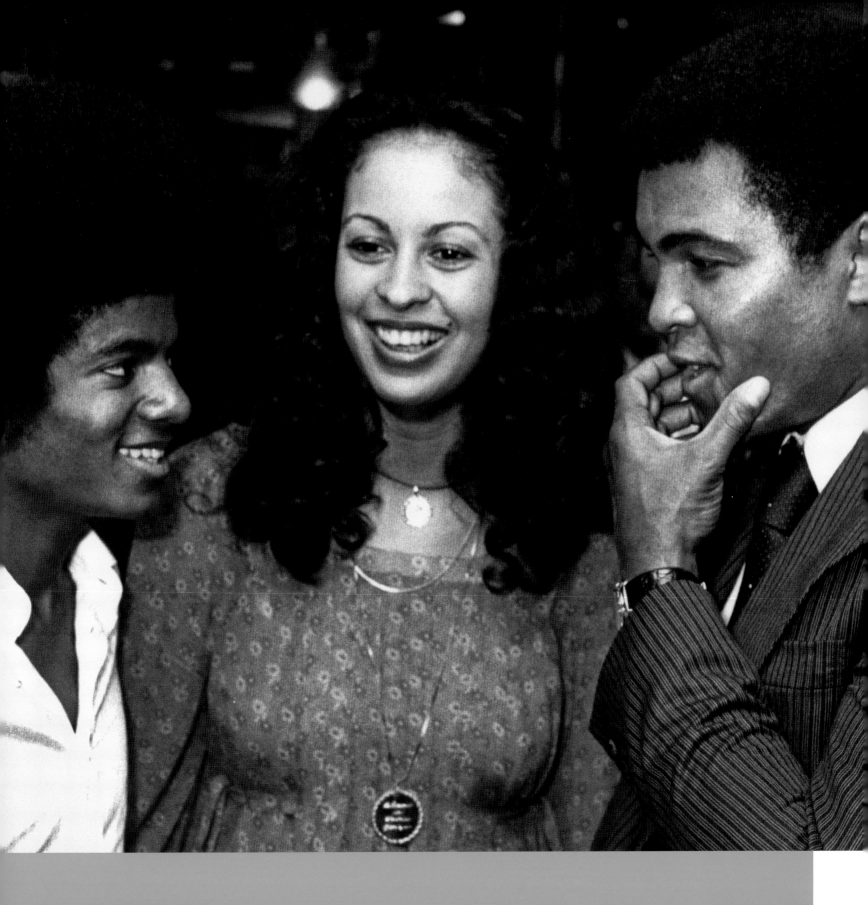

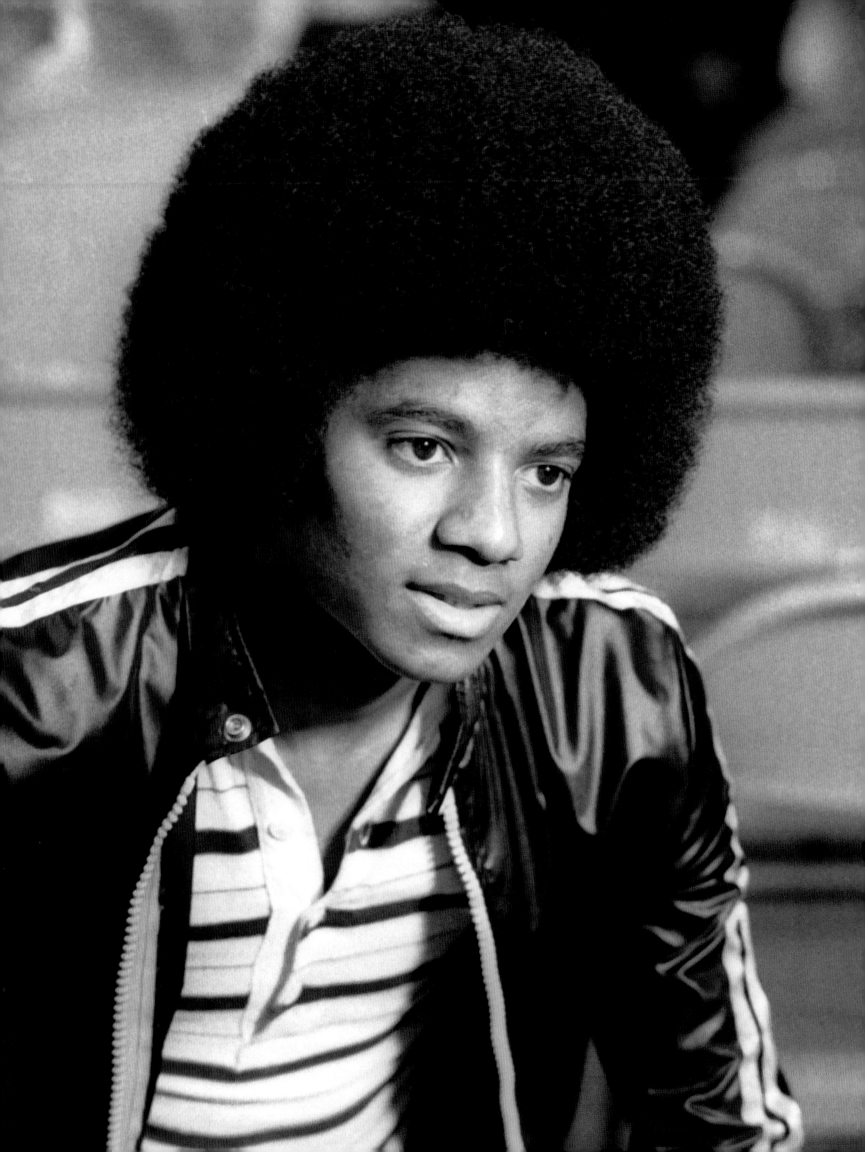

SUCCESS DEFINITELY BRINGS ON LONELINESS. PEOPLE THINK YOU'RE LUCKY, THAT YOU HAVE EVERYTHING. THEY THINK YOU CAN GO ANYWHERE AND DO ANYTHING, BUT THAT'S NOT THE POINT. ONE HUNGERS FOR THE BASIC STUFF.

YOU'RE NOT THE CUTE AND CHARMING CHILD THAT YOU WERE.

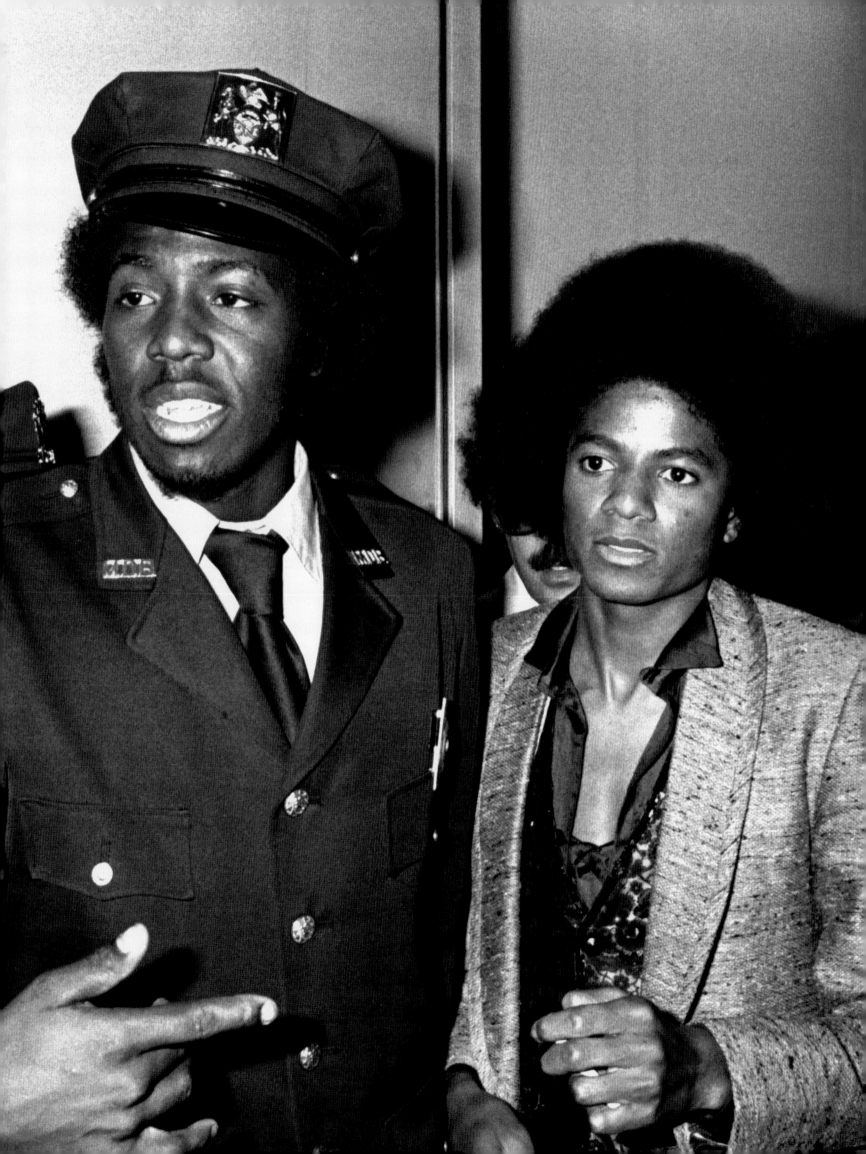

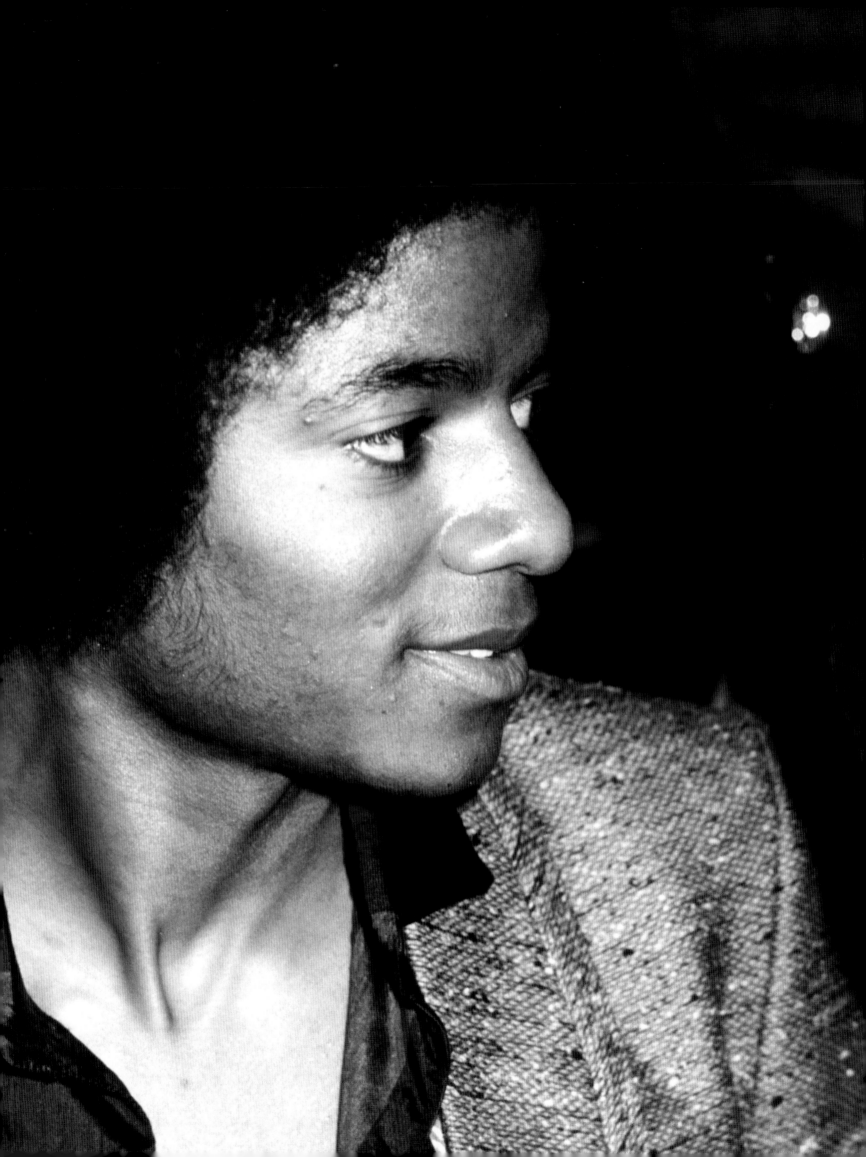

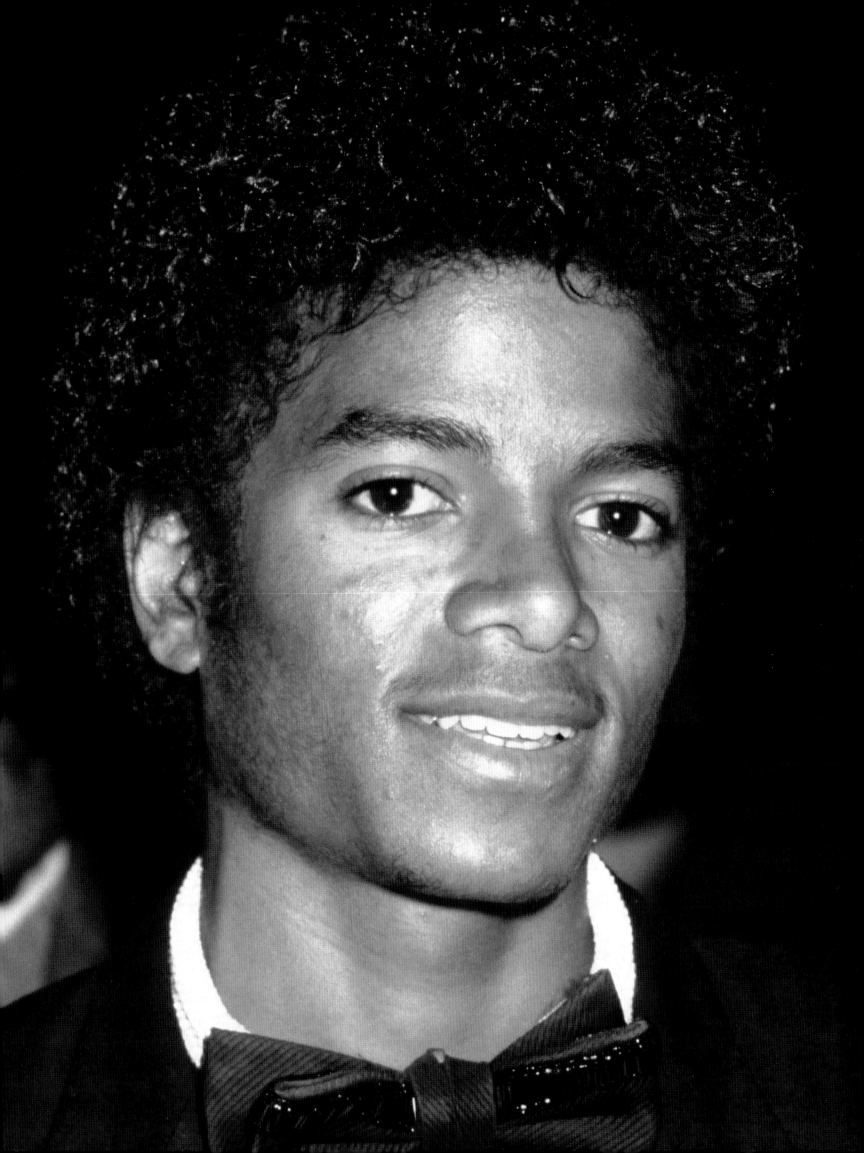

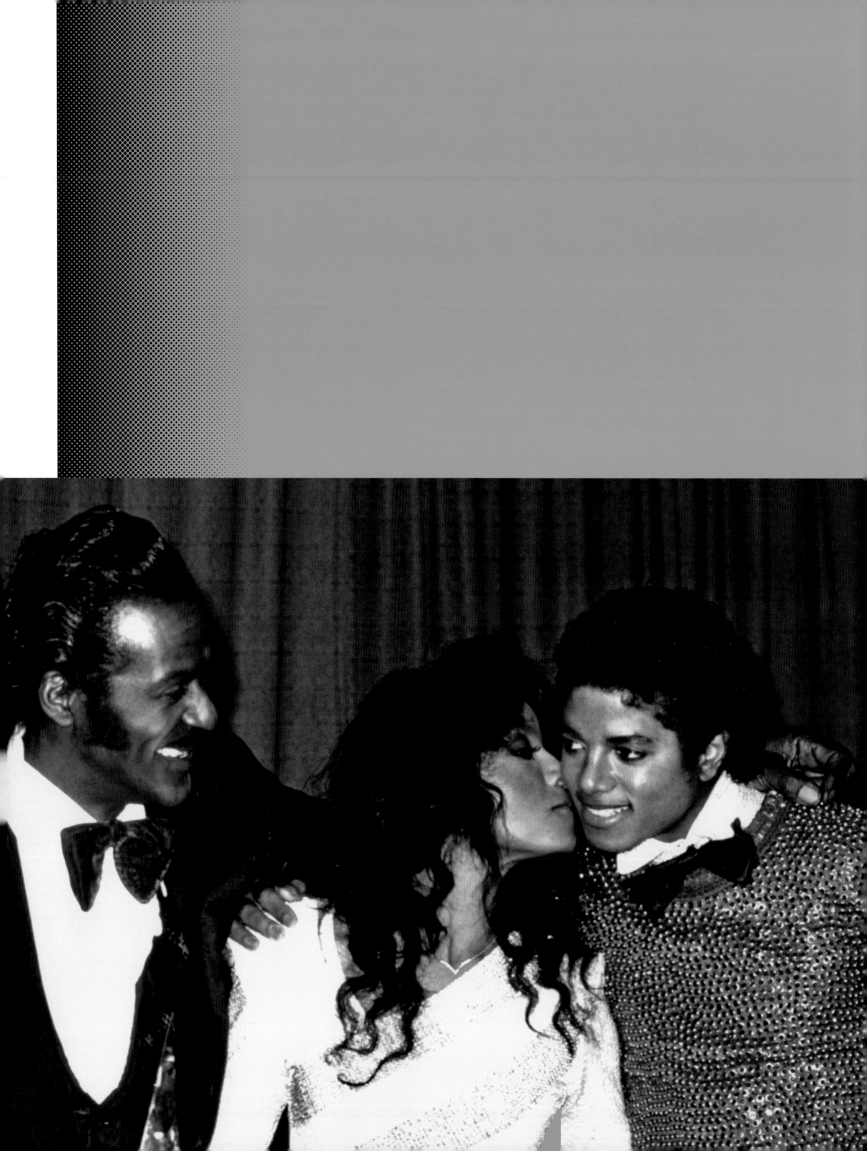

HE SPENDS A LOT OF TIME, TOO
MUCH TIME, BY HIMSELF. . .MICHAEL
HAS A LOT OF PEOPLE AROUND HIM,
BUT HE'S VERY AFRAID.

Diana Ross

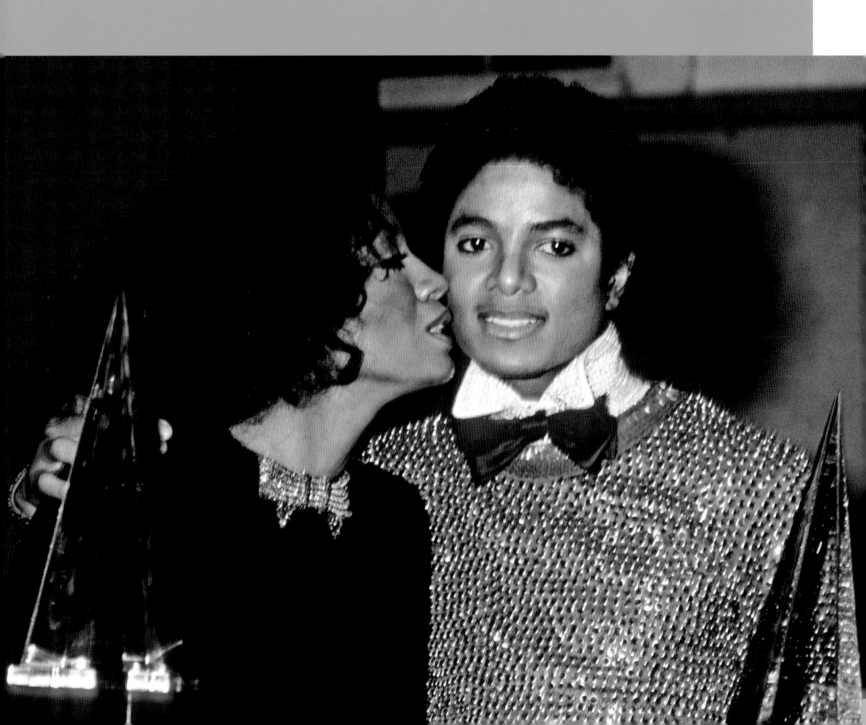

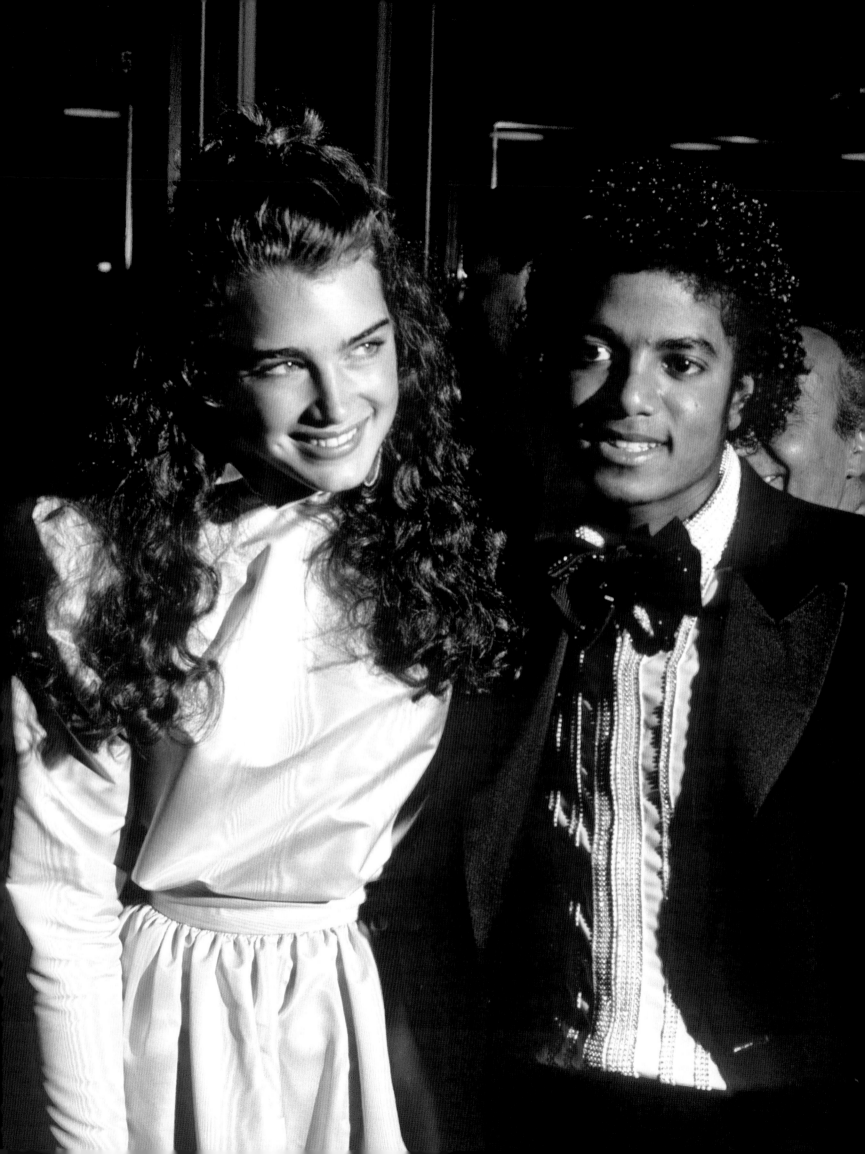

MY HEART IS OVERCOME WITH SADNESS FOR THE DEVASTATING LOSS OF MY TRUE FRIEND MICHAEL. HE WAS AN EXTRAORDINARY FRIEND, ARTIST, AND CONTRIBUTOR TO THE WORLD. I JOIN HIS FAMILY AND HIS FANS IN CELEBRATING HIS INCREDIBLE LIFE AND MOURNING HIS UNTIMELY PASSING.

Brooke Shields

I BEGAN PERFORMING AT THE TENDER AGE OF FIVE, AND EVER SINCE THEN I HAVEN'T STOPPED.

I USED TO LISTEN TO MY FATHER PLAY RAY CHARLES. I SAID, "THAT'S WHAT I WANT TO DO."

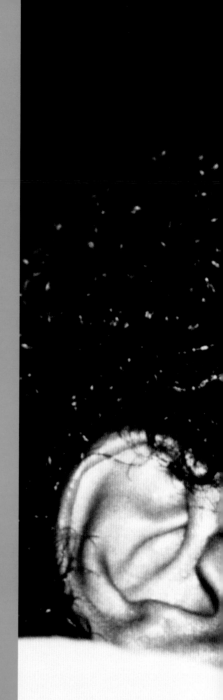

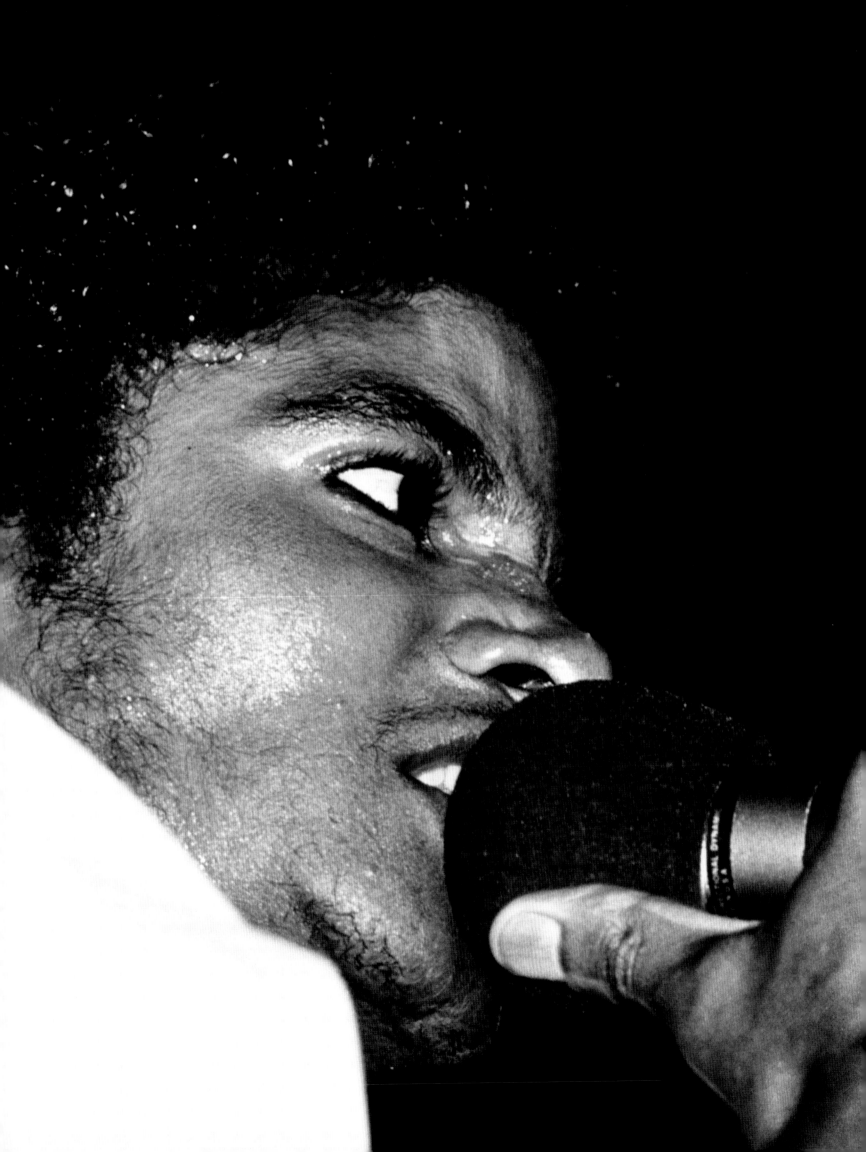

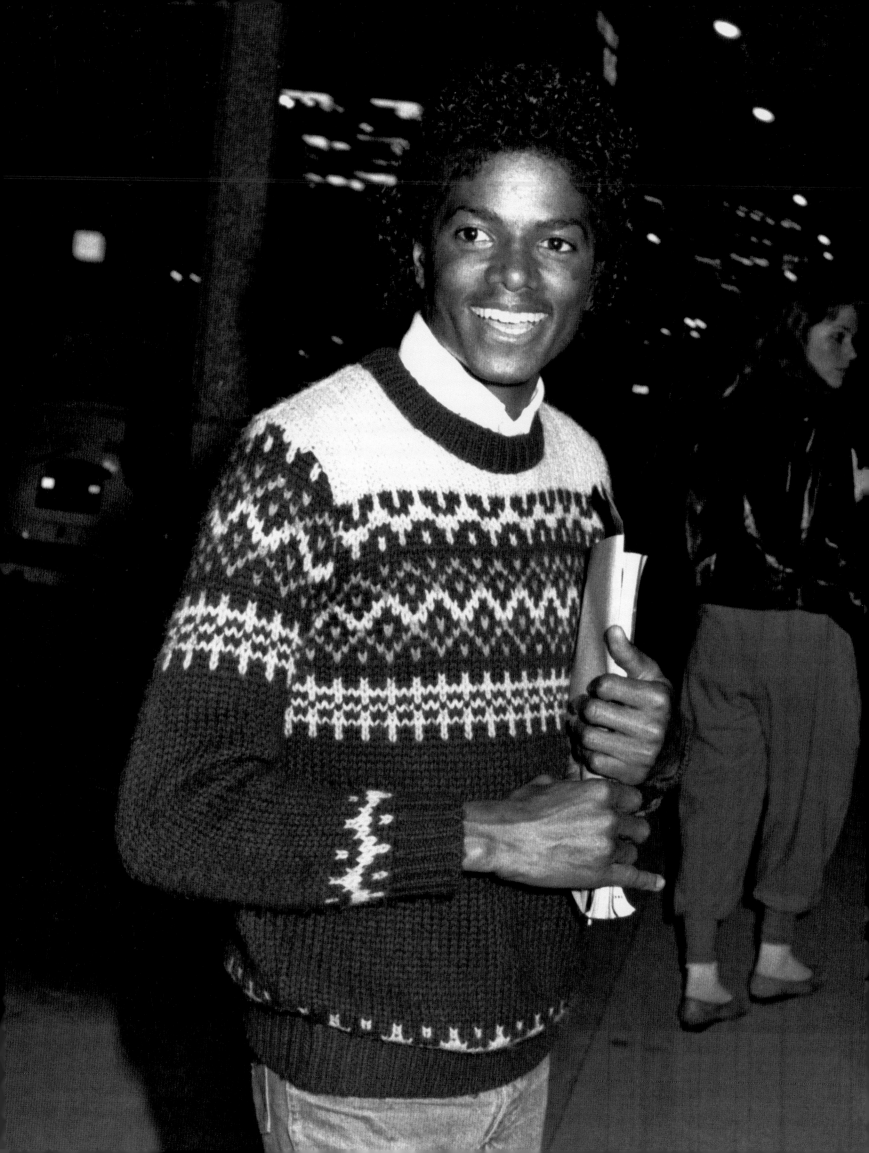

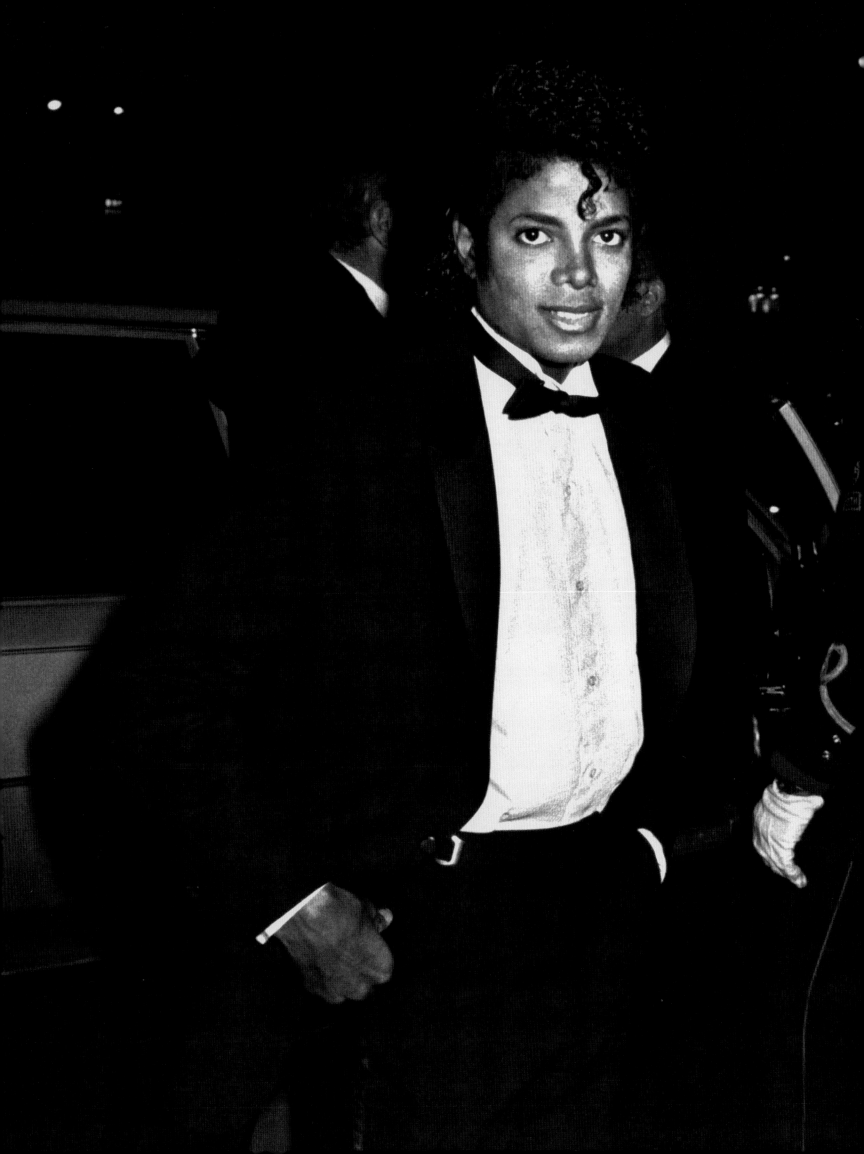

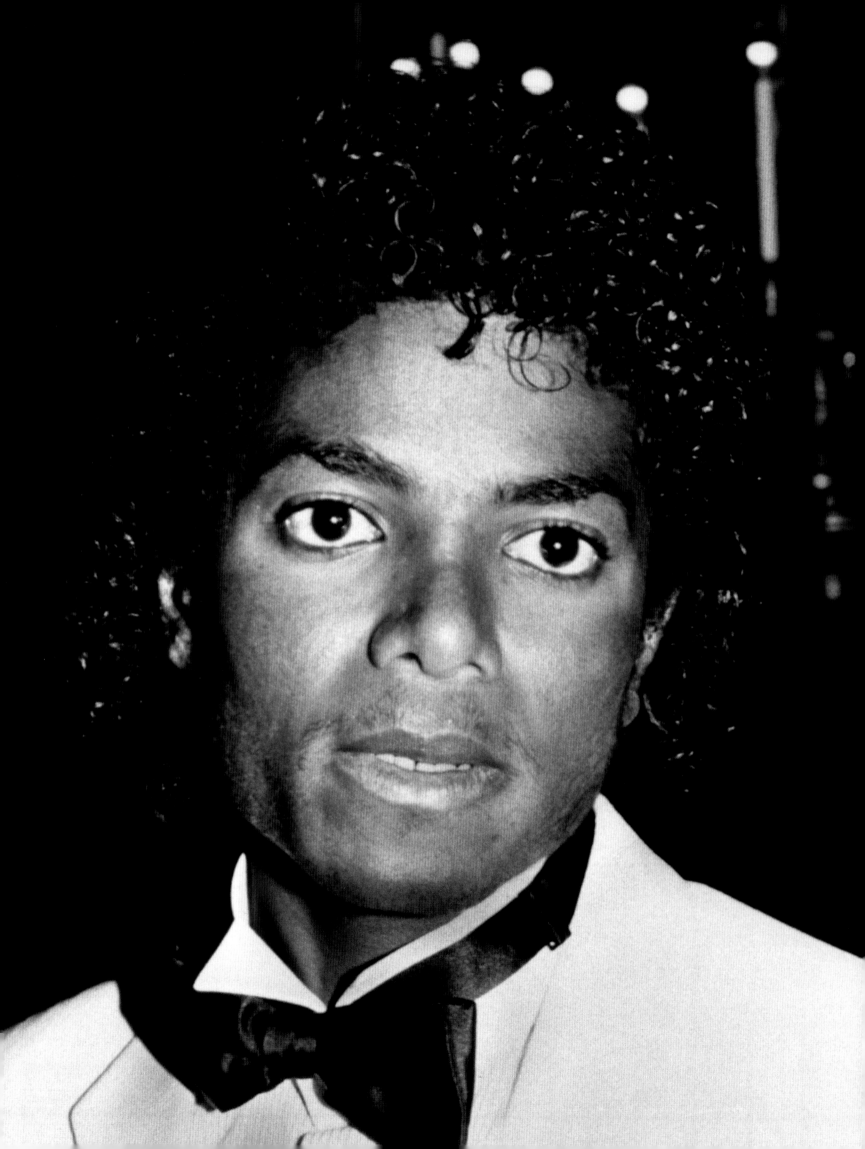

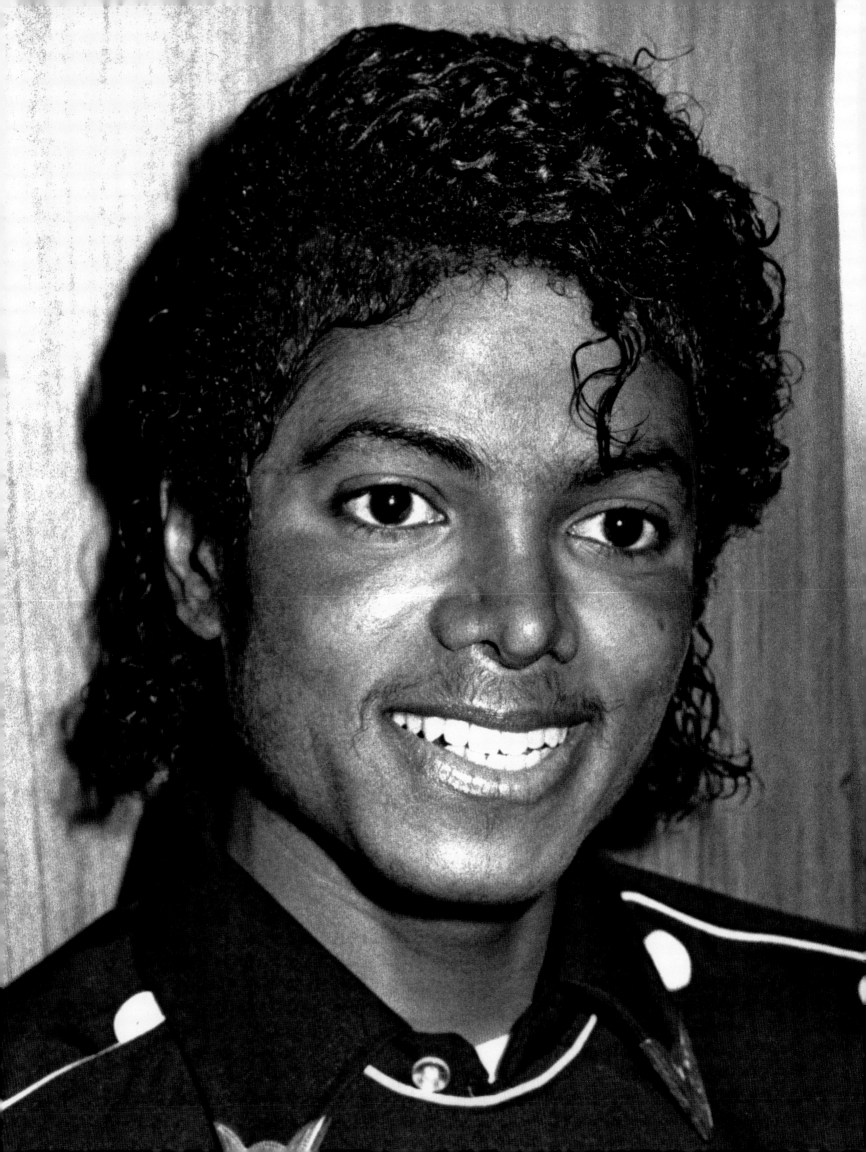

I AM STUNNED. MY FRIEND, MICHAEL JACKSON IS DEAD. HE LIVED WITH ME FOR A WEEK ON THE "GOLDEN POND" SET AFTER *THRILLER*.

Jane Fonda

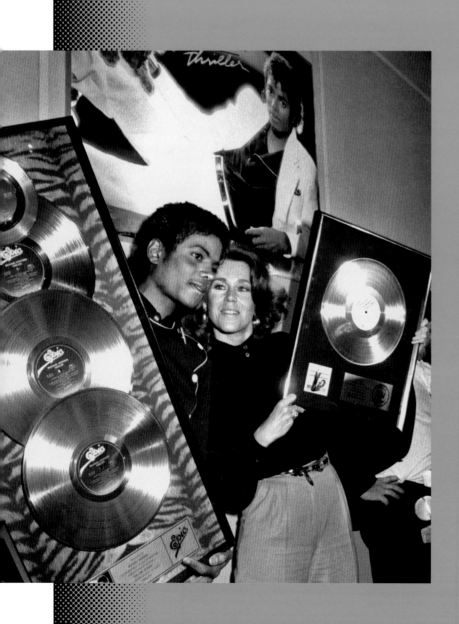

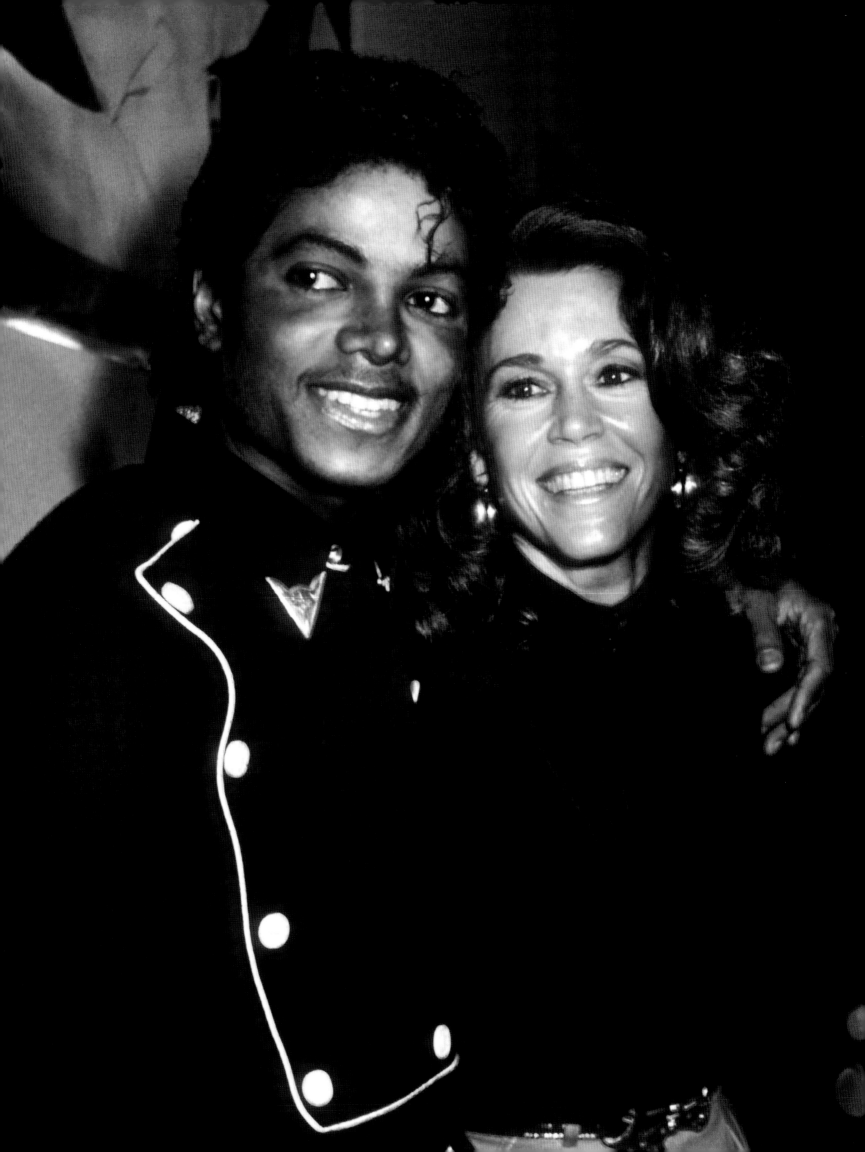

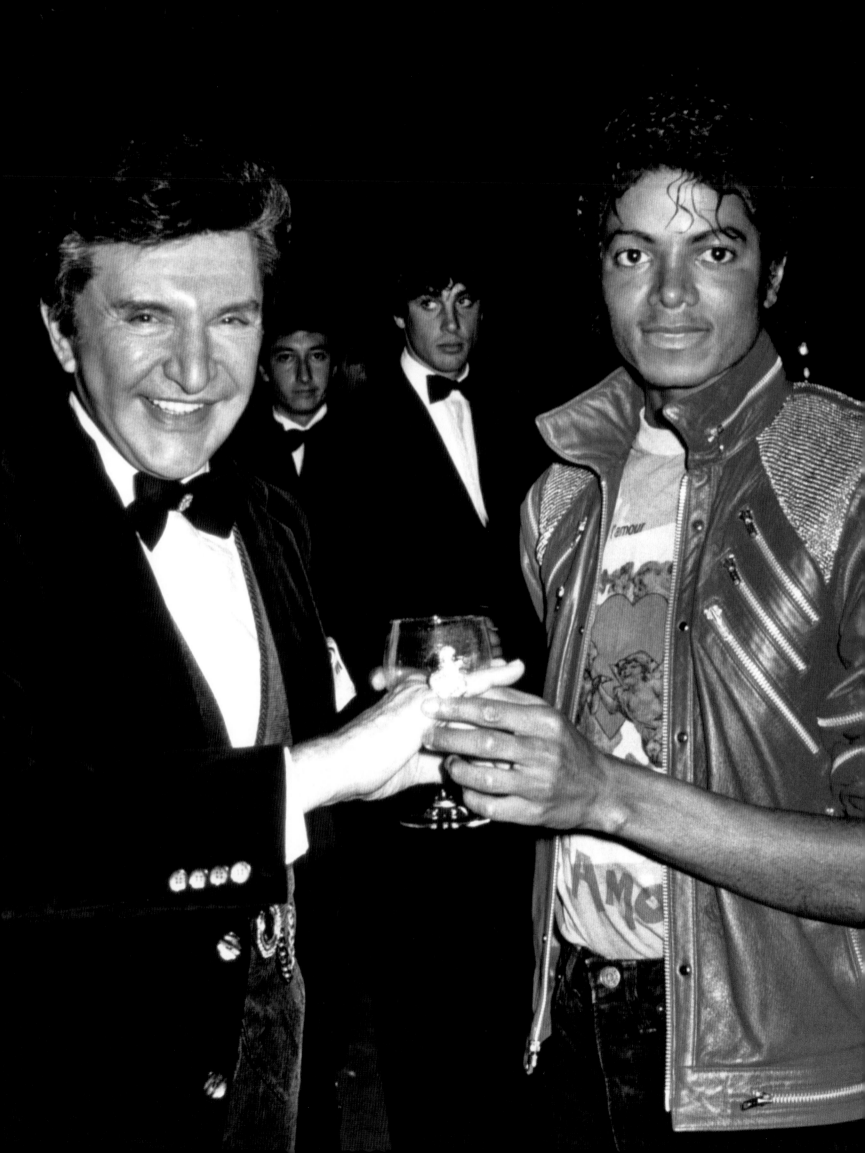

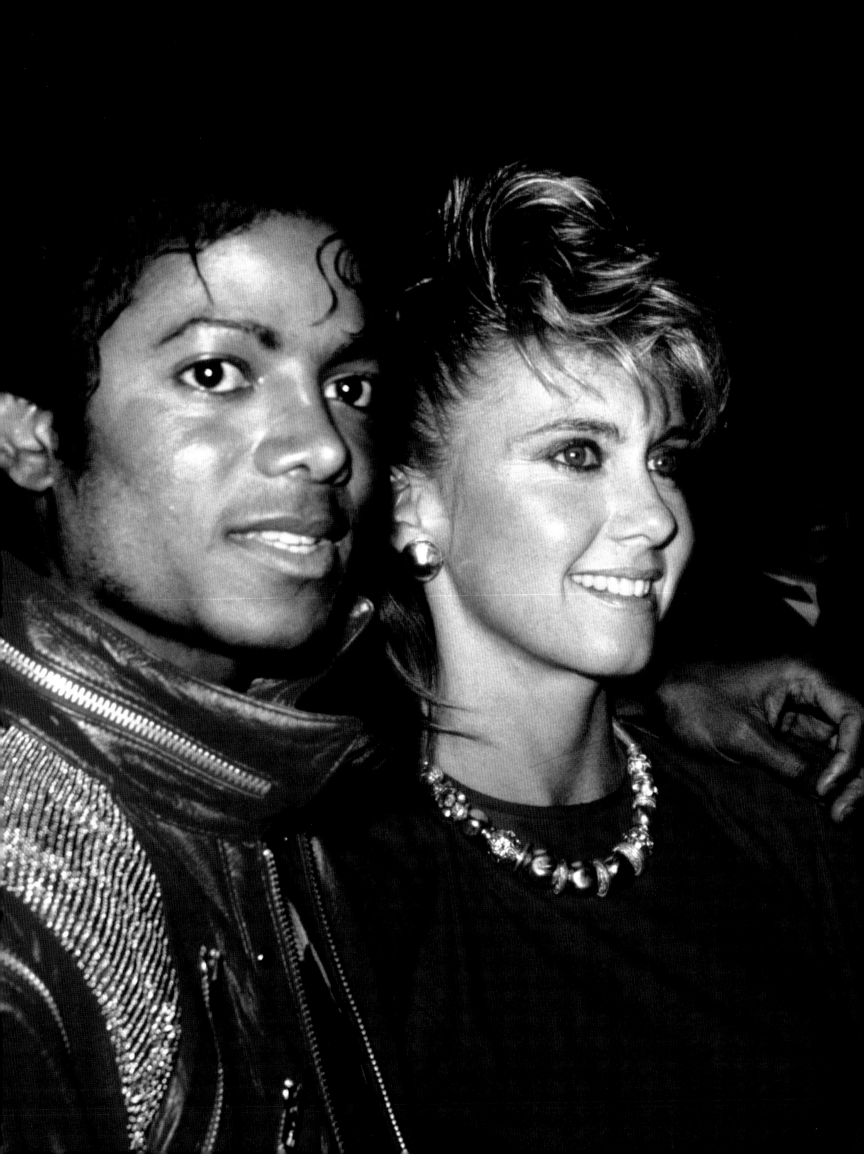

HE WAS A KIND, GENUINE, AND WONDERFUL MAN. HE WAS ALSO ONE OF THE GREATEST ENTERTAINERS THAT EVER LIVED. I LOVED HIM VERY MUCH AND I WILL MISS HIM EVERY REMAINING DAY OF MY LIFE.

Liza Minnelli

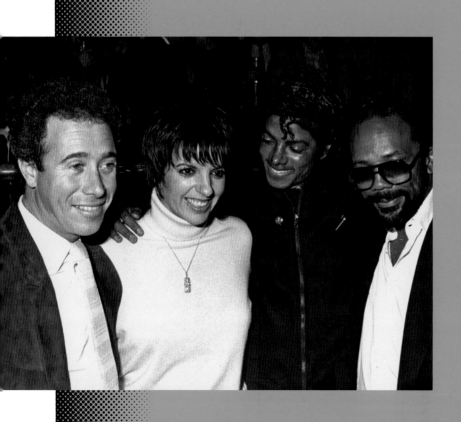

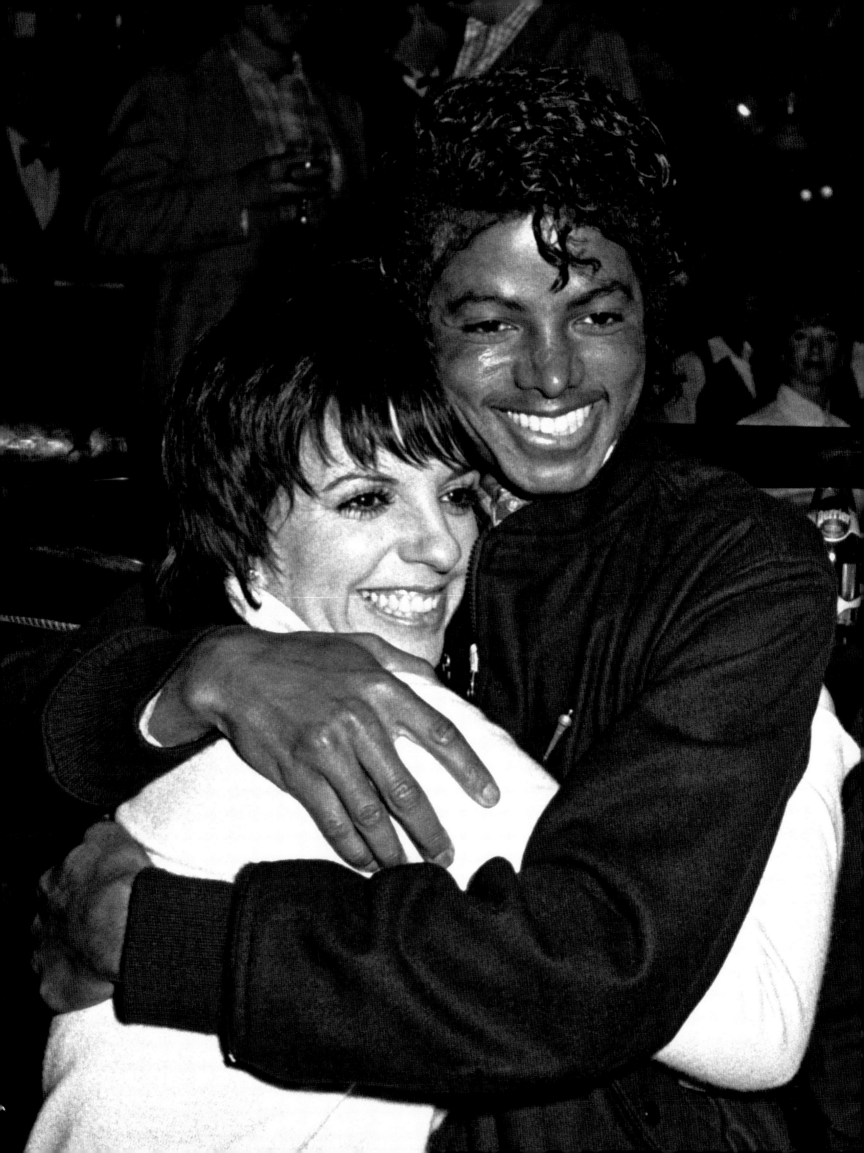

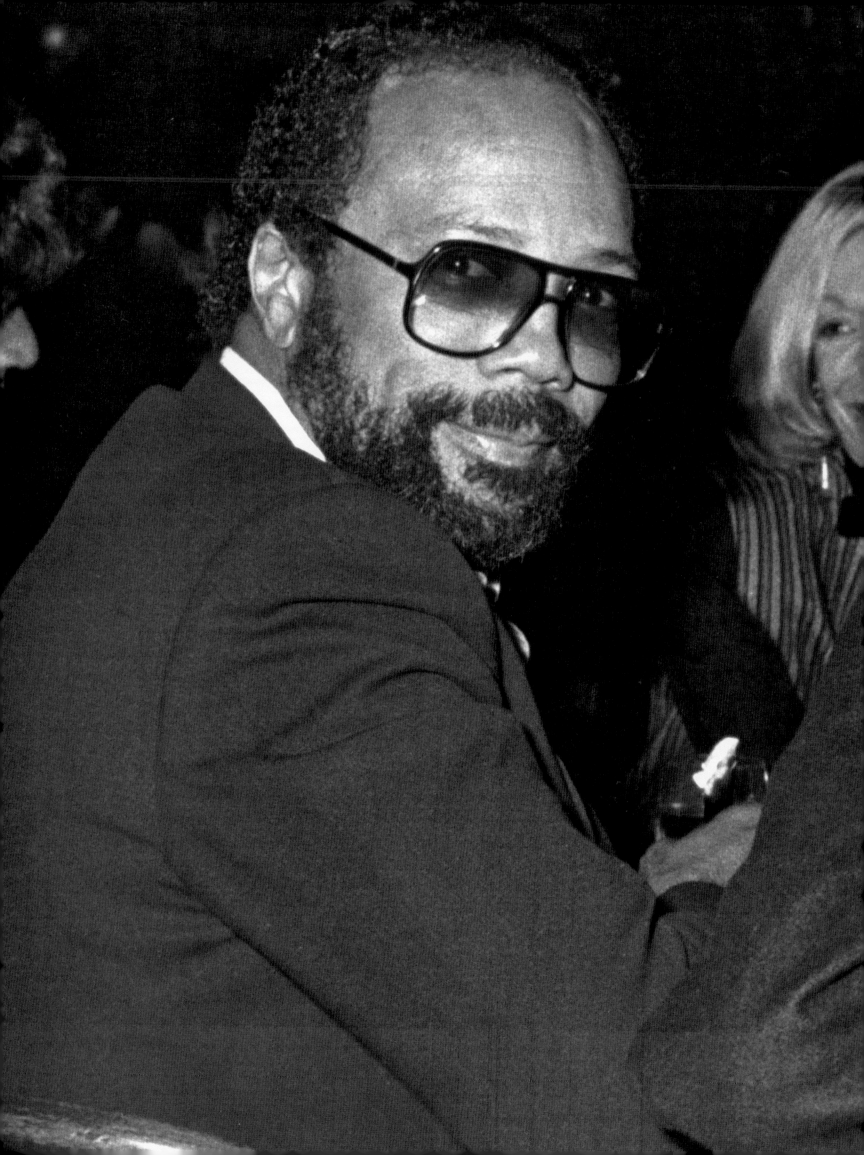

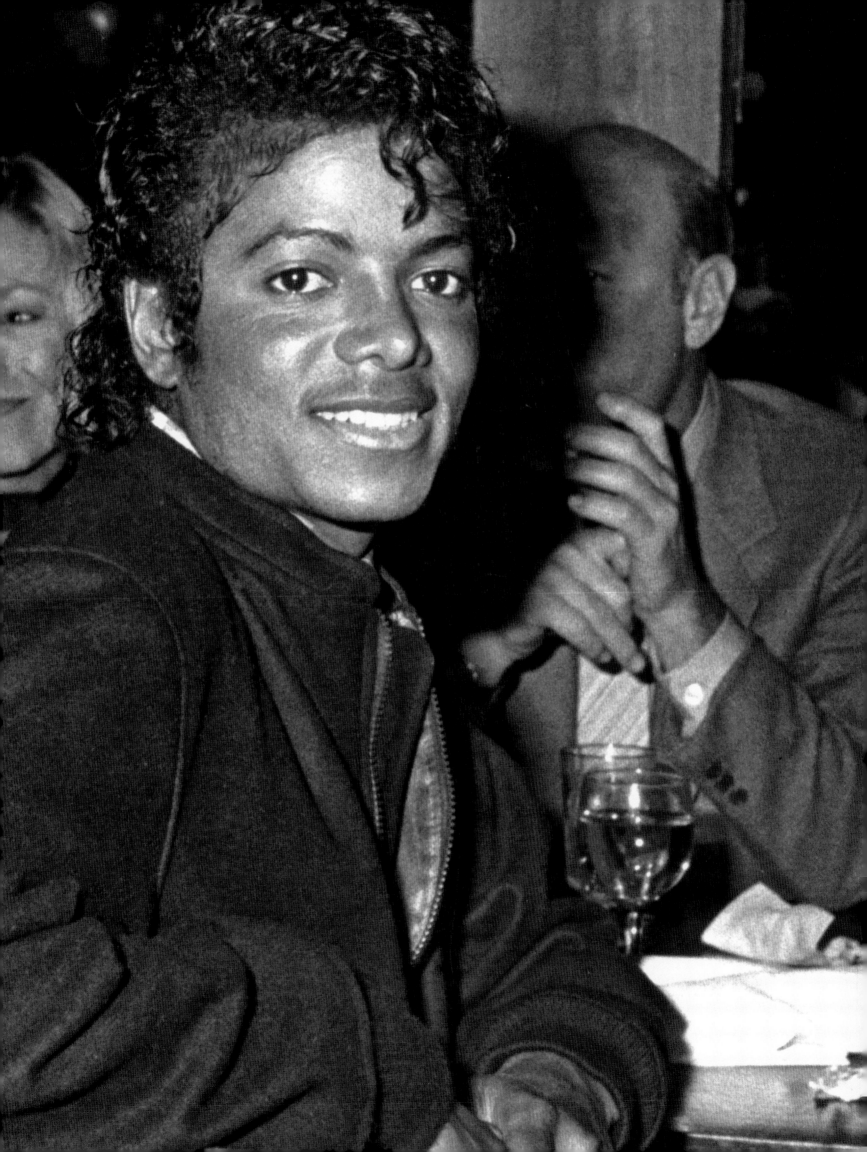

MICHAEL IS THE BEST FRIEND YOU COULD EVER HAVE. HE'S GENTLE, NOT ROUGH LIKE OTHER GUYS. I CAN COUNT ON HIM ANY TIME, AND HE CAN COUNT ON ME.

Emmanuel Lewis

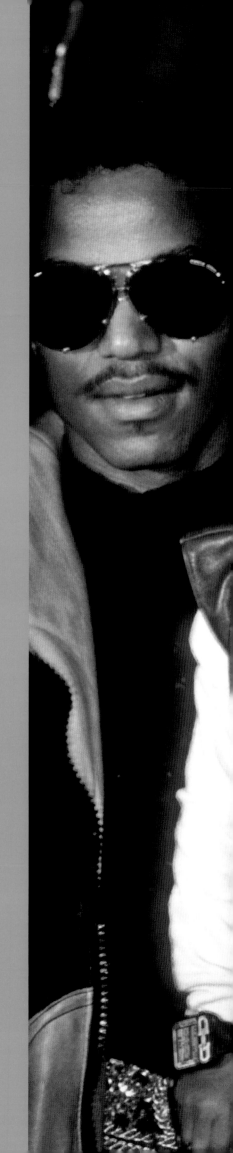

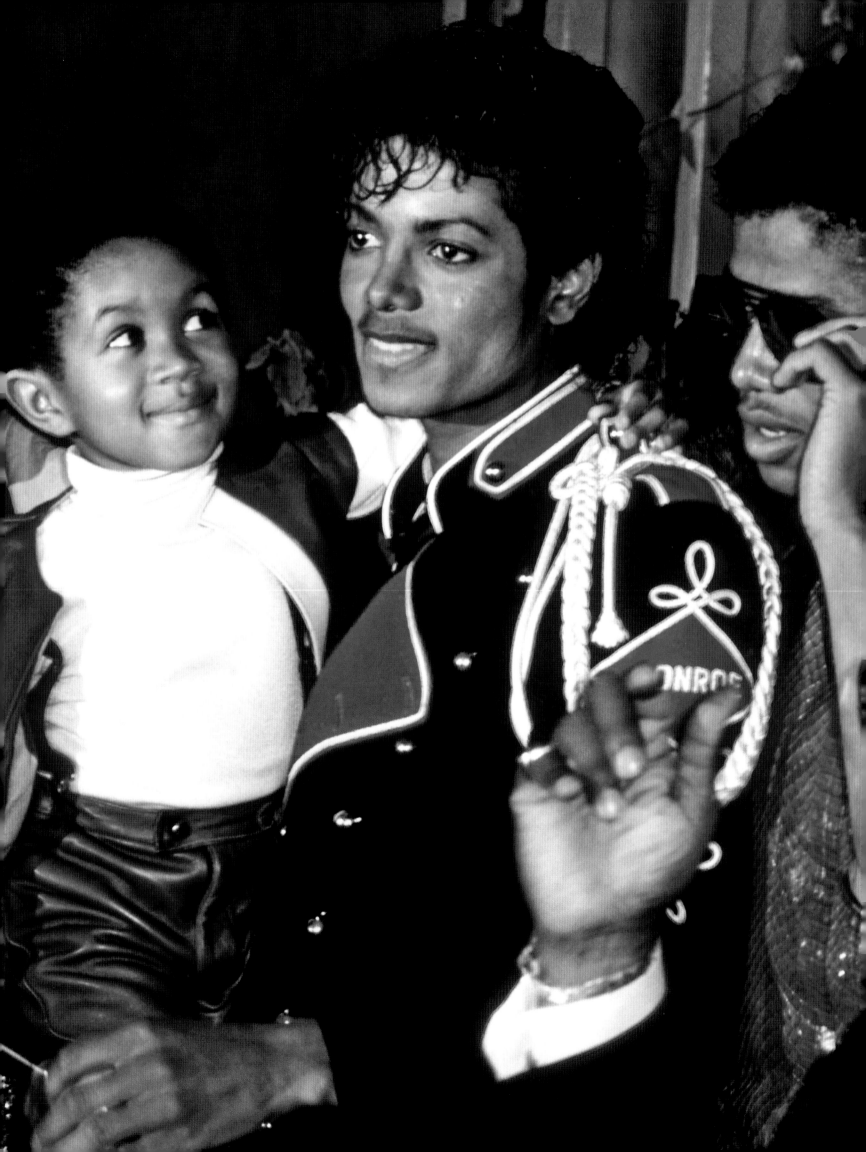

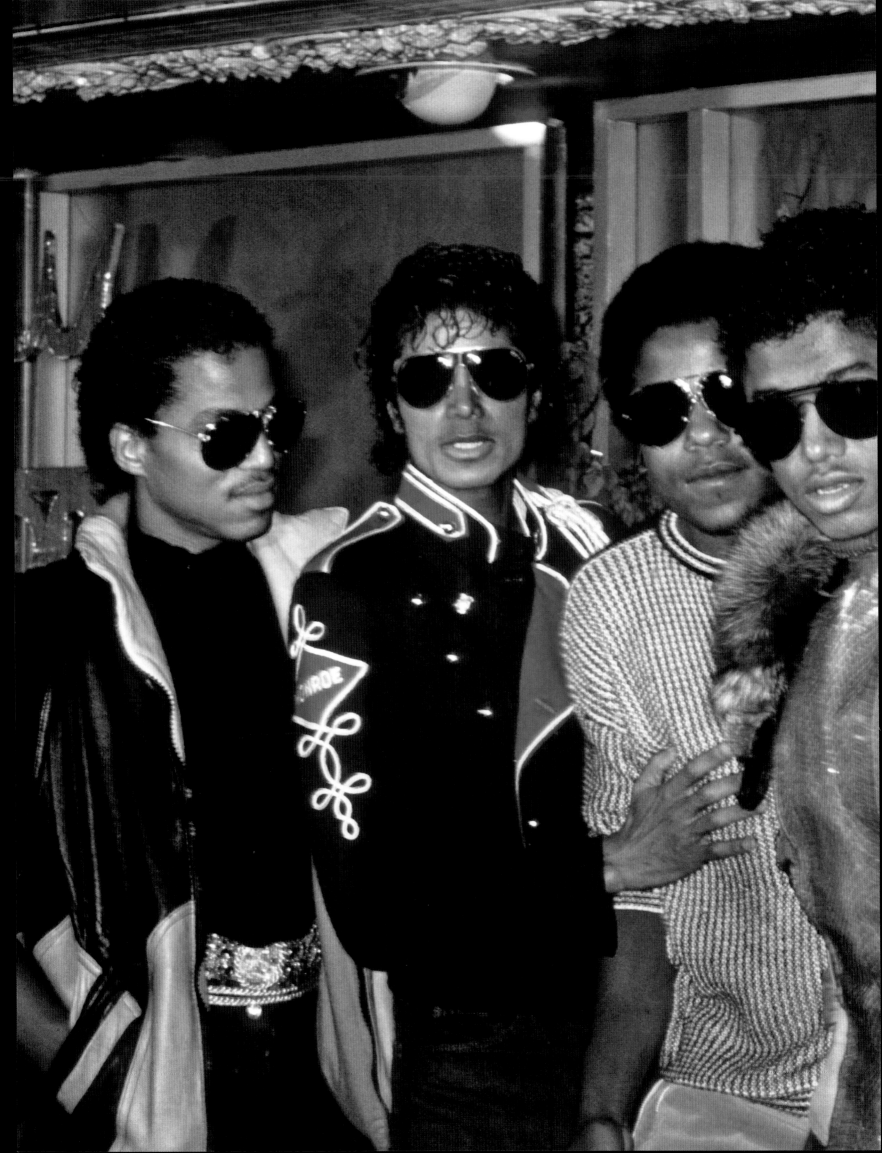

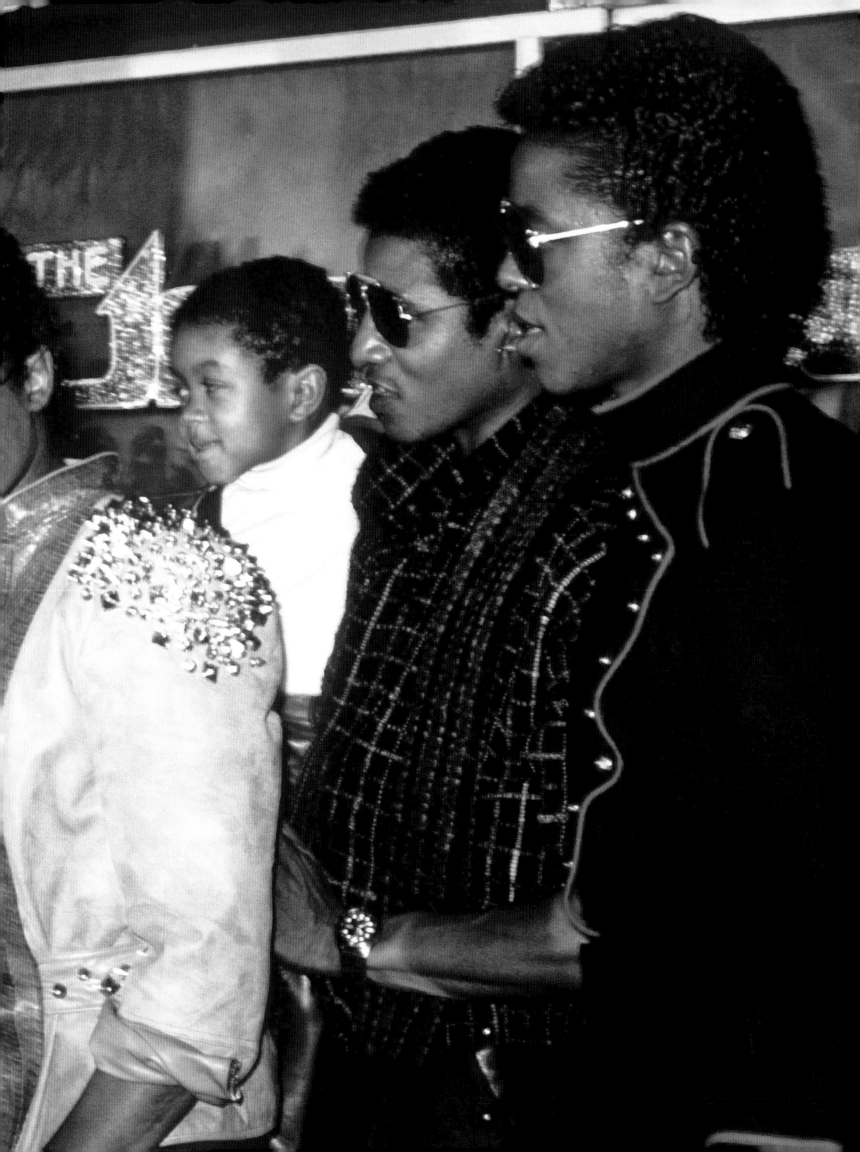

THERE WAS AN IDENTIFICATION BETWEEN MICHAEL JACKSON AND I. I WAS OLDER. HE KIND OF IDOLIZED ME, AND HE WANTED TO SING LIKE ME.

Diana Ross

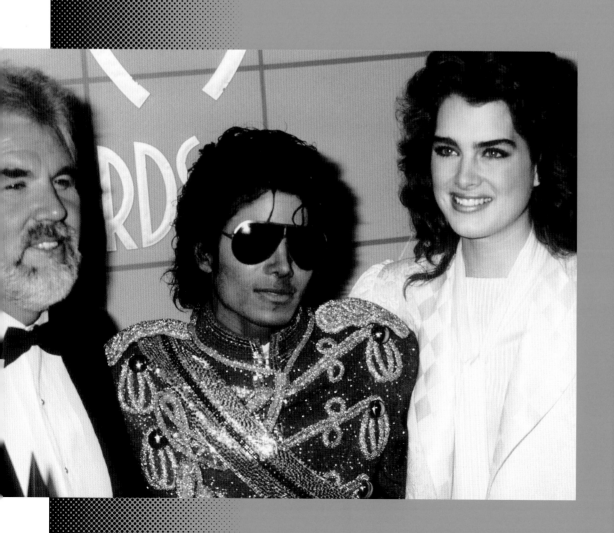

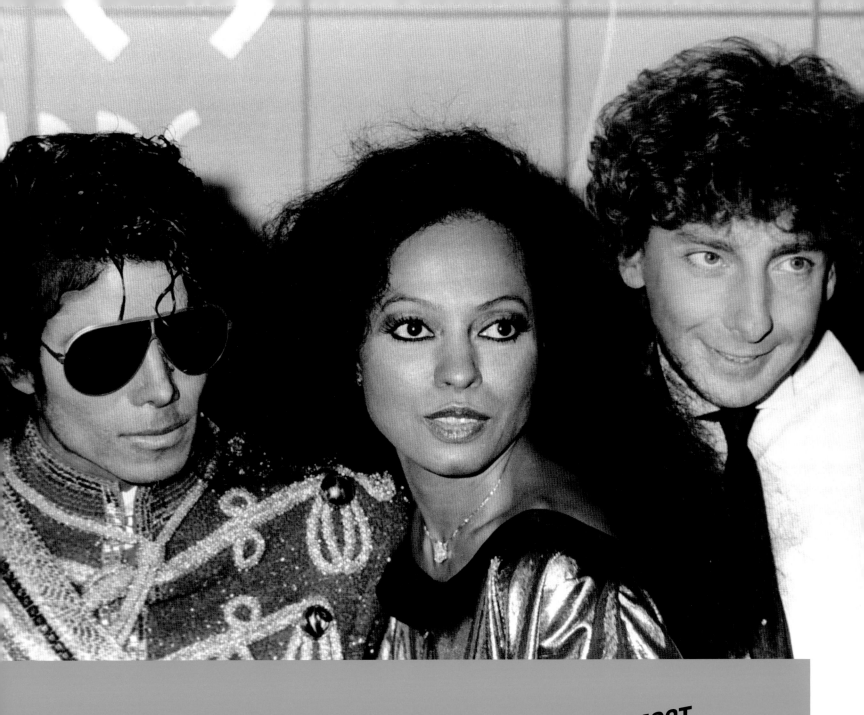

HE WAS ONE OF THE MOST GIFTED AND ORIGINAL TALENTS THE WORLD HAS EVER KNOWN. HE INSPIRED A GENERATION OF YOUNG PEOPLE AND AMAZED THE REST OF THE WORLD. THERE WILL NEVER BE ANOTHER MICHAEL JACKSON.

Barry Manilow

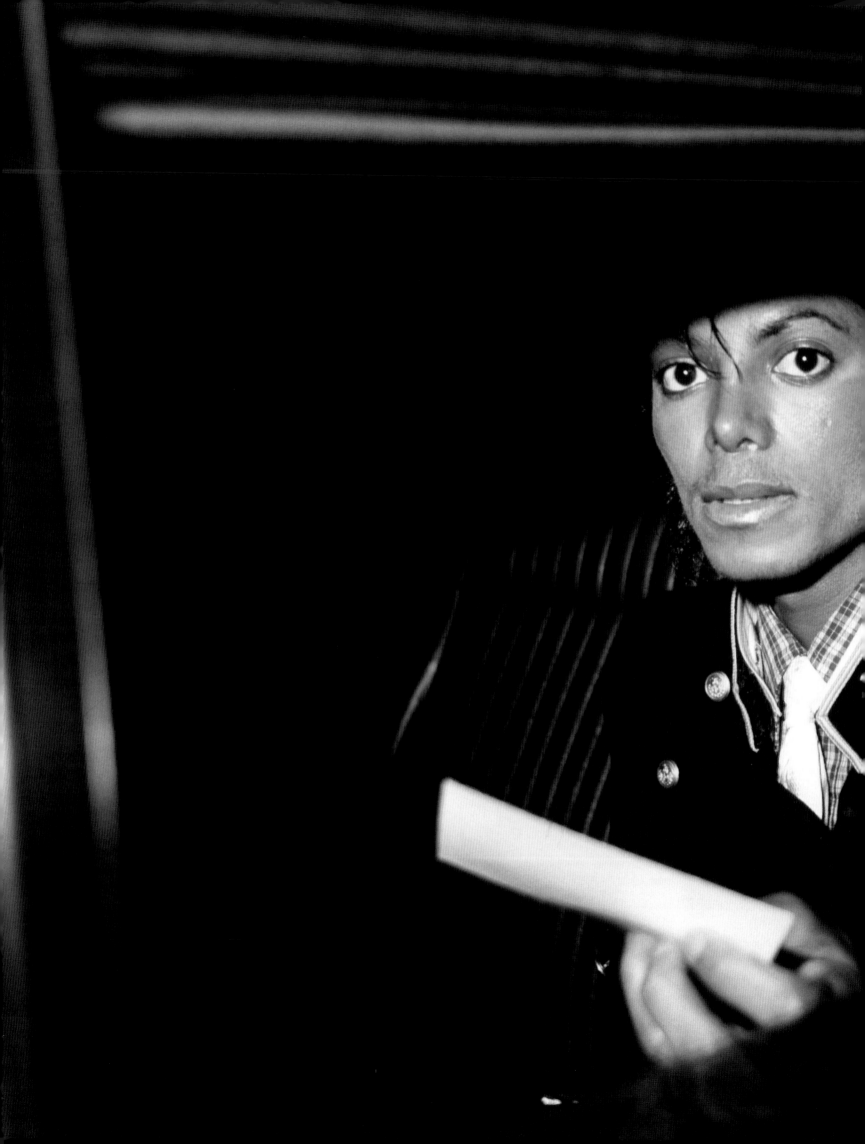

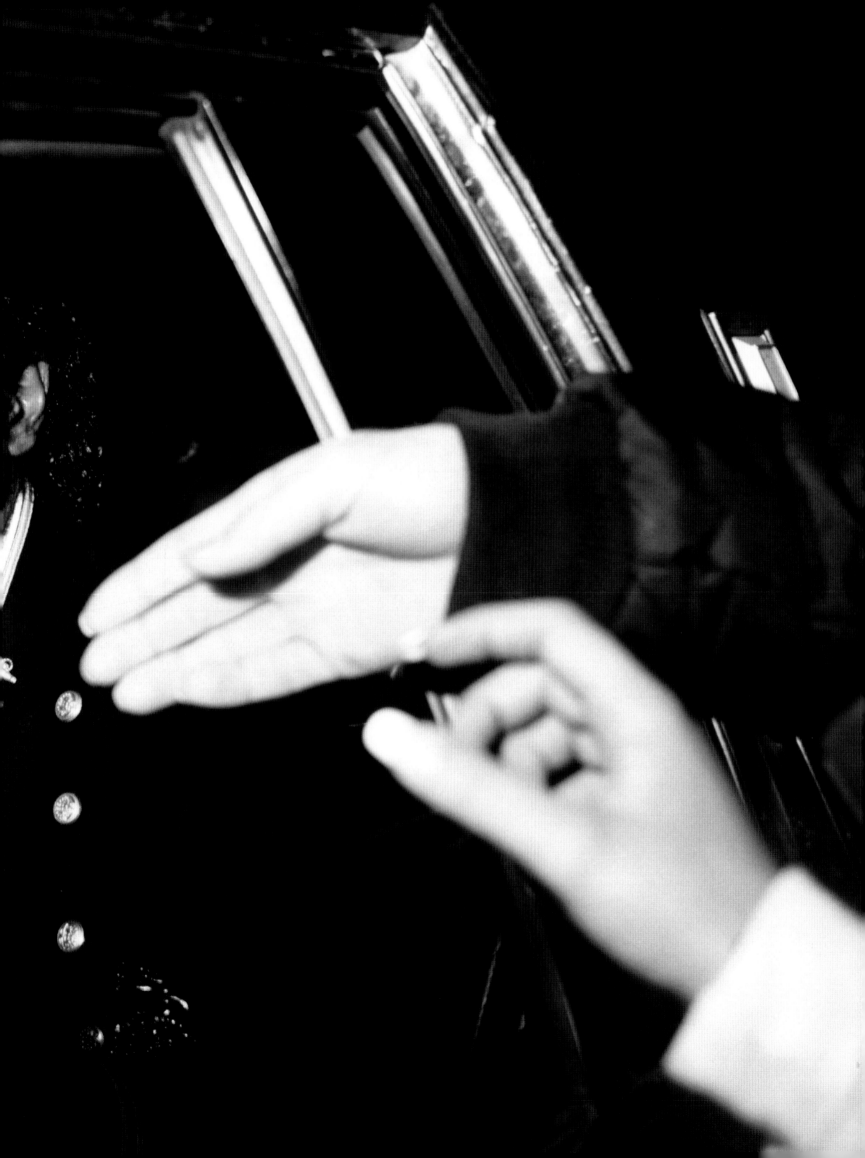

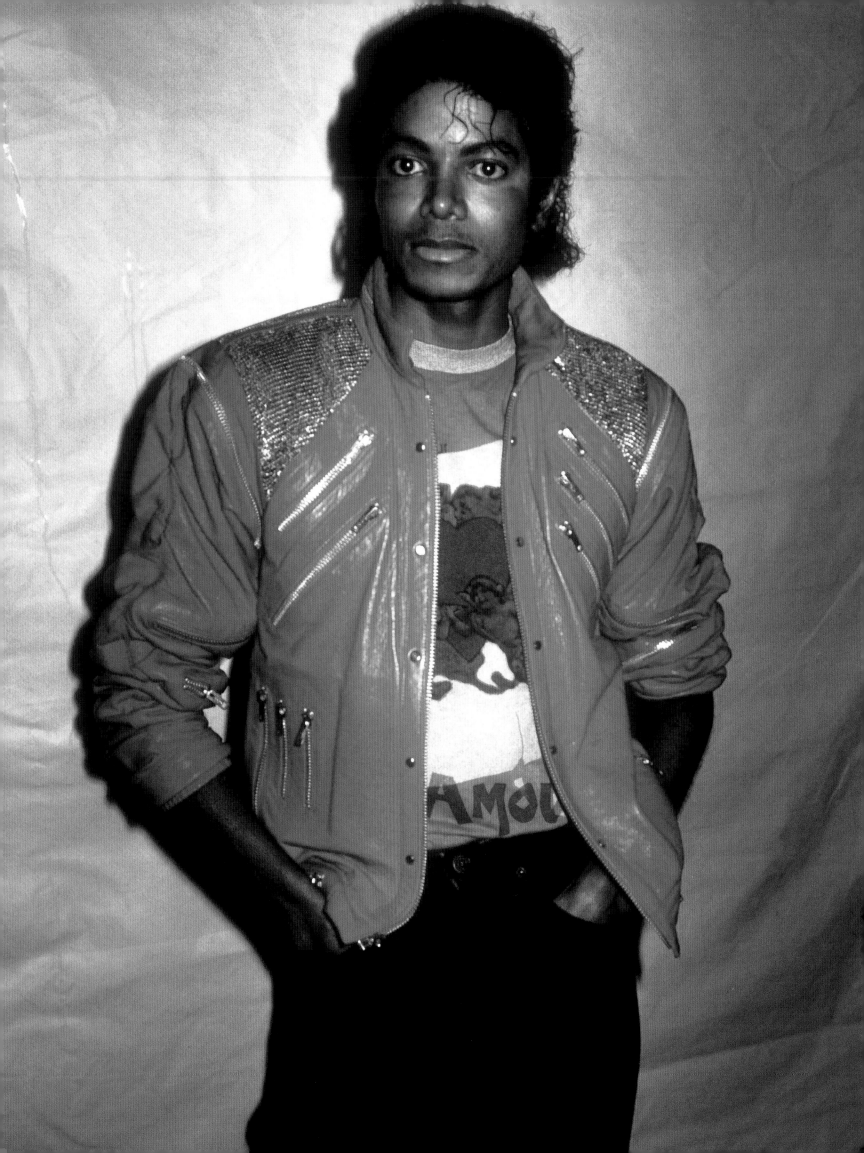

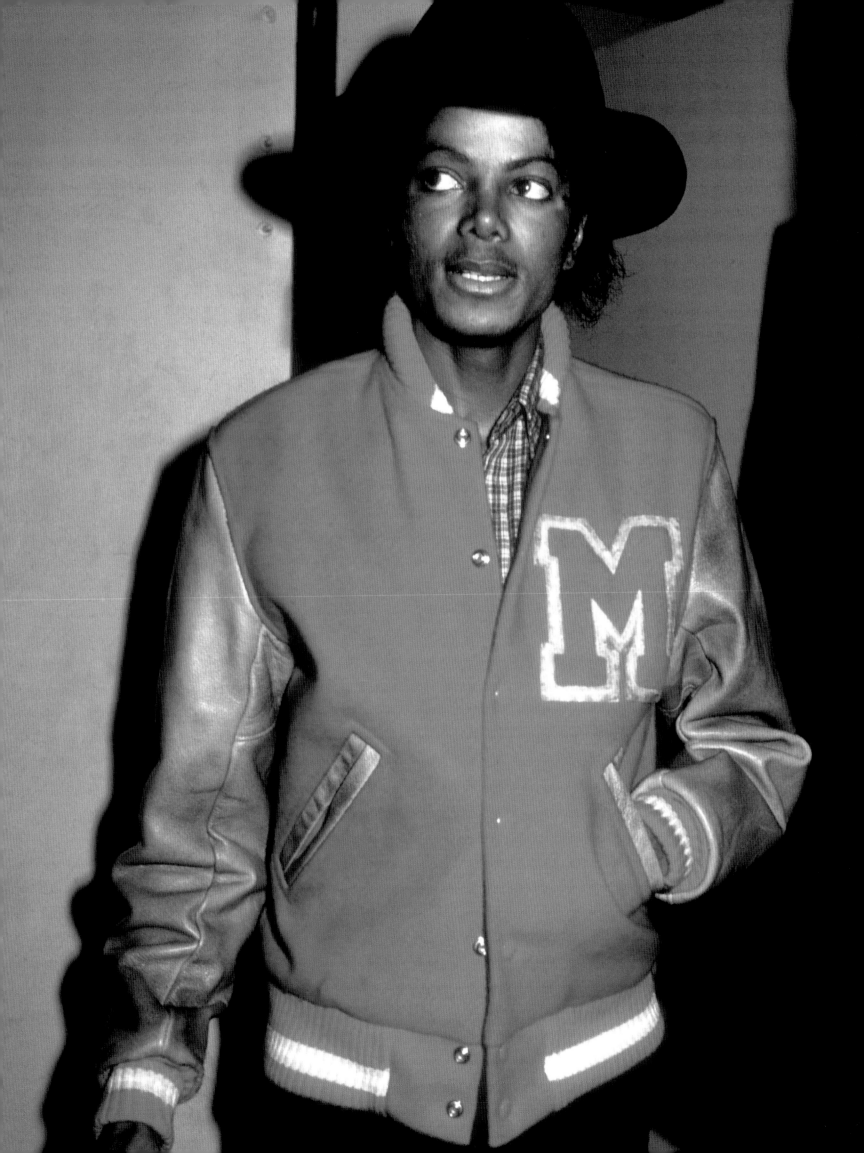

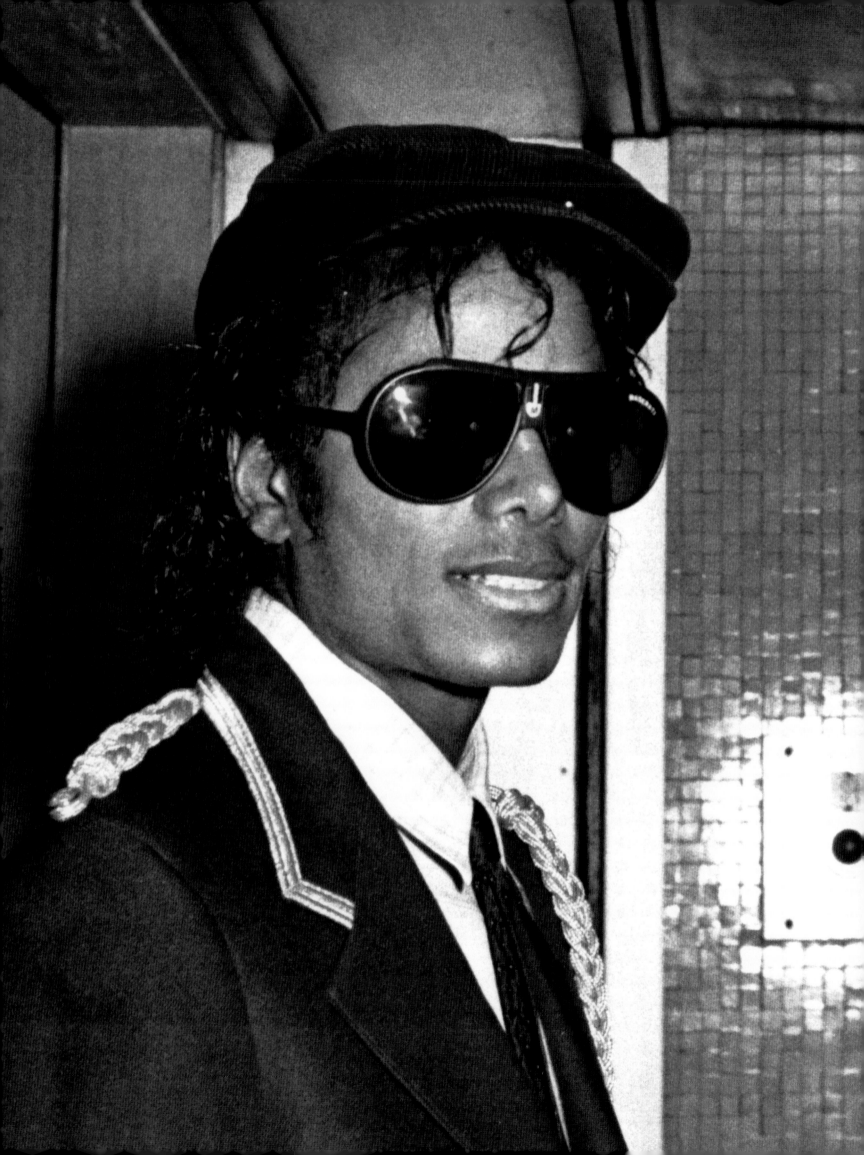

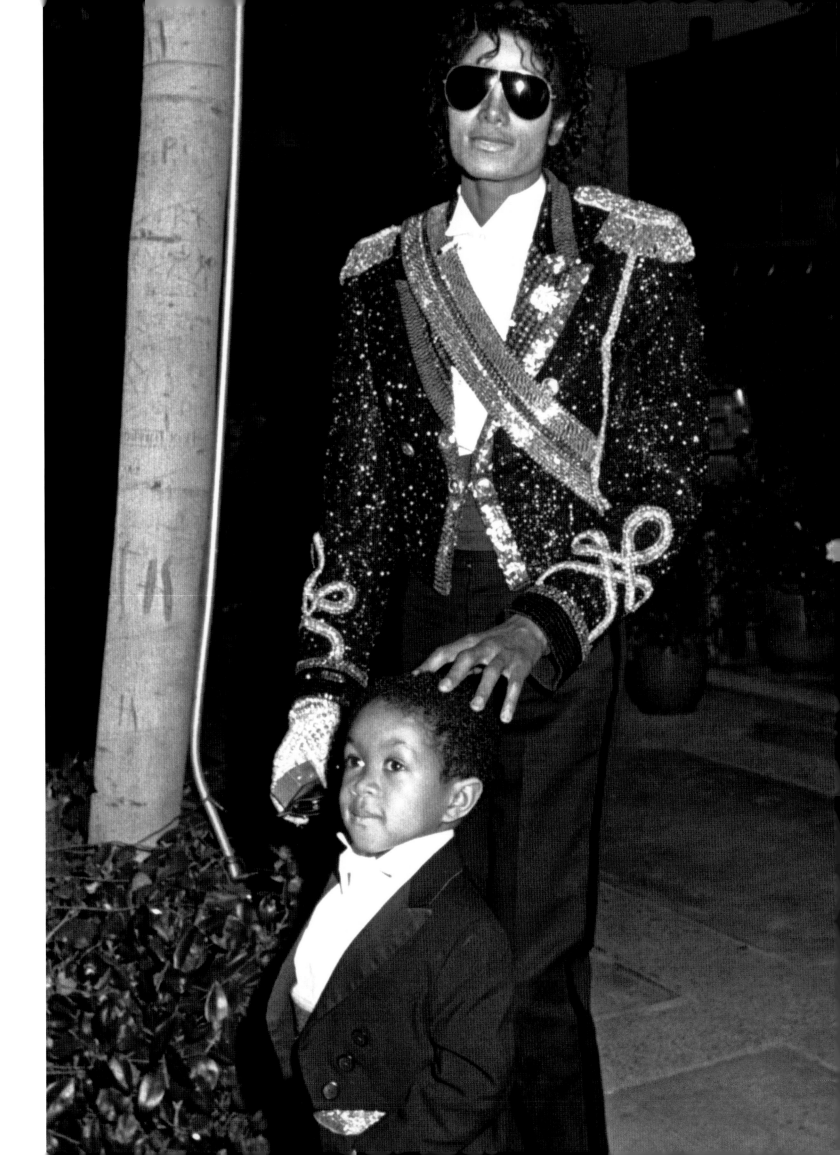

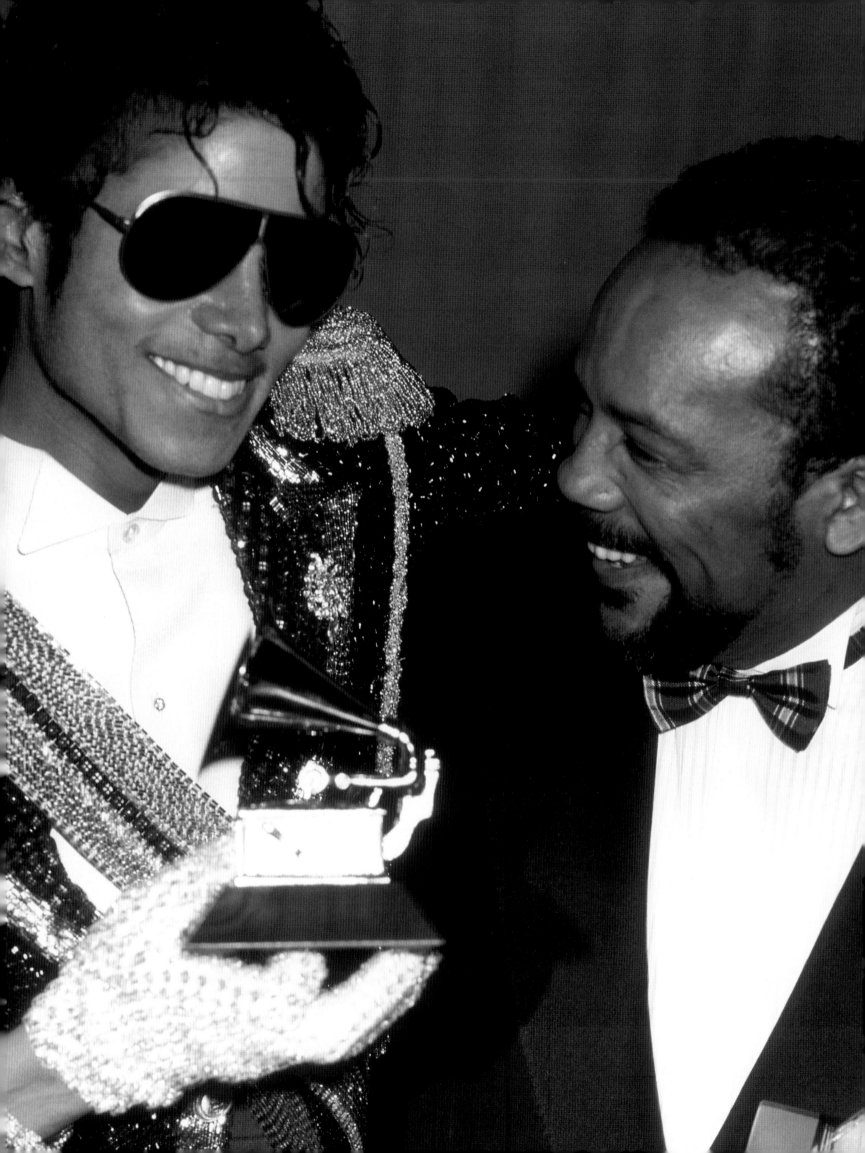

MICHAEL'S A TRUTH MACHINE.
HE'S GOT A BALANCE BETWEEN
THE WISDOM OF A 60-YEAR-
OLD AND THE ENTHUSIASM OF
A CHILD.
Quincy Jones

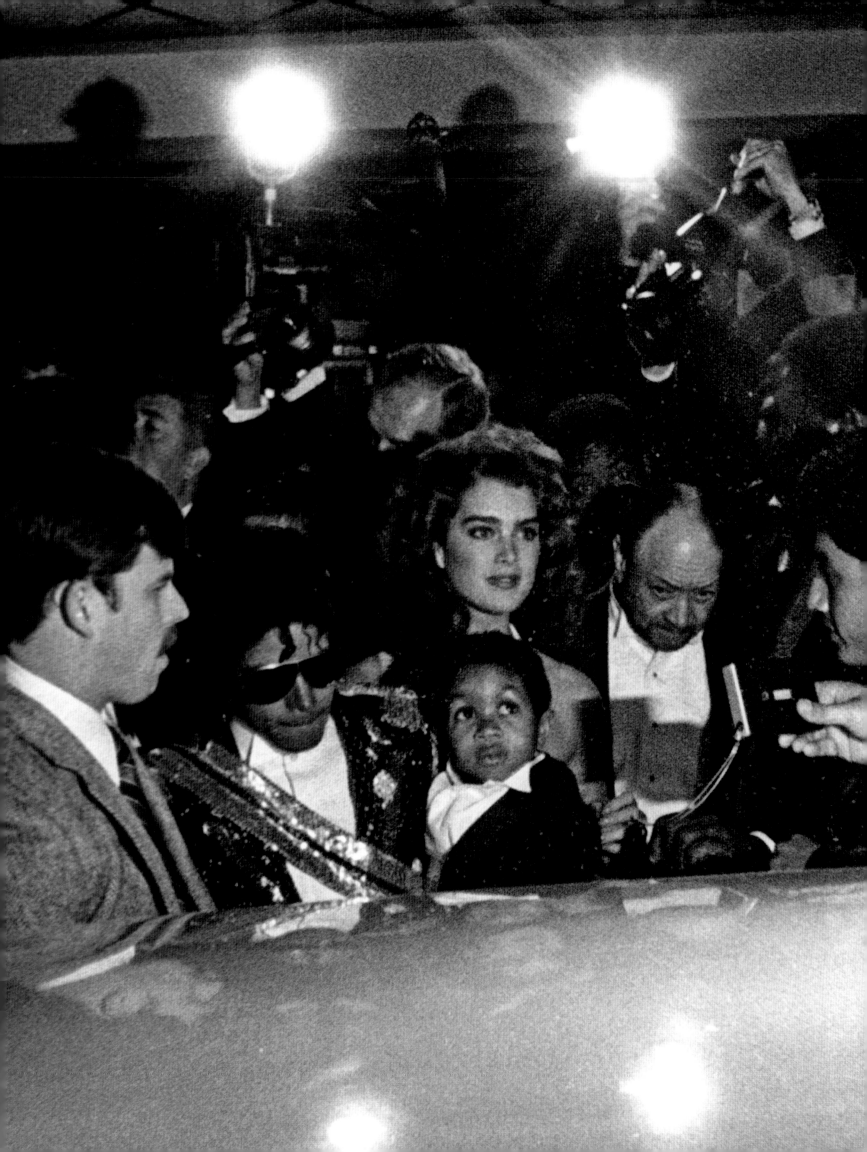

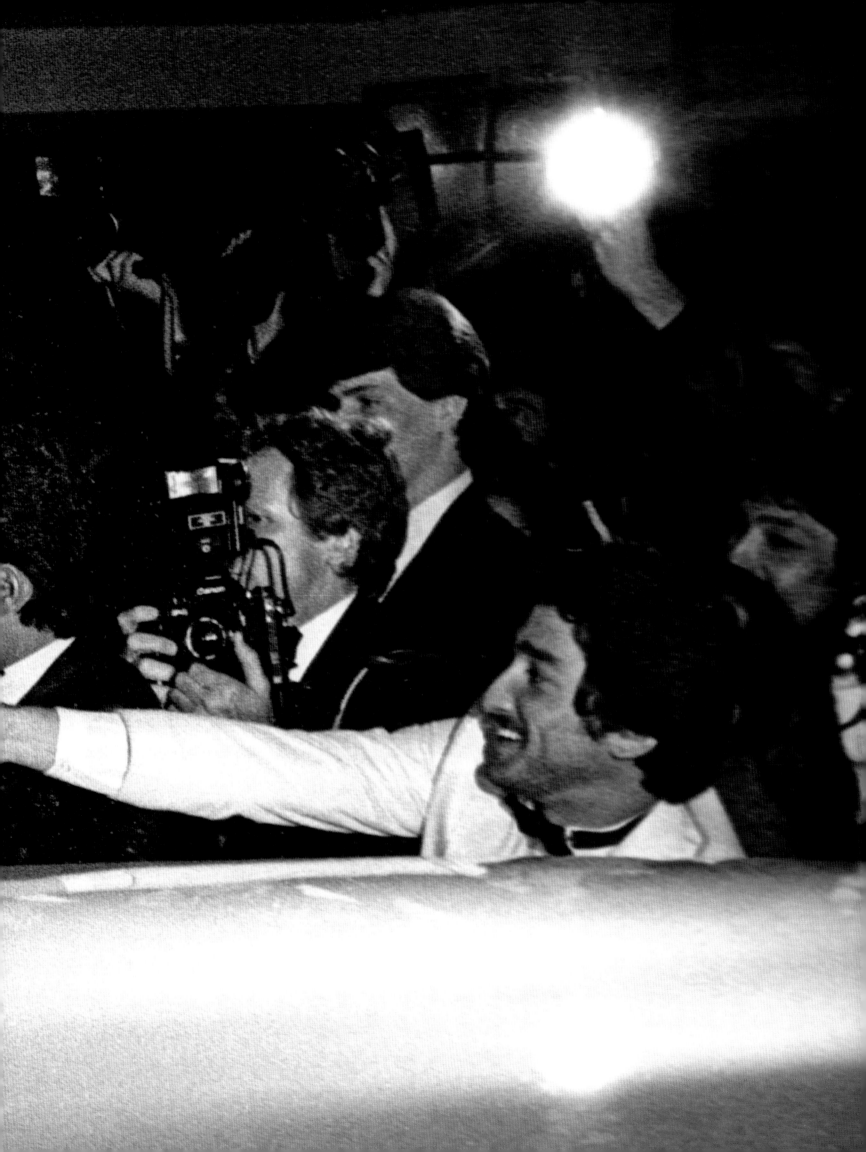

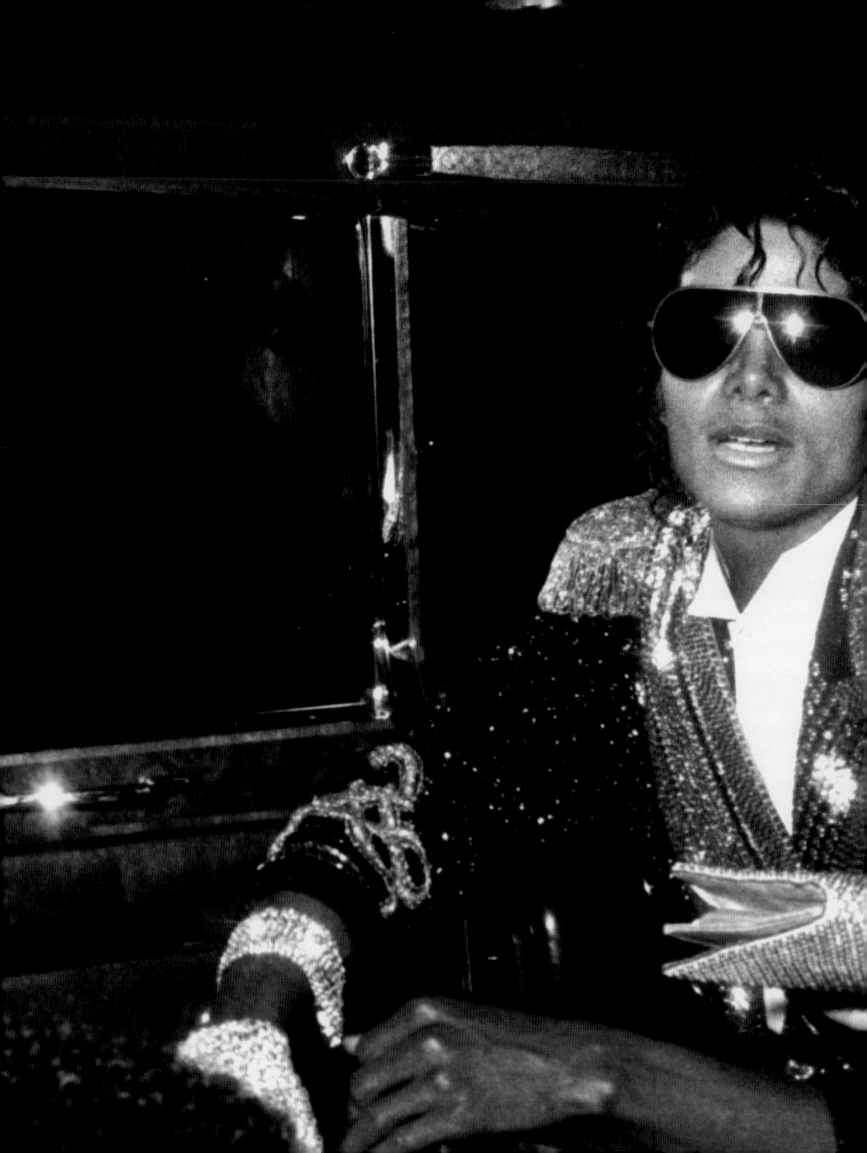

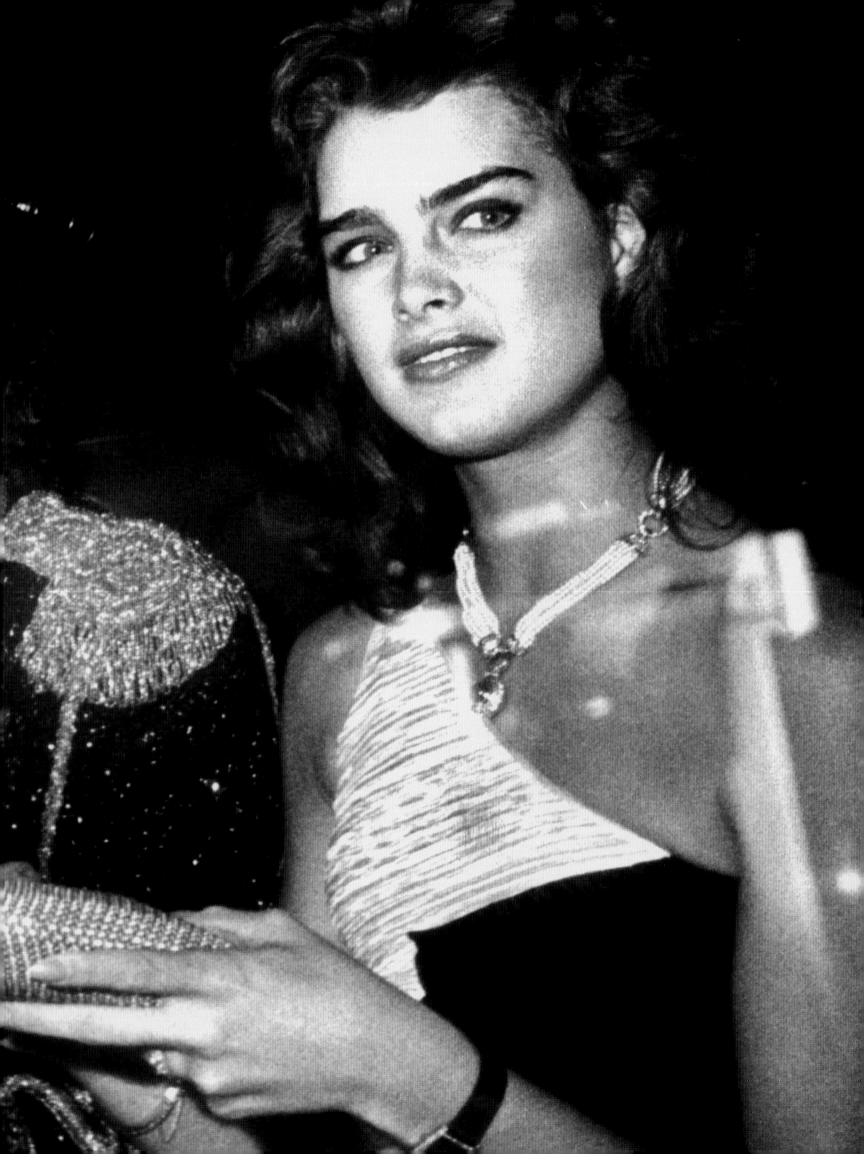

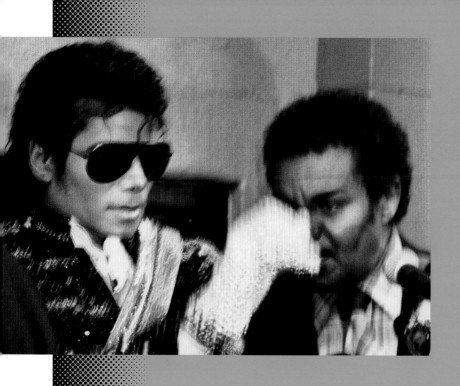

THERE'S A LOT OF SADNESS ABOUT MY PAST AND ADOLESCENCE, ABOUT MY FATHER AND ALL OF THOSE THINGS... HE WAS VERY STRICT, VERY HARD, VERY STERN. JUST A LOOK WOULD SCARE YOU.

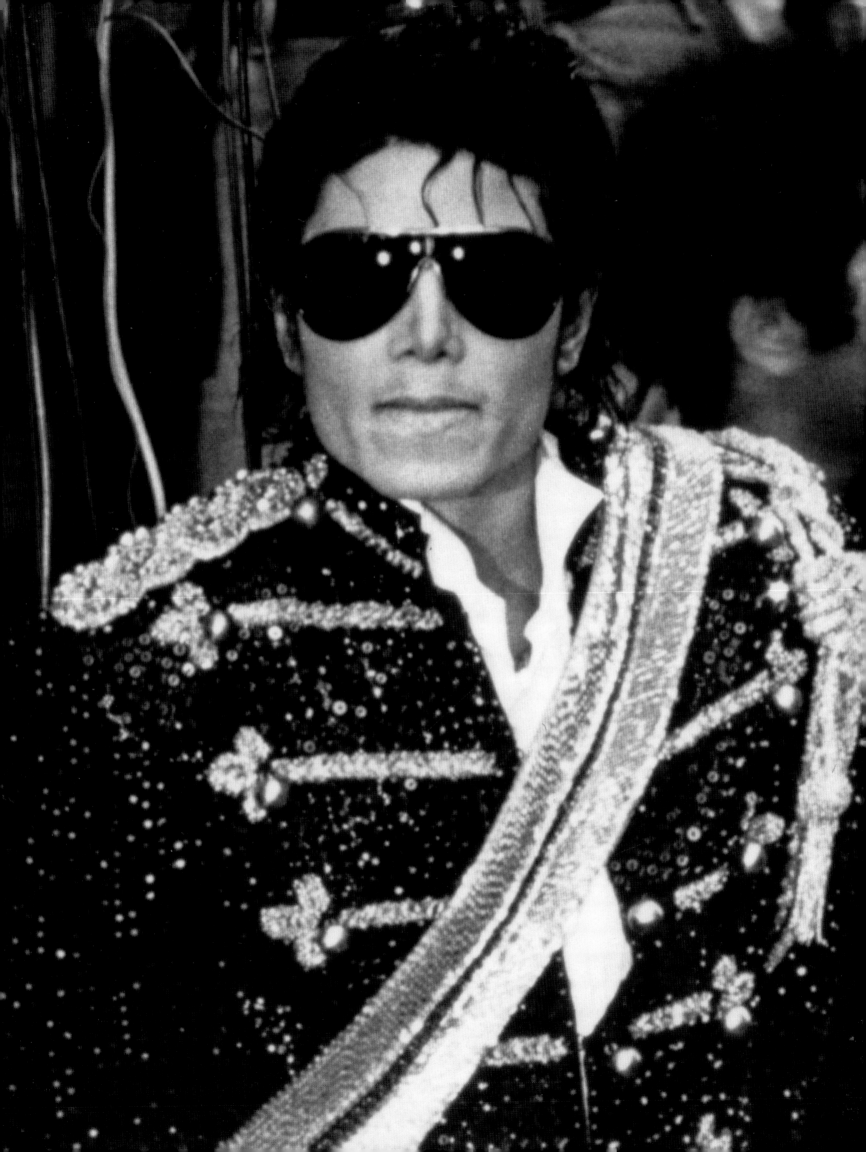

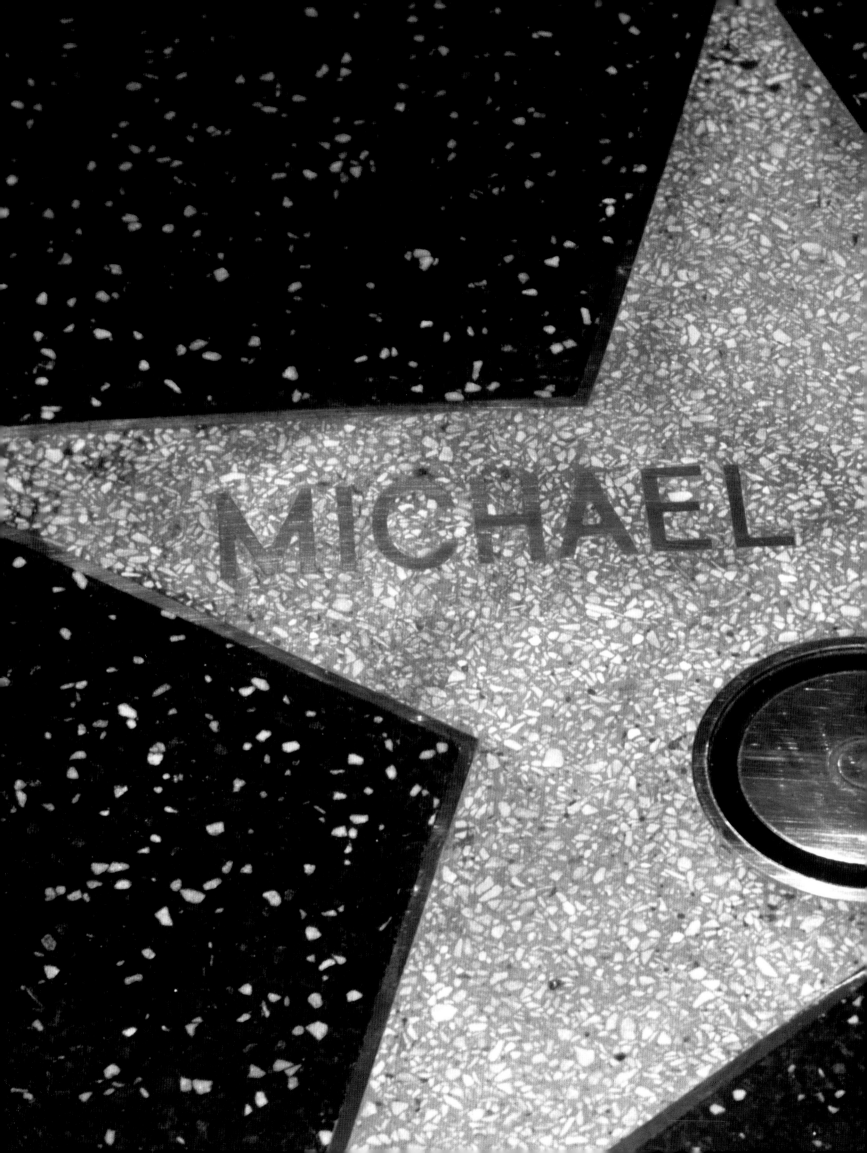

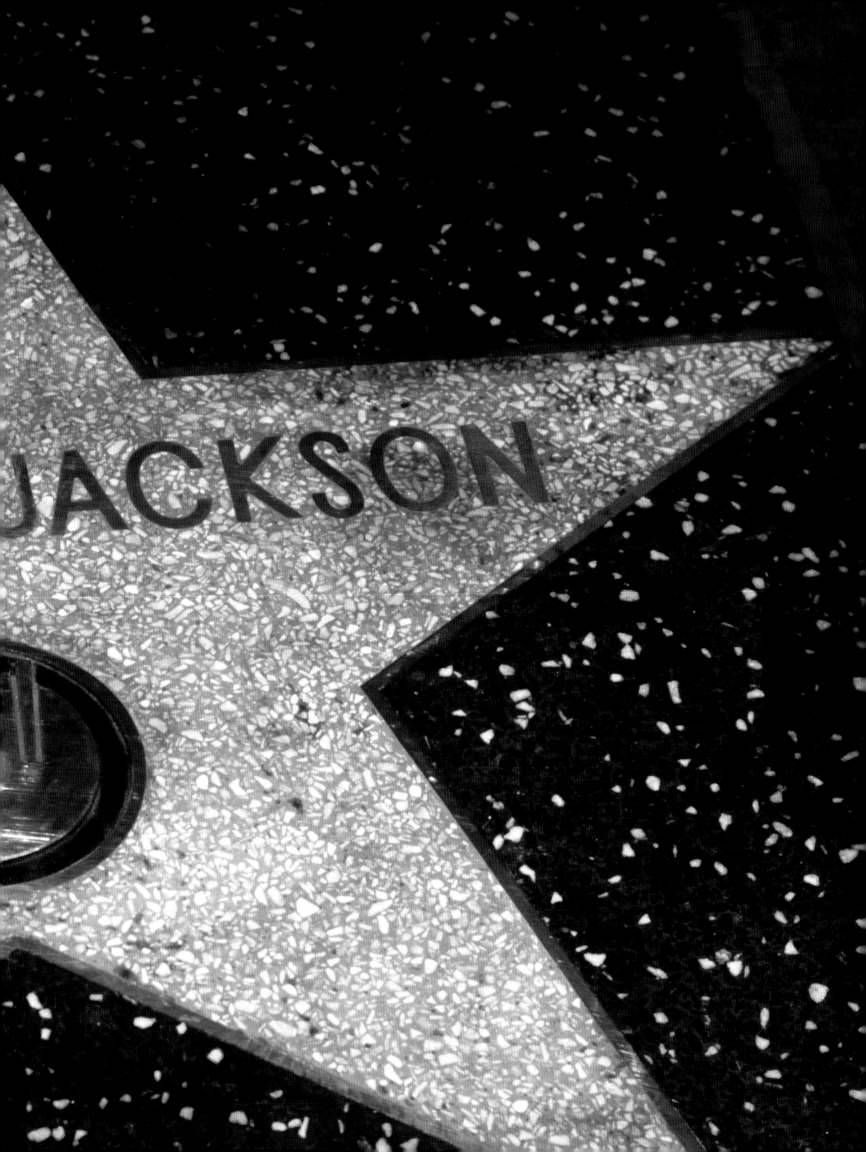

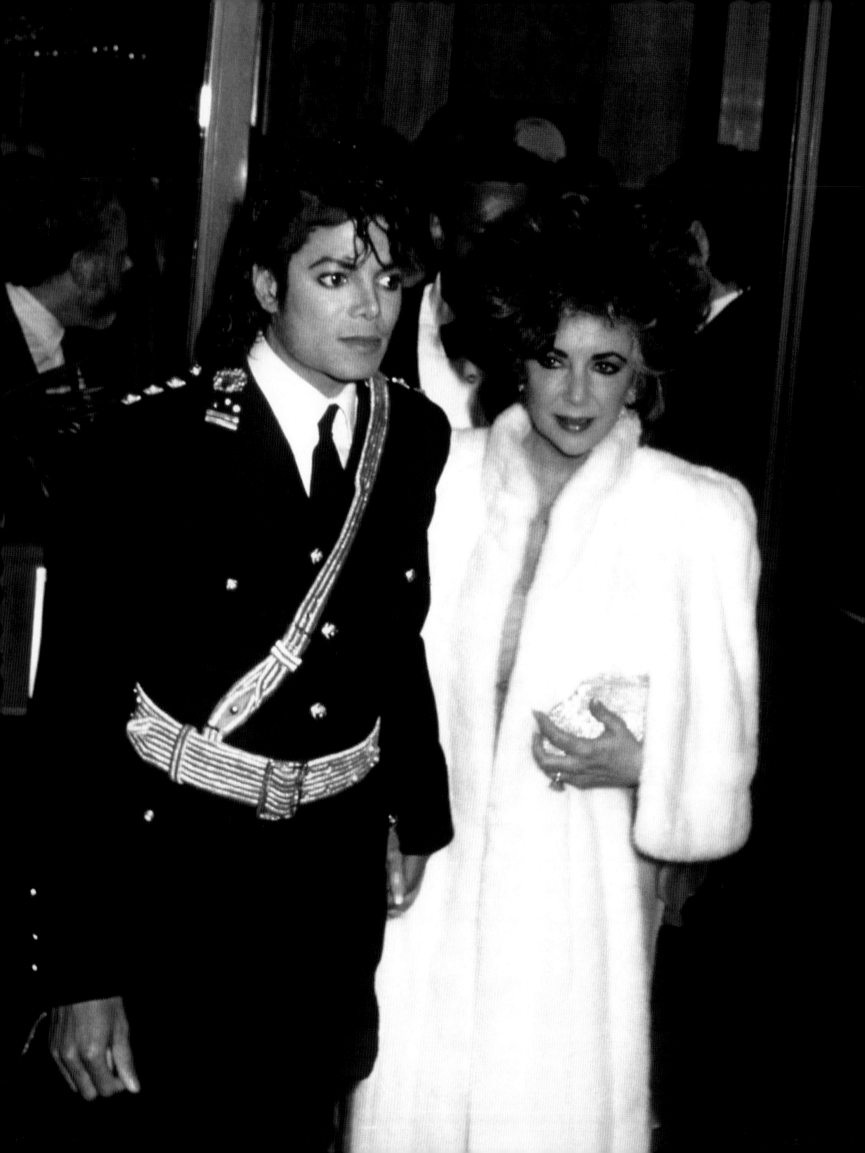

I'VE NEVER SELF-PROCLAIMED MYSELF TO BE ANYTHING. IF I CALLED UP ELIZABETH TAYLOR RIGHT NOW, SHE WOULD TELL YOU THAT SHE COINED THE PHRASE. SHE WAS INTRODUCING ME, I THINK AT THE AMERICAN MUSIC AWARDS, AND SAID IN HER OWN WORDS—IT WASN'T IN THE SCRIPT—"I'M A PERSONAL FAN, AND IN MY OPINION HE IS THE KING OF POP, ROCK, AND SOUL." THEN THE PRESS STARTED SAYING "KING OF POP" AND THE FANS STARTED. THIS SELF-PROCLAIMED GARBAGE, I DON'T KNOW WHO SAID THAT.

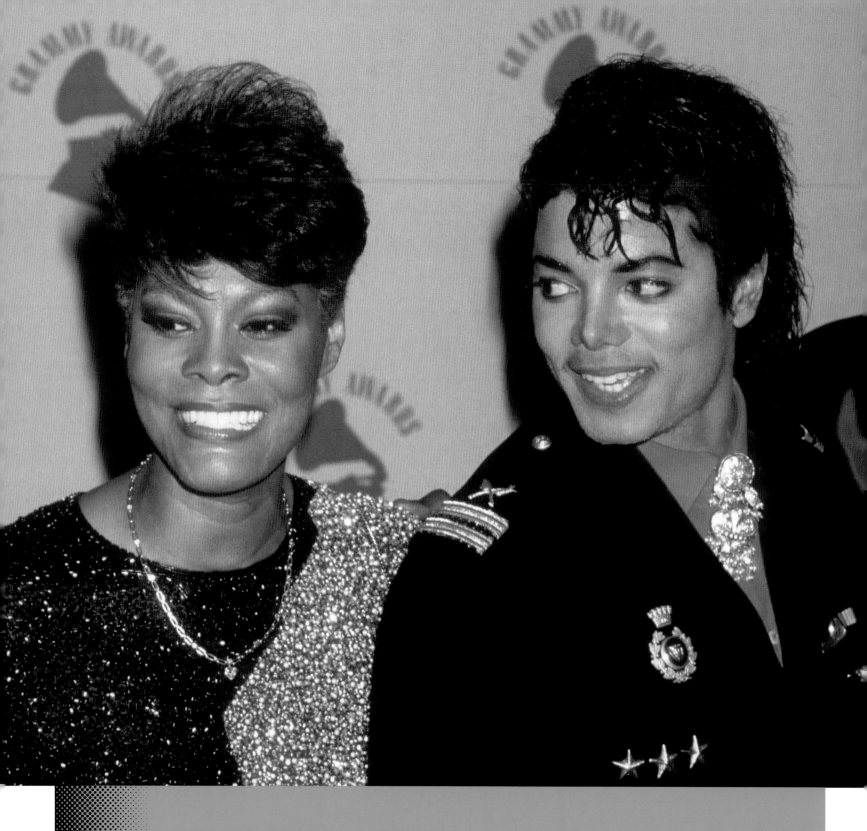

HE WAS MY BABY.
Dionne Warwick

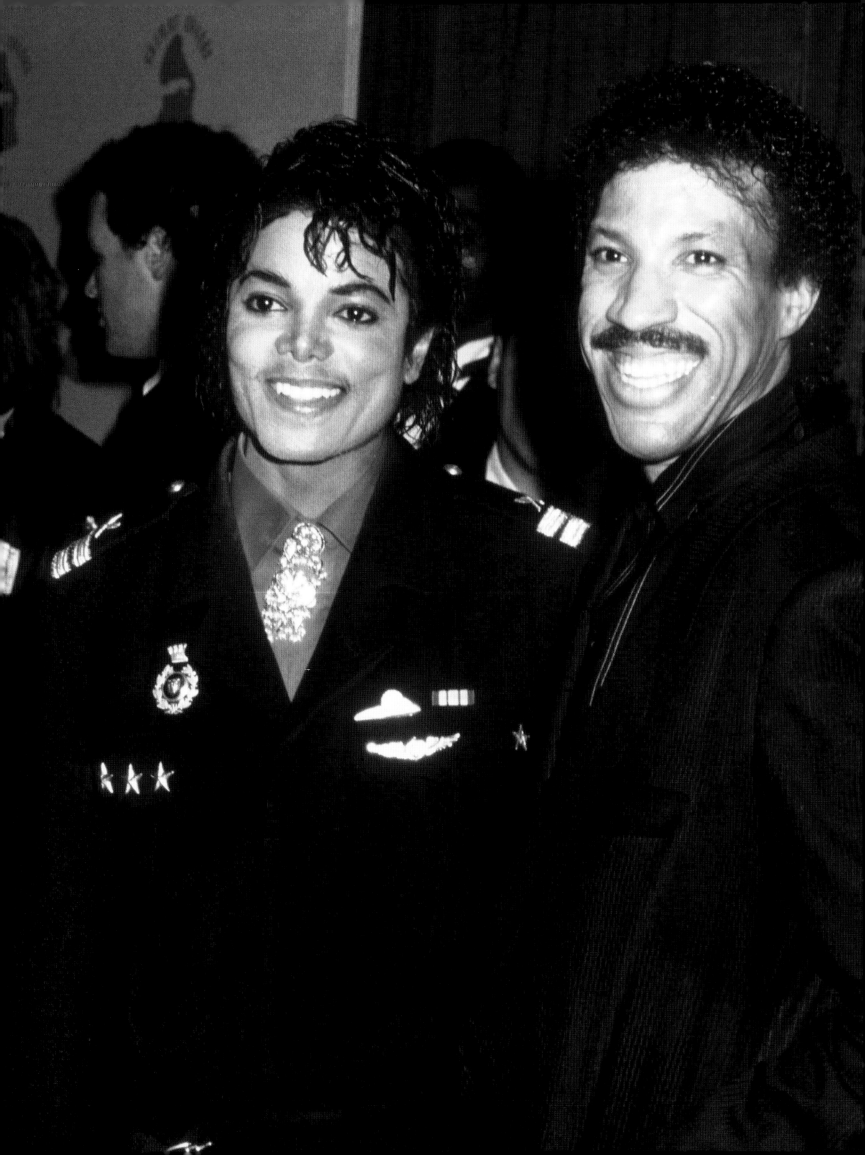

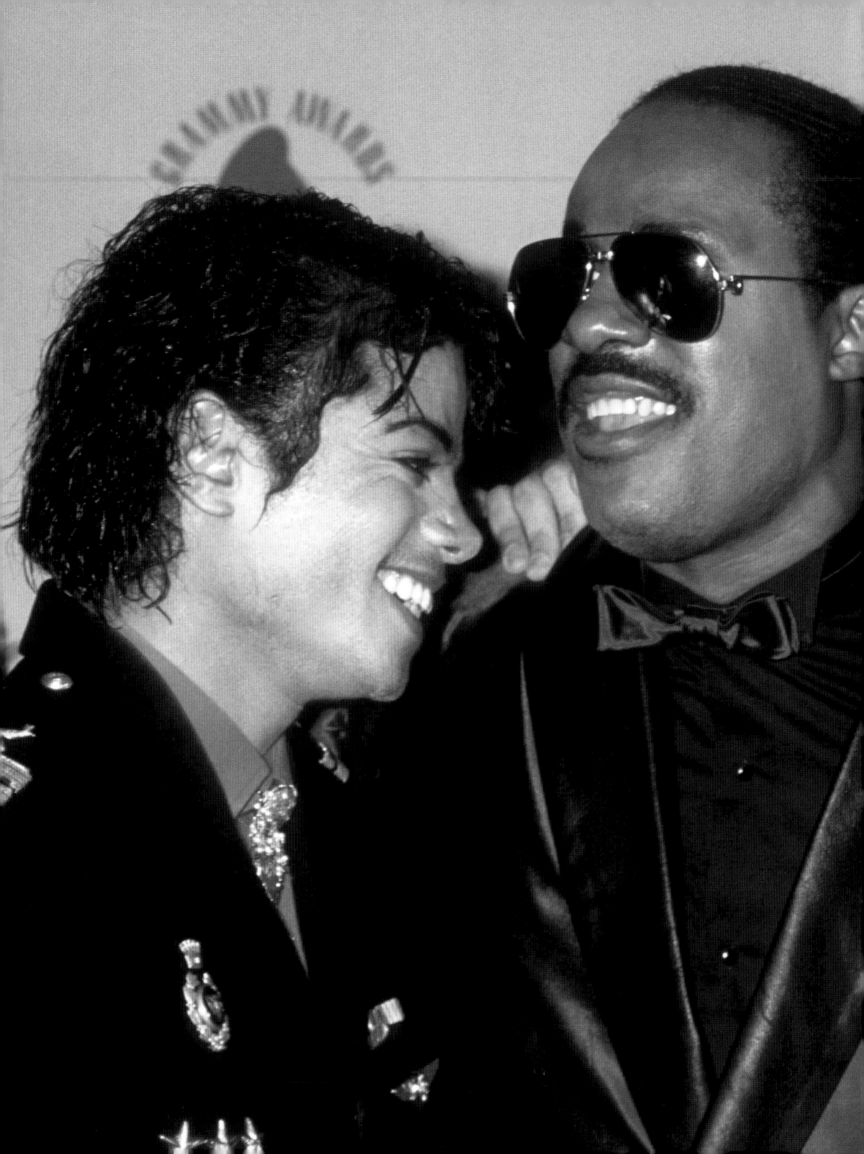

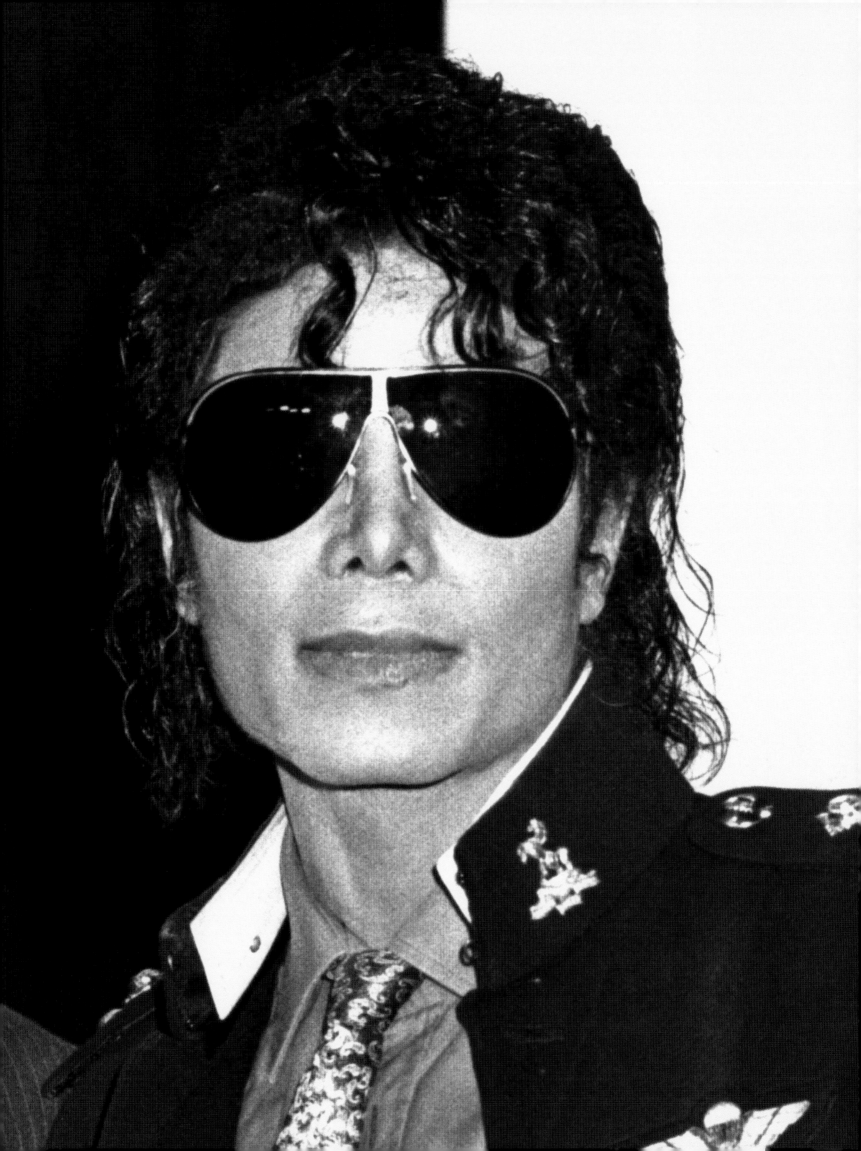

RIDING THROUGH HARLEM, I REMEMBER IN THE LATE 70s EARLY 80s, I WOULD SEE THESE KIDS DANCING ON THE STREET...I TOOK A MENTAL PICTURE OF IT.

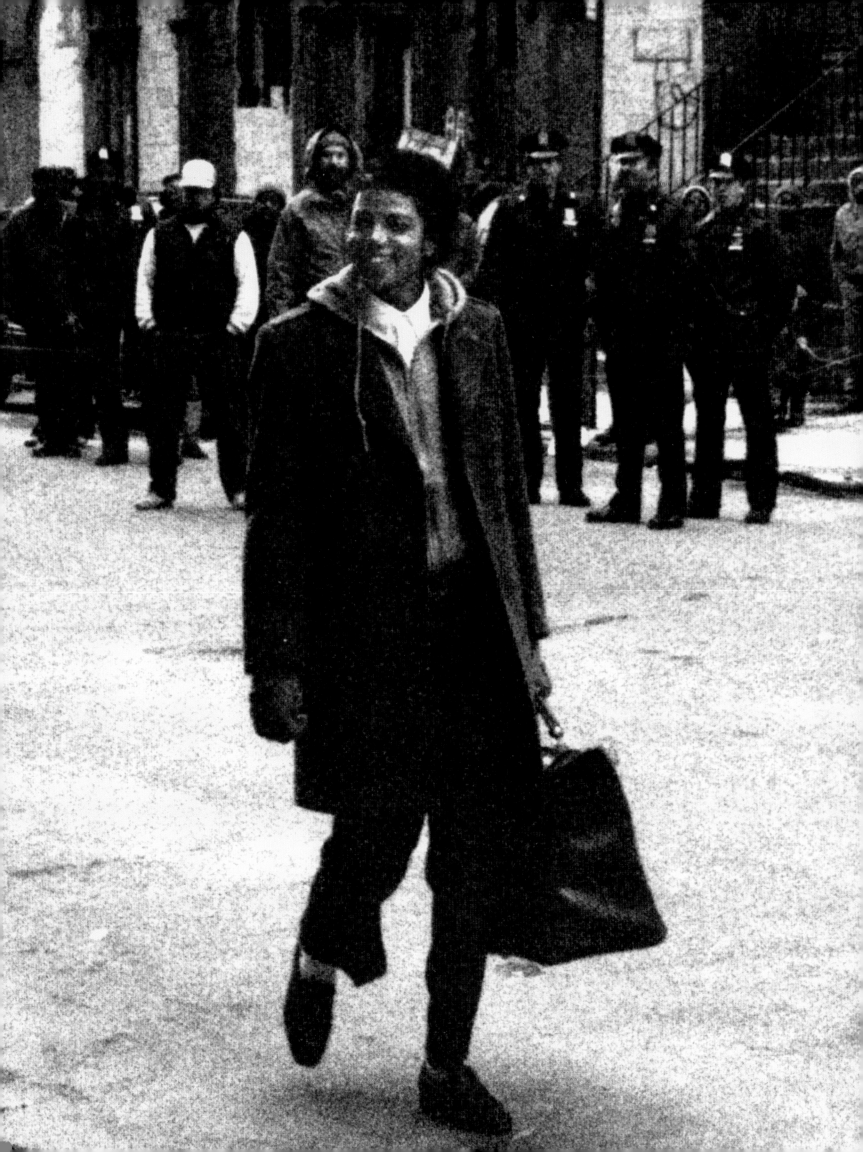

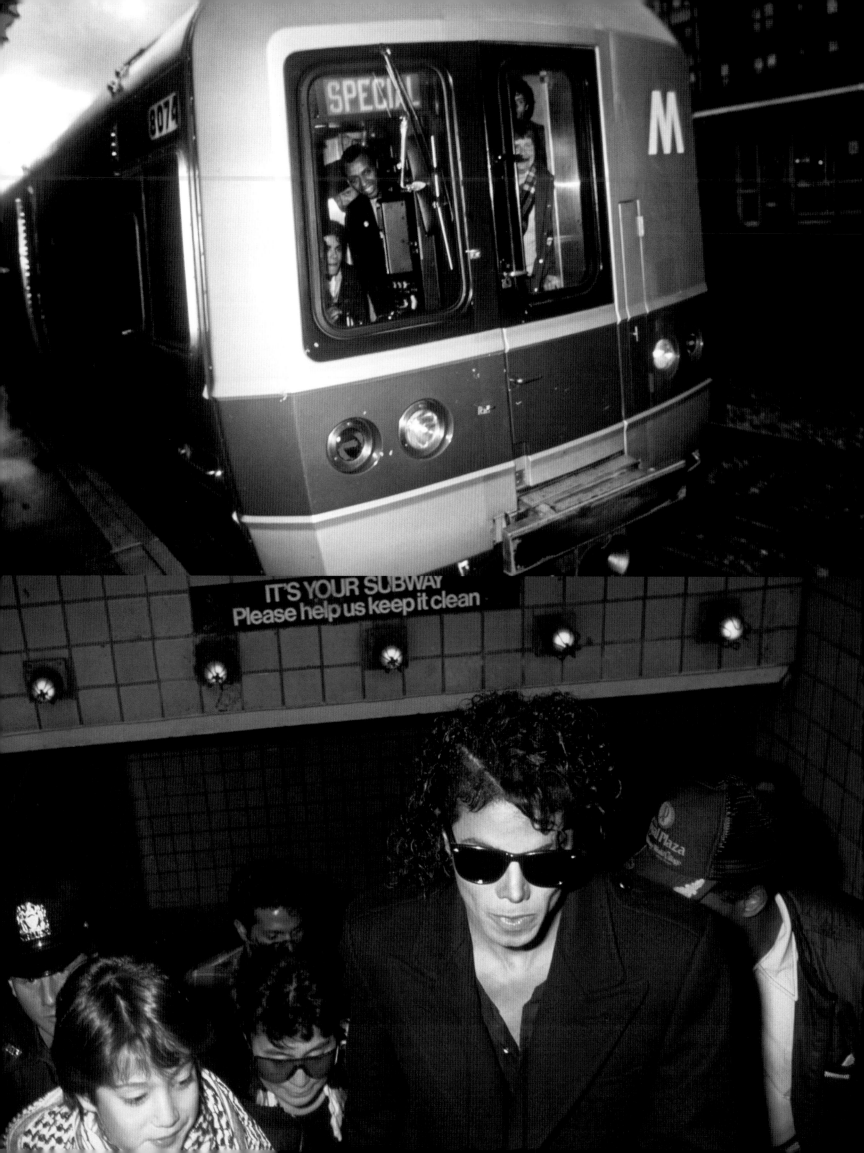

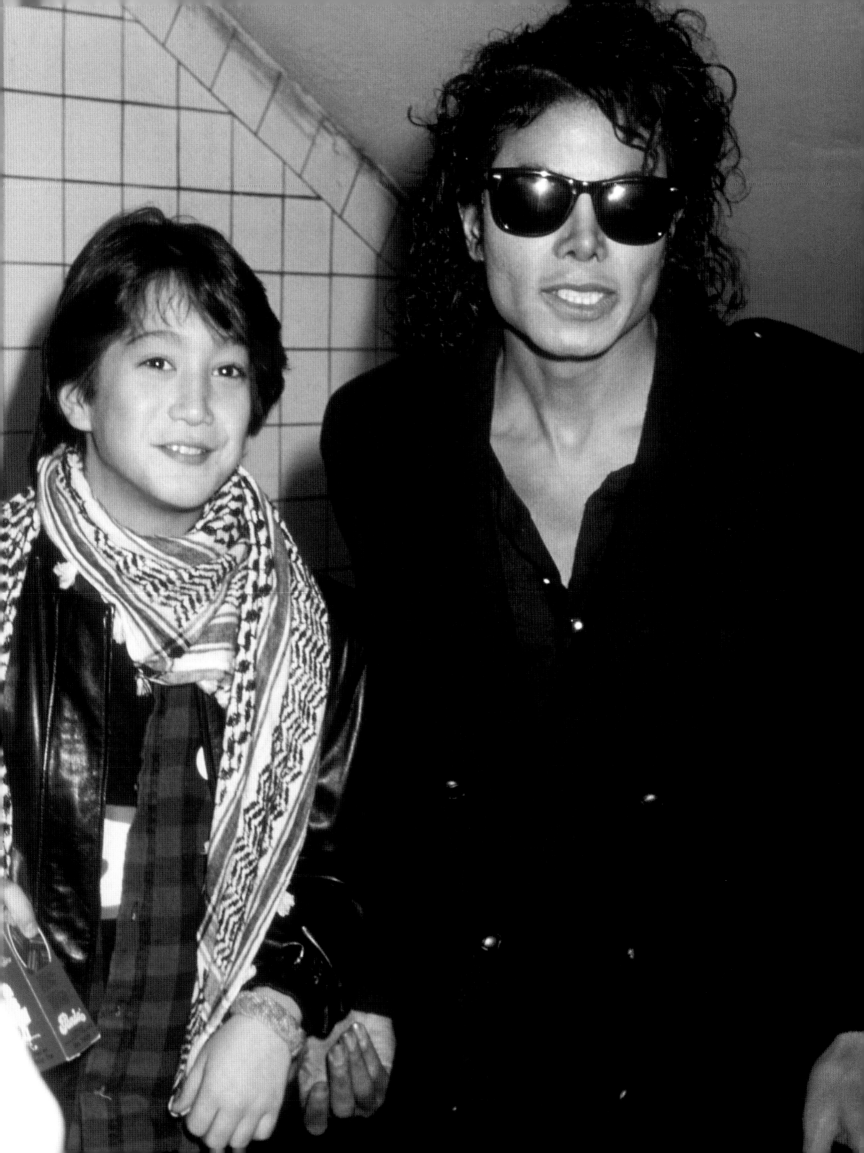

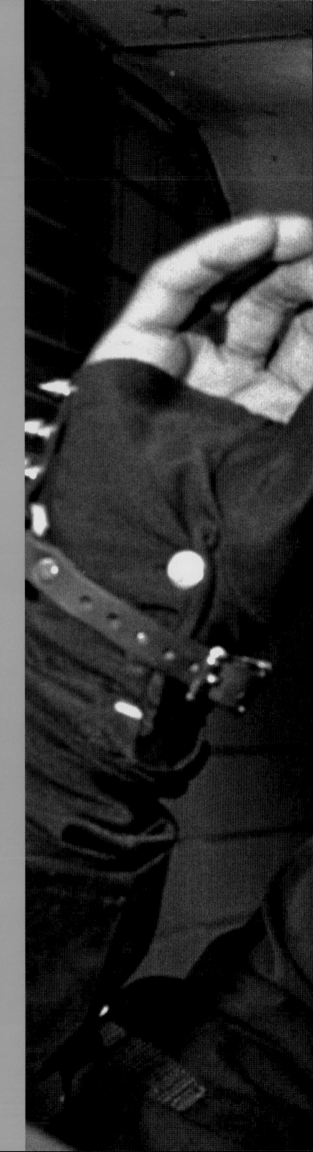

I STARTED DOING THAT WITH *BAD*. MARTIN SCORSESE DIRECTED THAT SHORT FILM IN THE SUBWAYS OF NEW YORK. I LET THE MUSIC TELL ME WHAT TO DO. I REMEMBER HIM SAYING, "THAT WAS A GREAT TAKE! I WANT YOU TO SEE IT." SO WE PUSHED PLAYBACK, AND I WENT, "AAAH!" I DIDN'T REALIZE I WAS DOING THAT. BUT THEN EVERYONE ELSE STARTED DOING THAT, AND MADONNA, TOO, BUT IT'S NOT SEXUAL AT ALL.

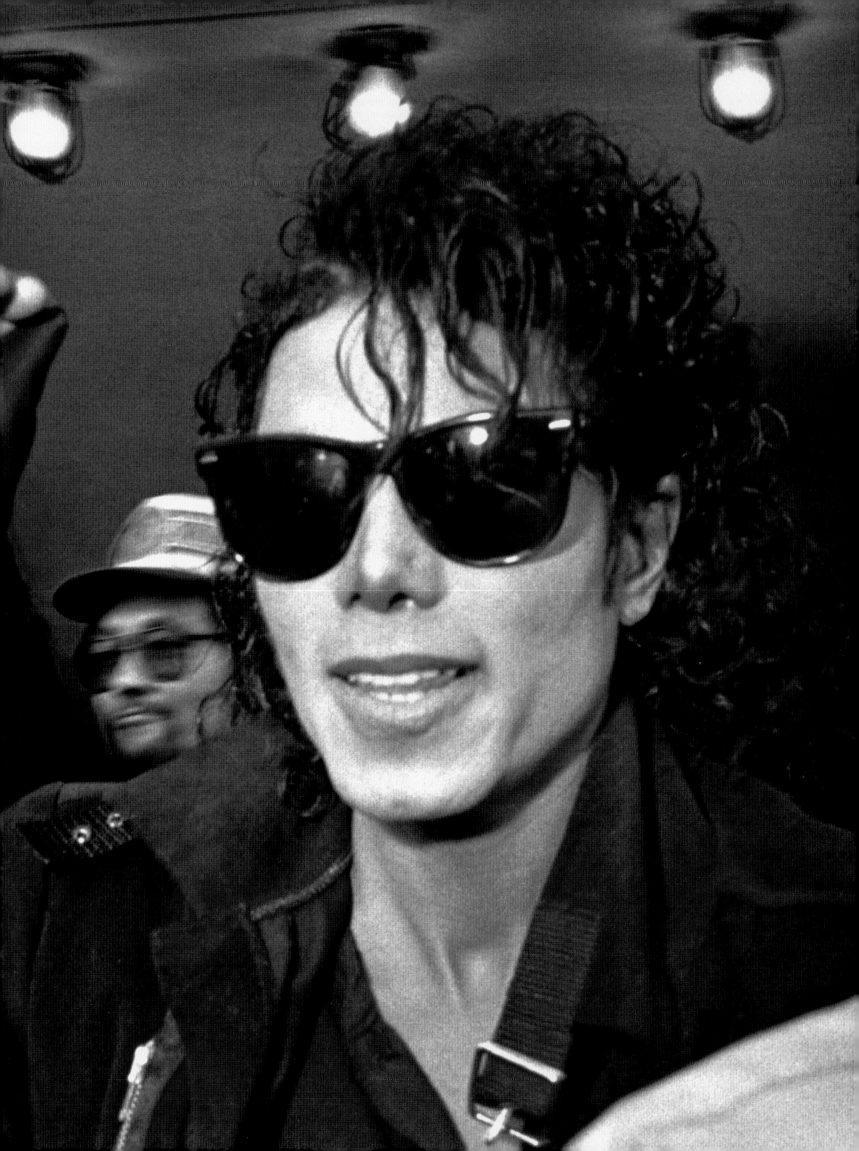

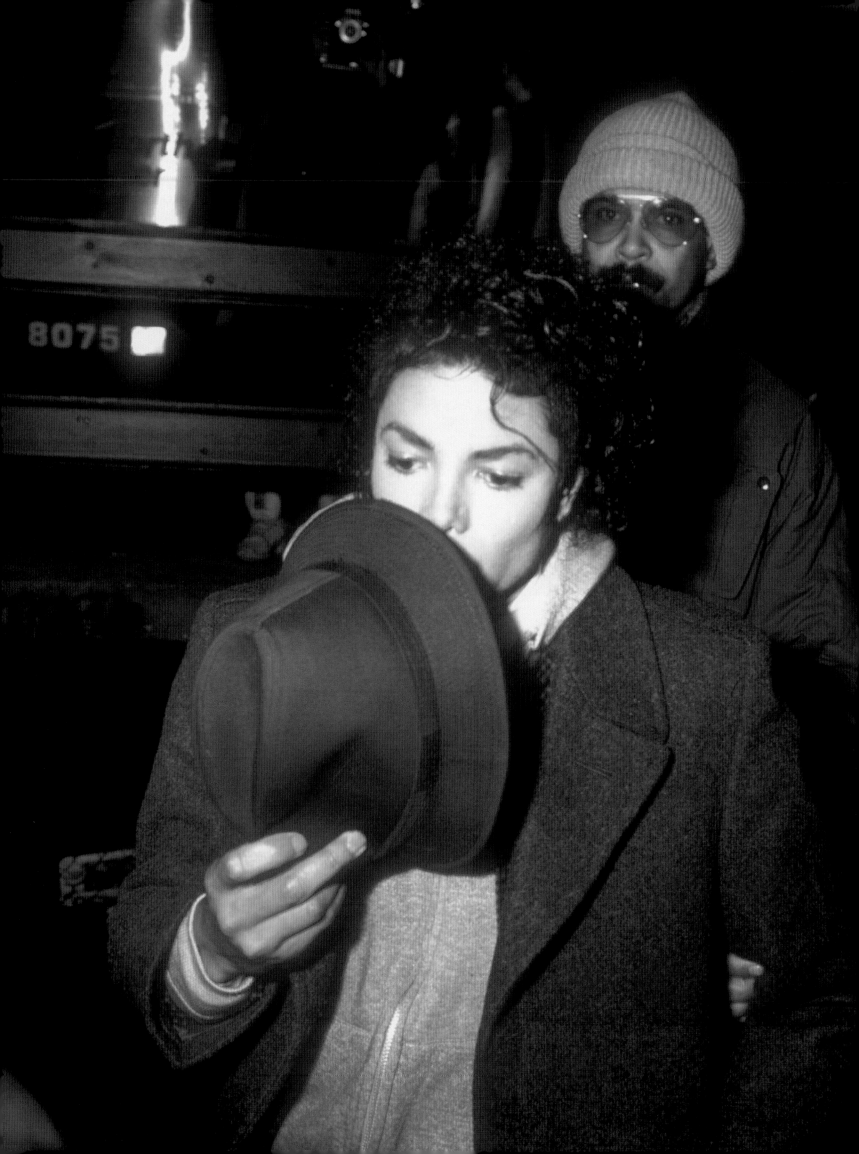

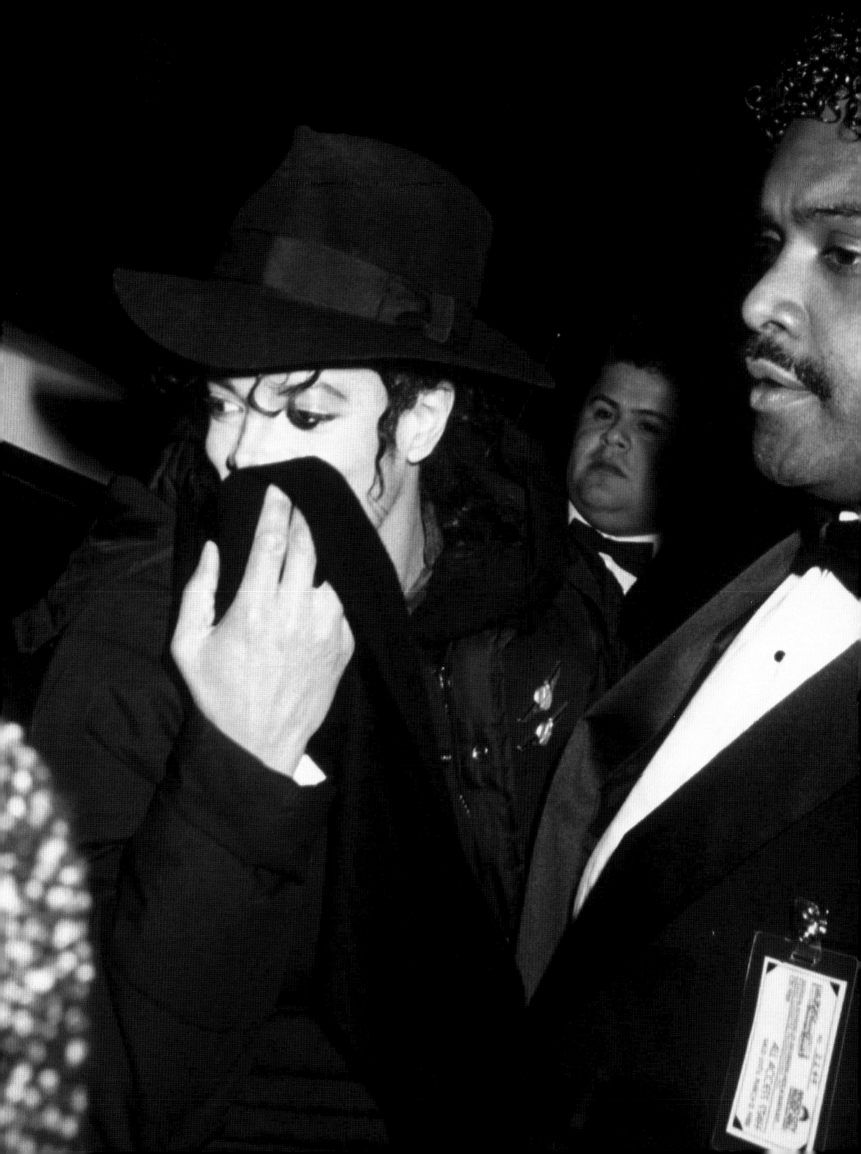

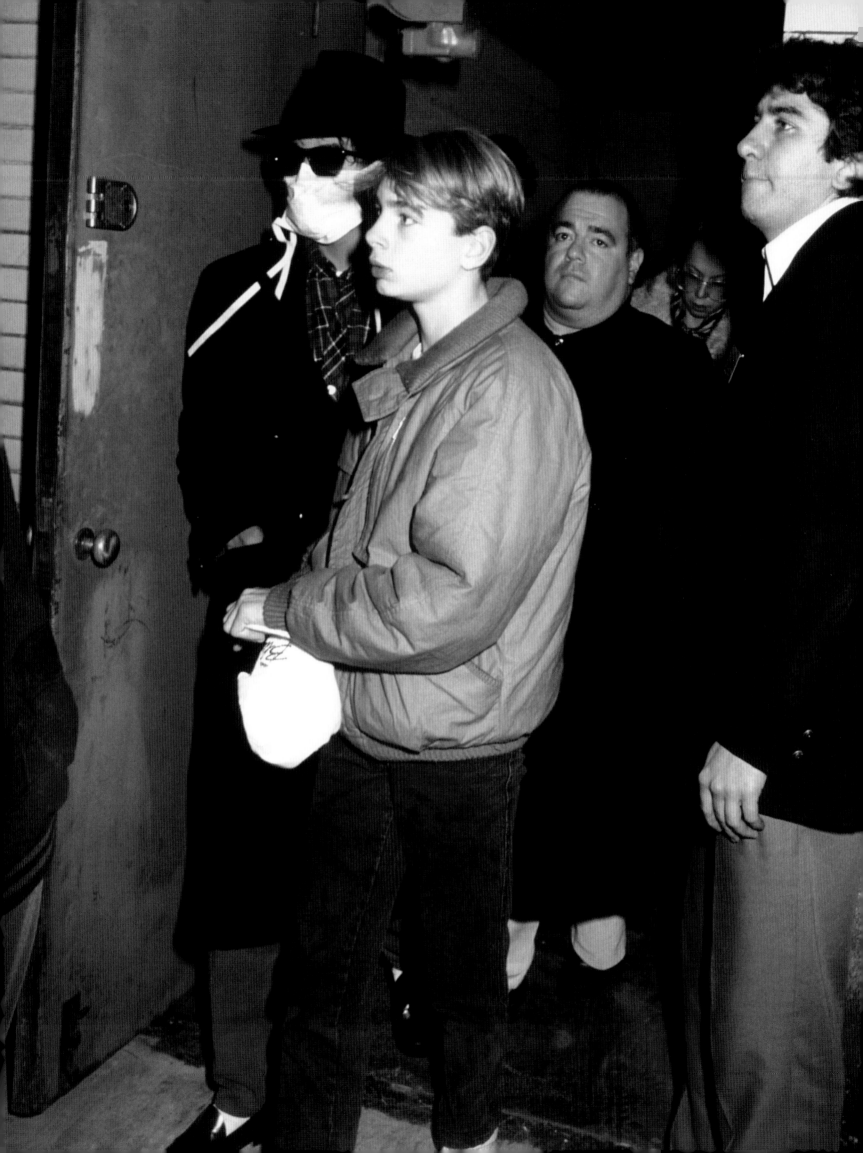

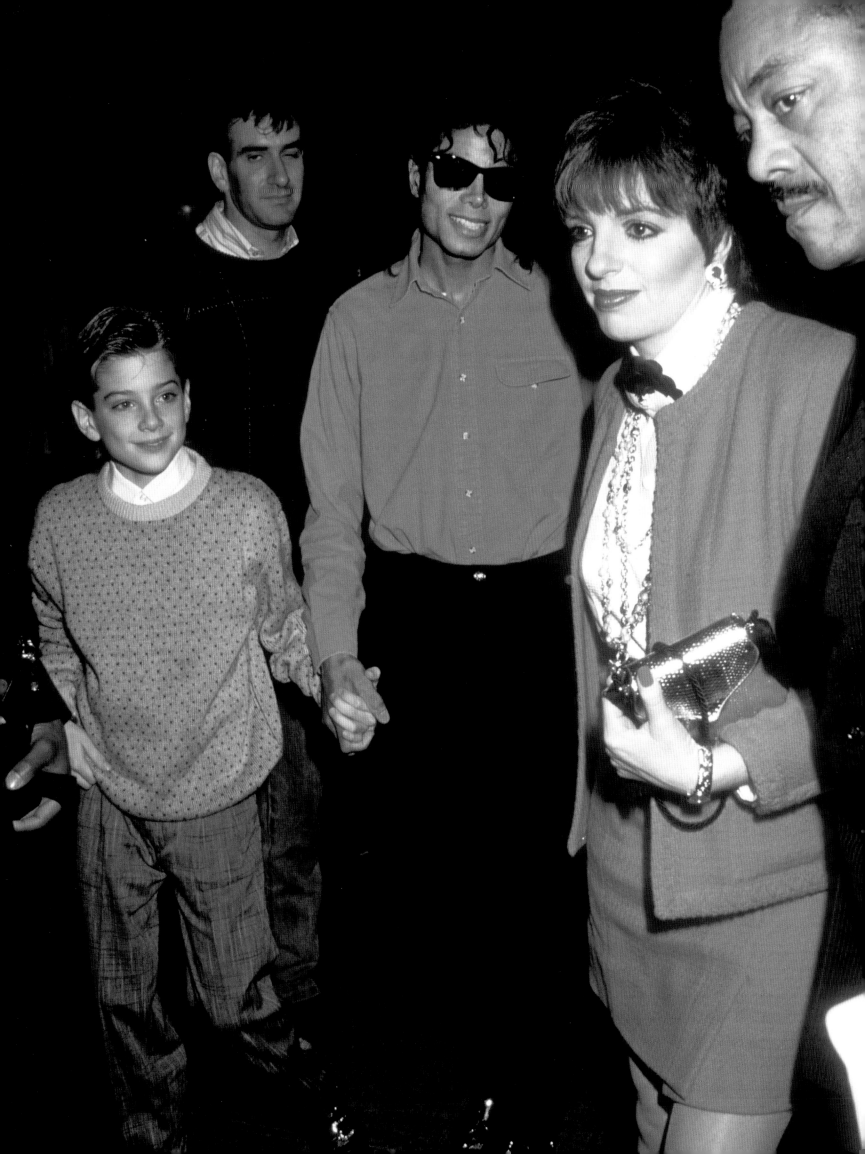

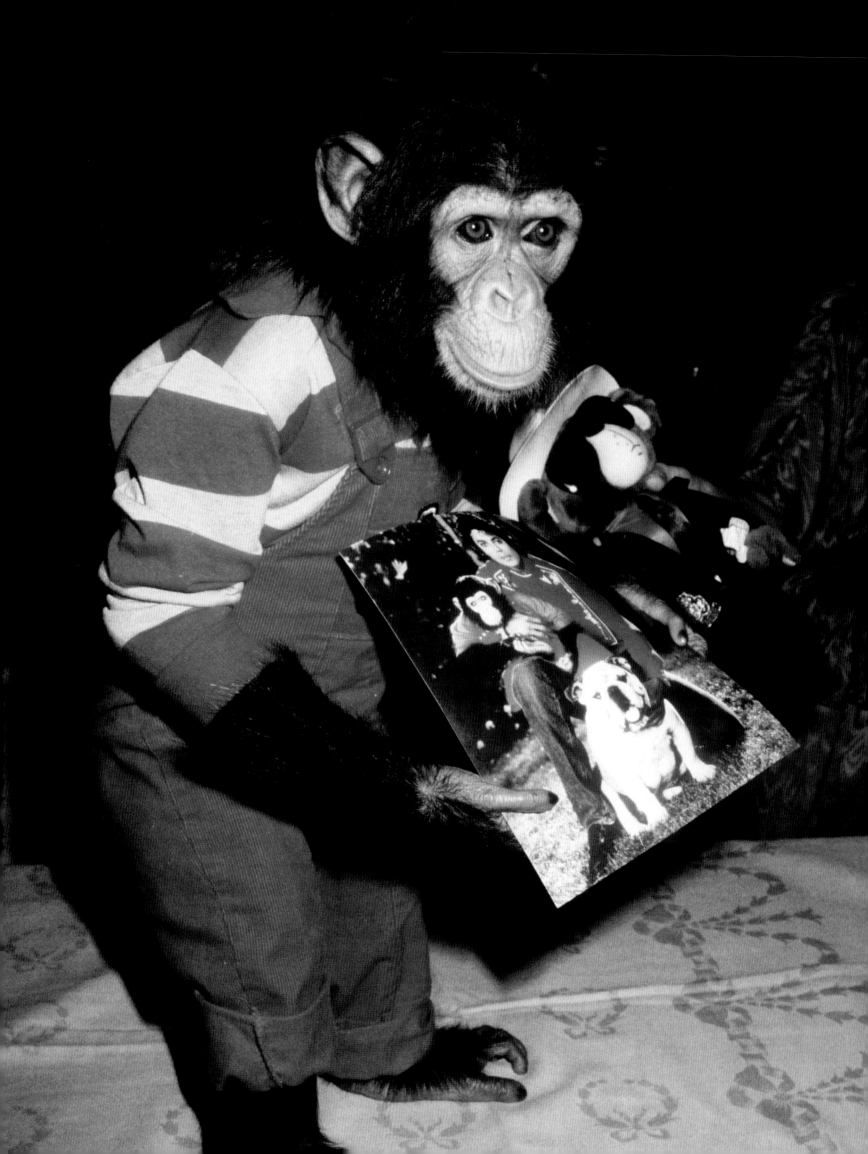

I'M CRAZY ABOUT MONKEYS, ESPECIALLY CHIMPS. MY CHIMP BUBBLES IS A CONSTANT DELIGHT. I REALLY ENJOY TAKING HIM WITH ME ON TRIPS OR EXCURSIONS. HE'S A WONDERFUL DISTRACTION AND A GREAT PET.

THE WORLD HAS LOST AN
ICON AND MUSIC HAS LOST
TREASURES. . .I HOPE THAT
MICHAEL WILL FIND THAT PEACE
THAT MAYBE HE DID NOT HAVE IN
THE LAST 15 YEARS.

Sophia Loren

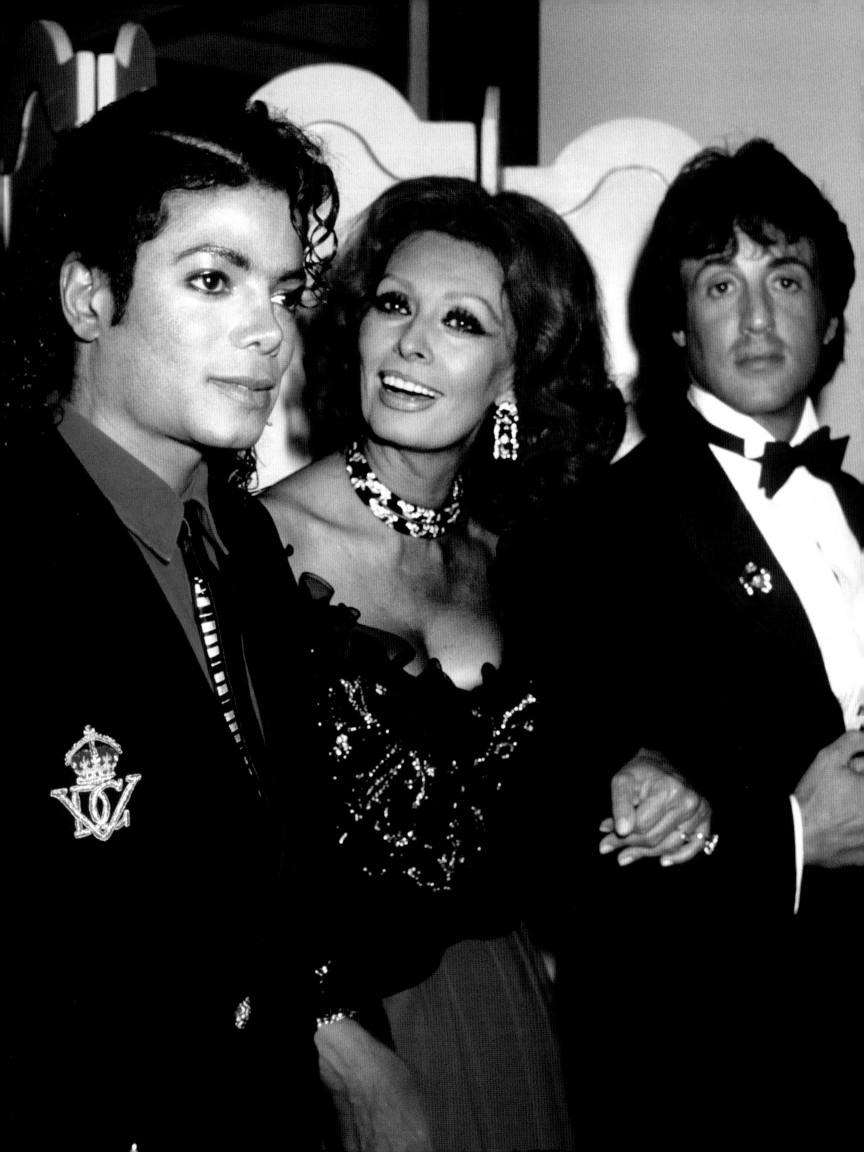

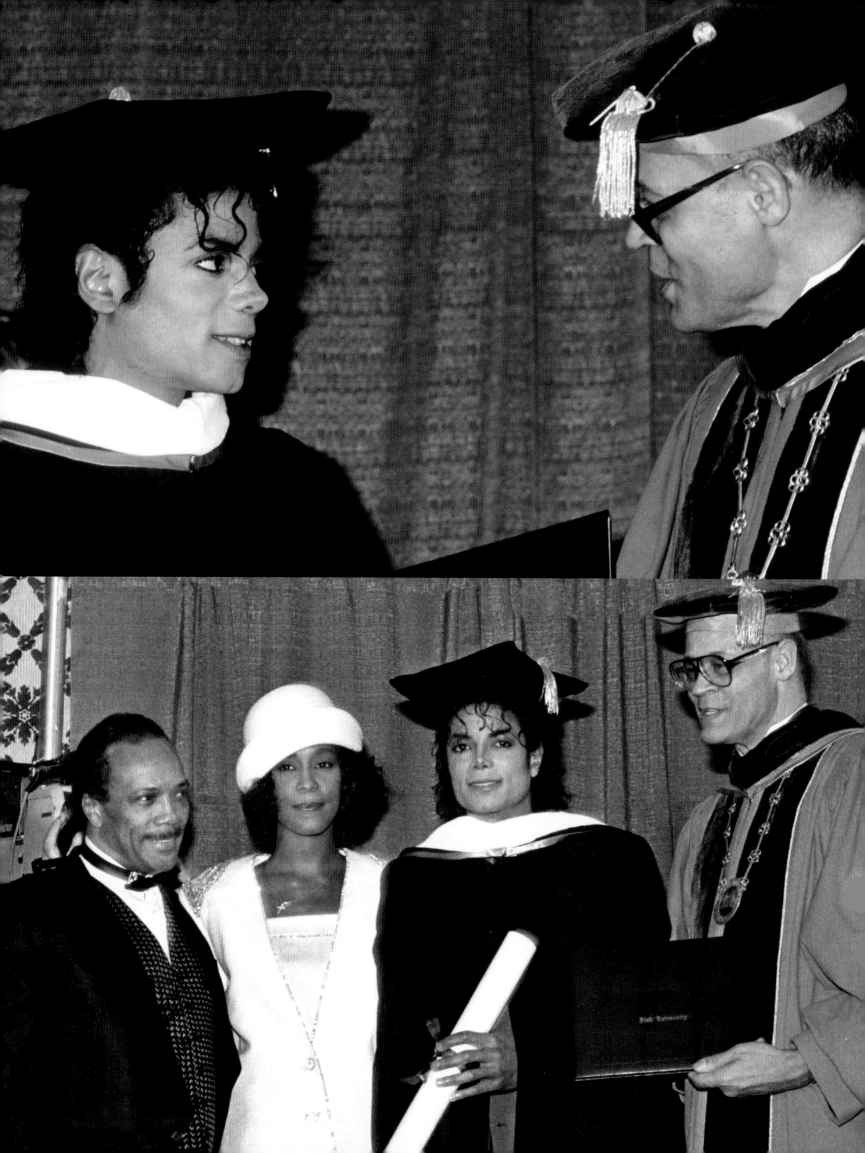

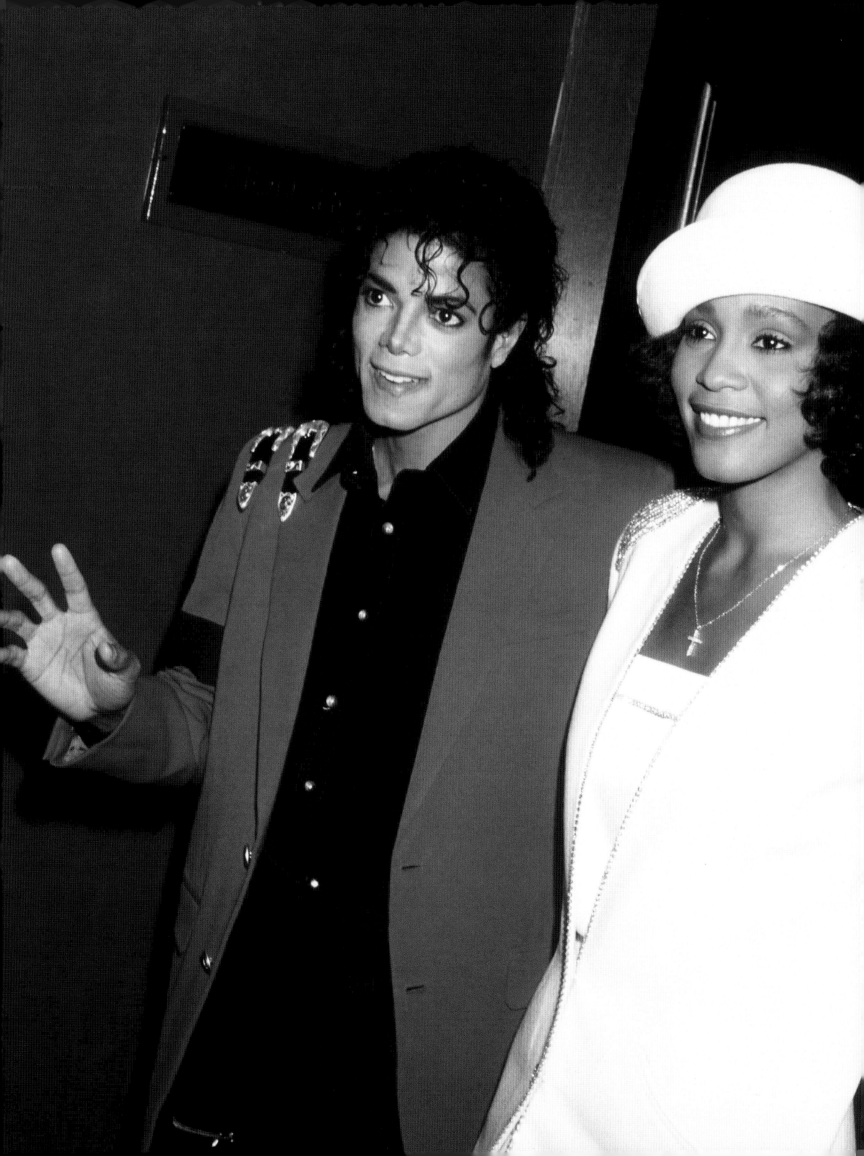

WE'VE LIVED THE SAME LIVES. . . .WE LOOK AT EACH OTHER, AND IT'S LIKE LOOKING IN A MIRROR. ELIZABETH HAS THIS LITTLE GIRL INSIDE OF HER WHO NEVER HAD A CHILDHOOD. SHE WAS ON THE SET EVERY DAY. SHE LOVES PLAYING WITH A NEW GADGET OR TOY, AND SHE'S TOTALLY AWE-INSPIRED BY IT. SHE'S A WONDERFUL HUMAN BEING.

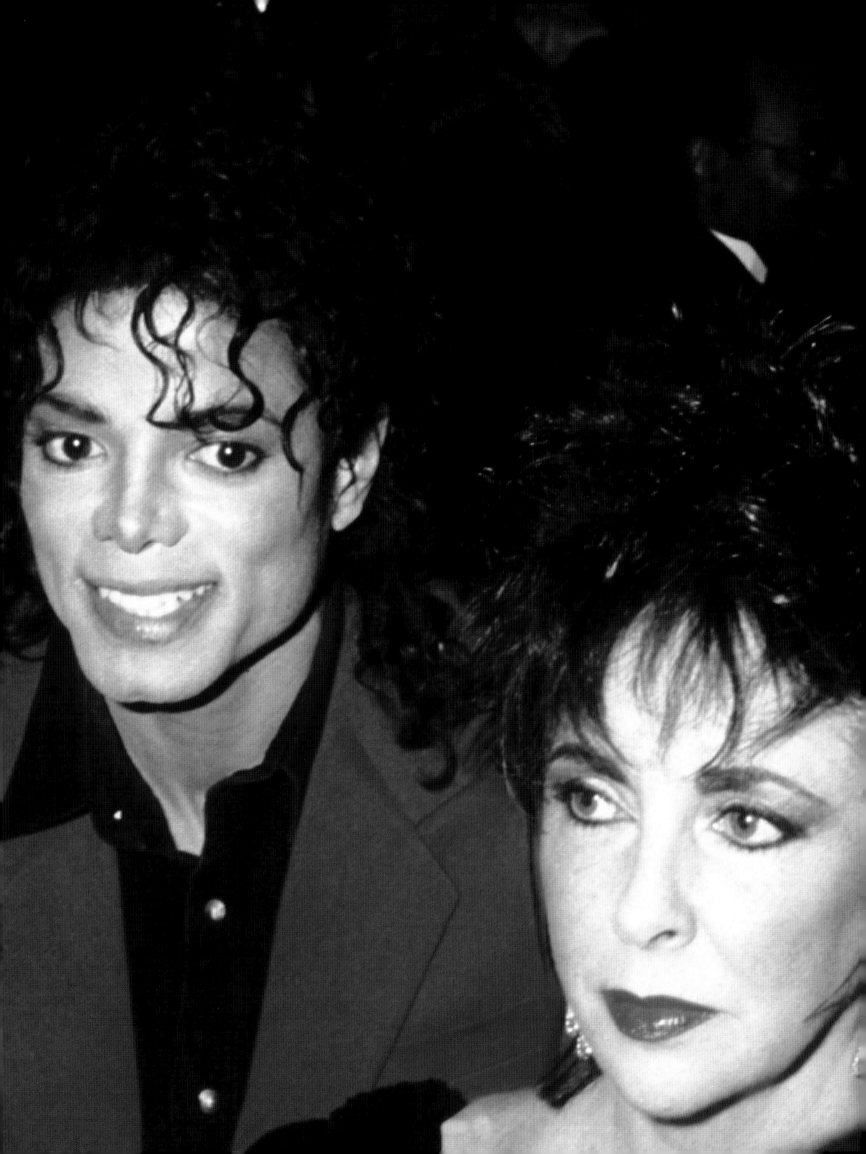

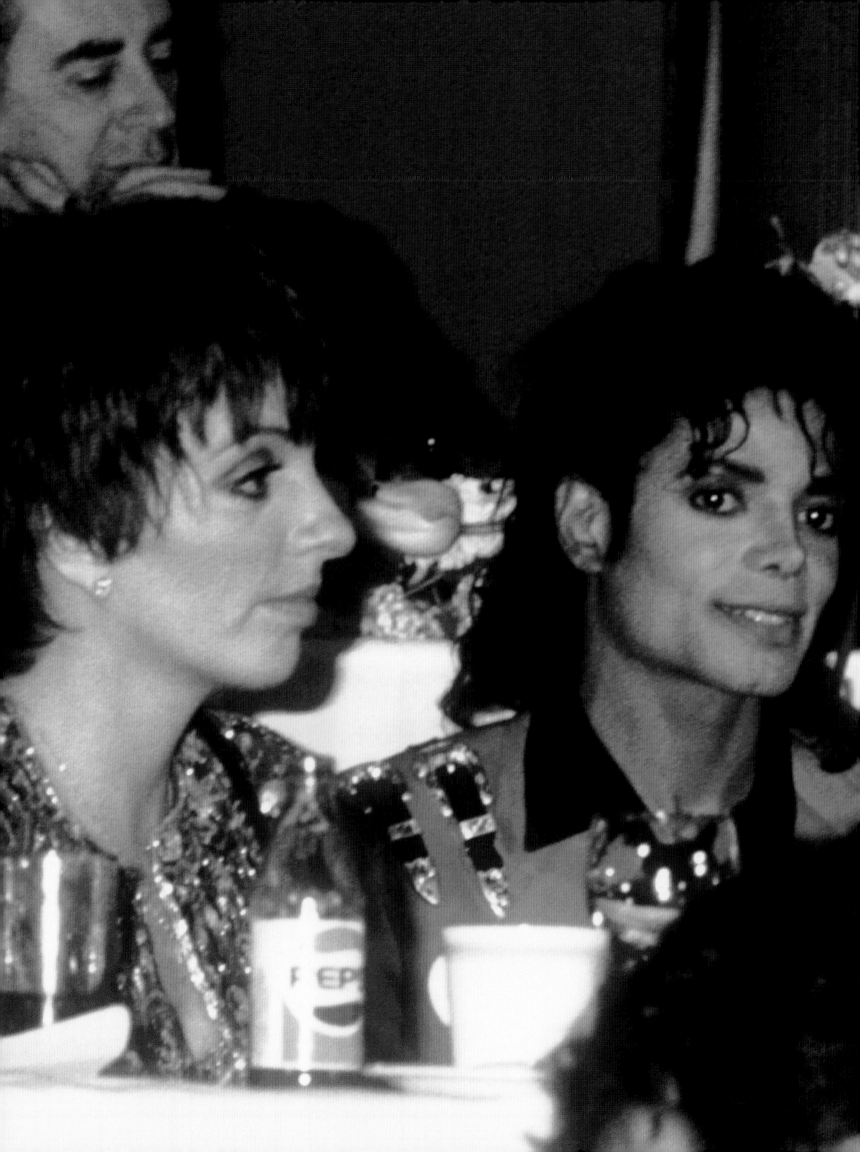

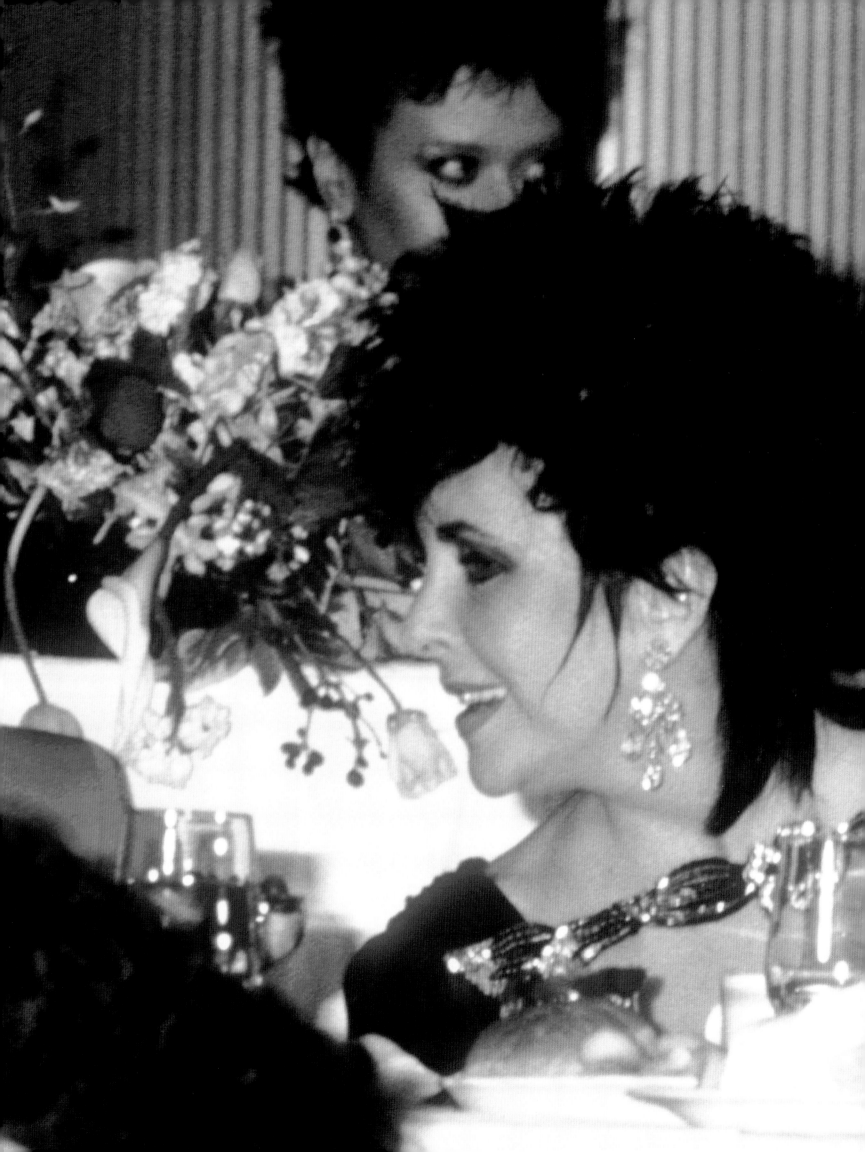

I FEEL COMPELLED TO
GIVE PEOPLE SOME
SENSE OF ESCAPISM...
I THINK IT'S THE
REASON I'M HERE.

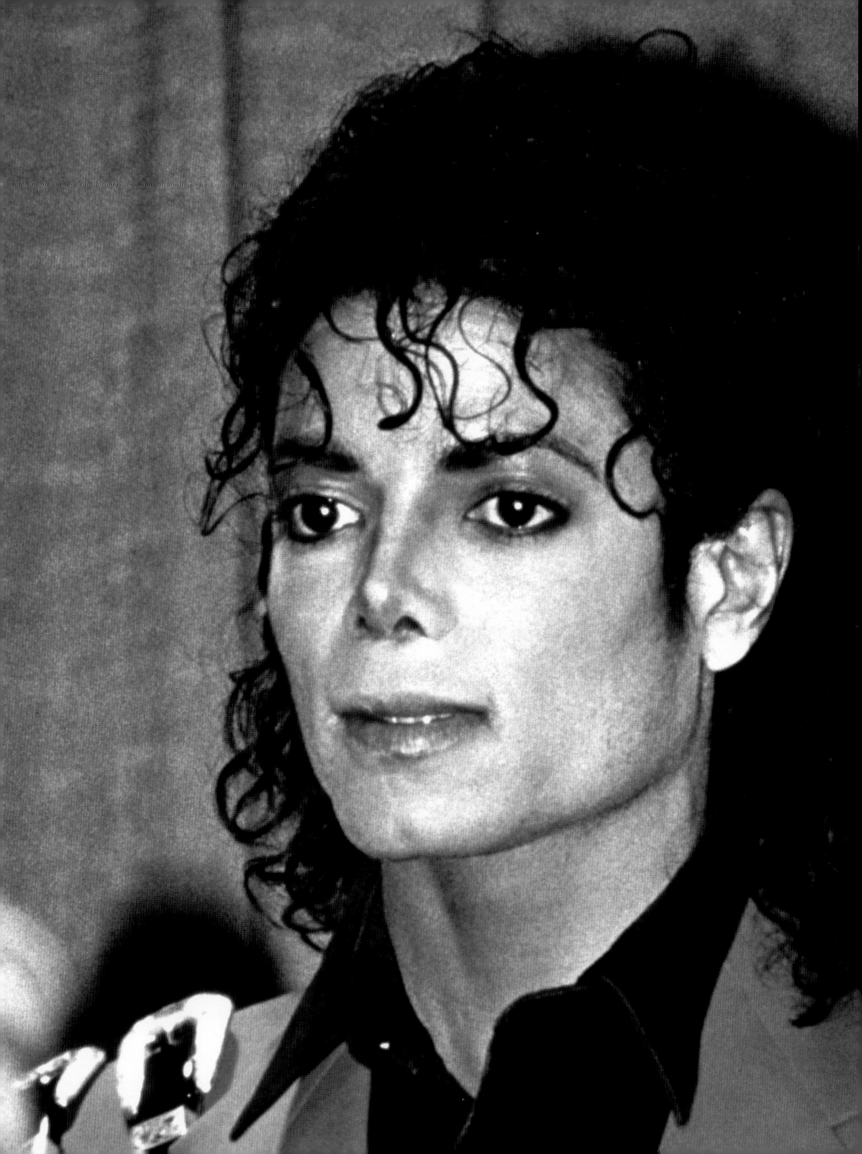

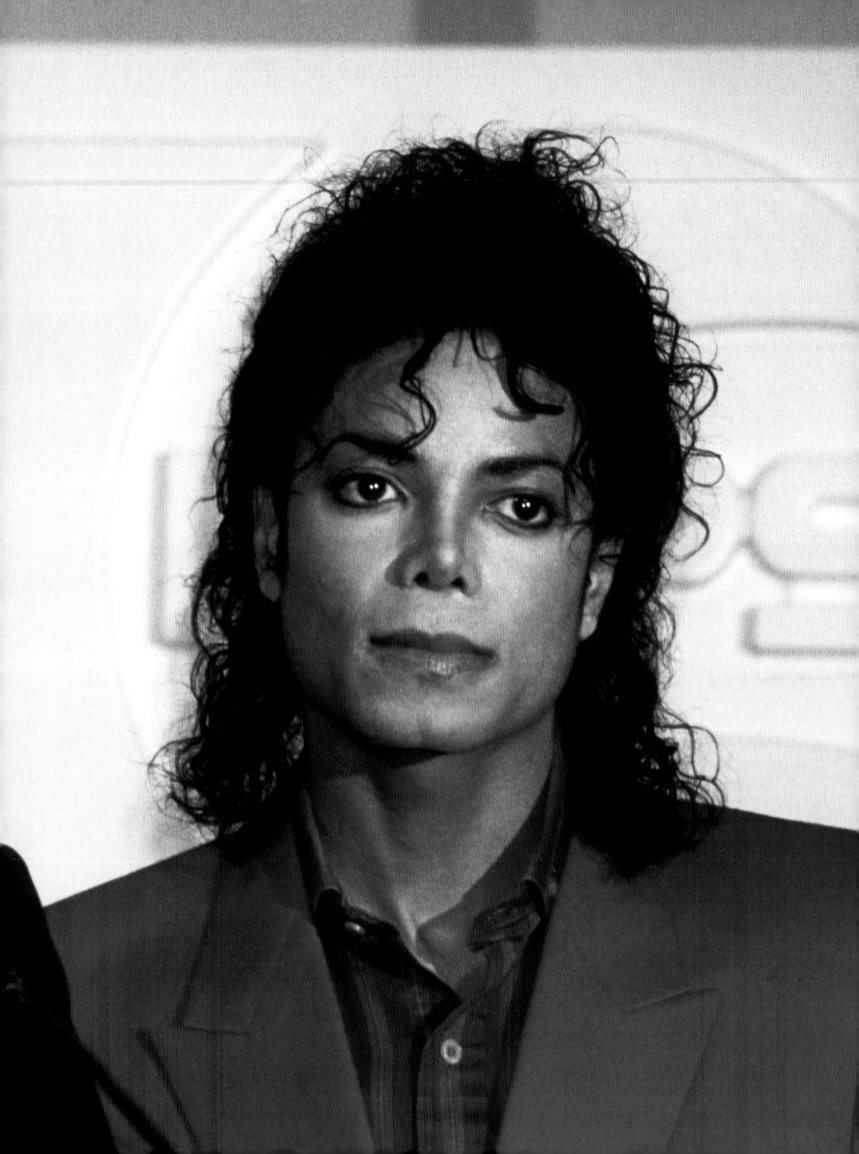

PEOPLE CAN ALWAYS HAVE A JUDGMENT ABOUT ANYTHING YOU DO. SO IT DOESN'T BOTHER ME. EVERYTHING CAN BE STRANGE TO SOMEONE.

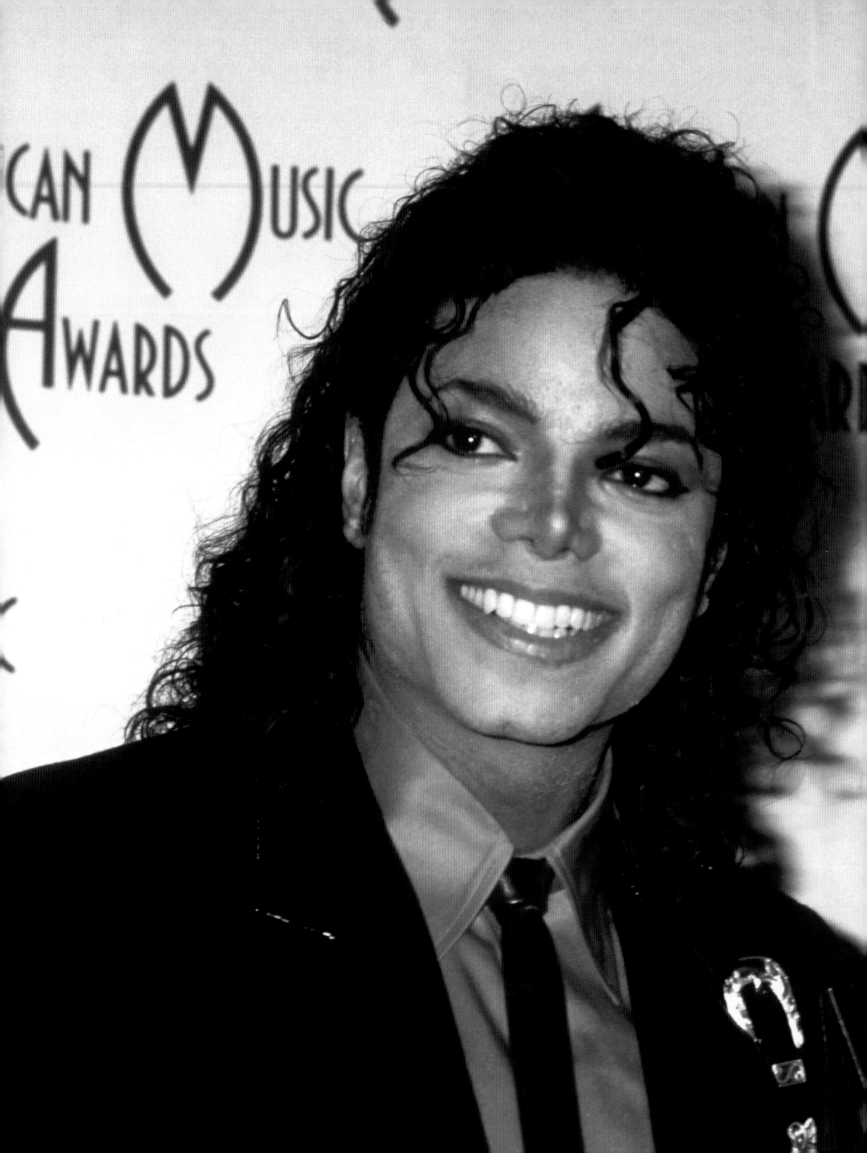

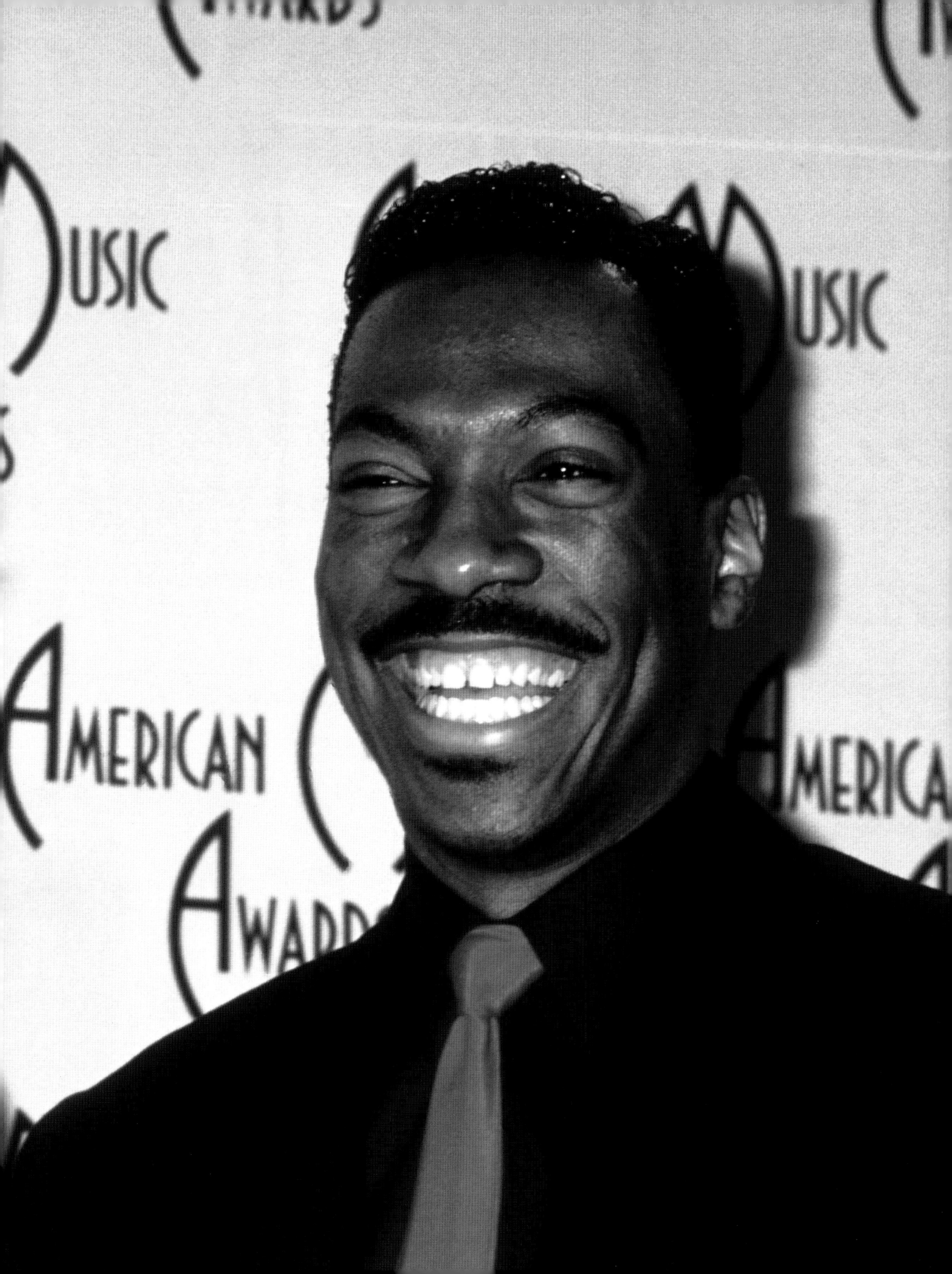
MUSIC
AMERICAN

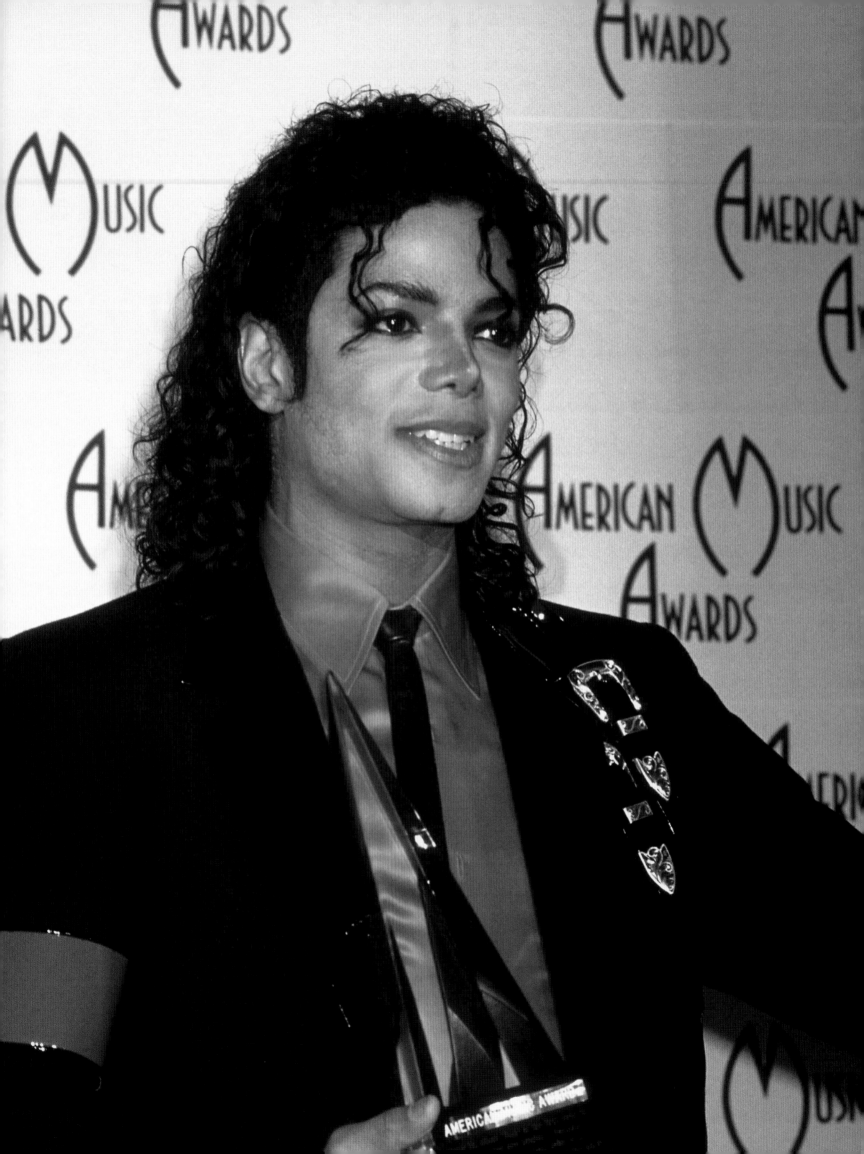

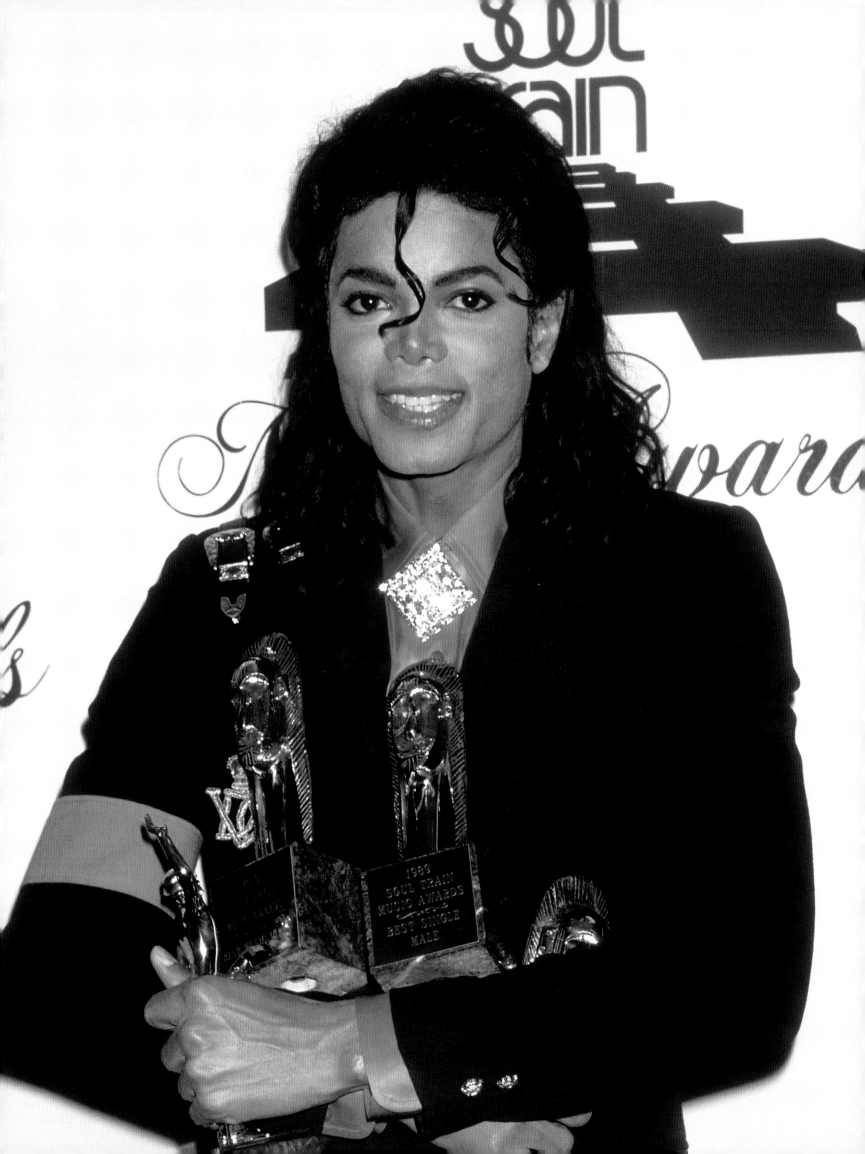

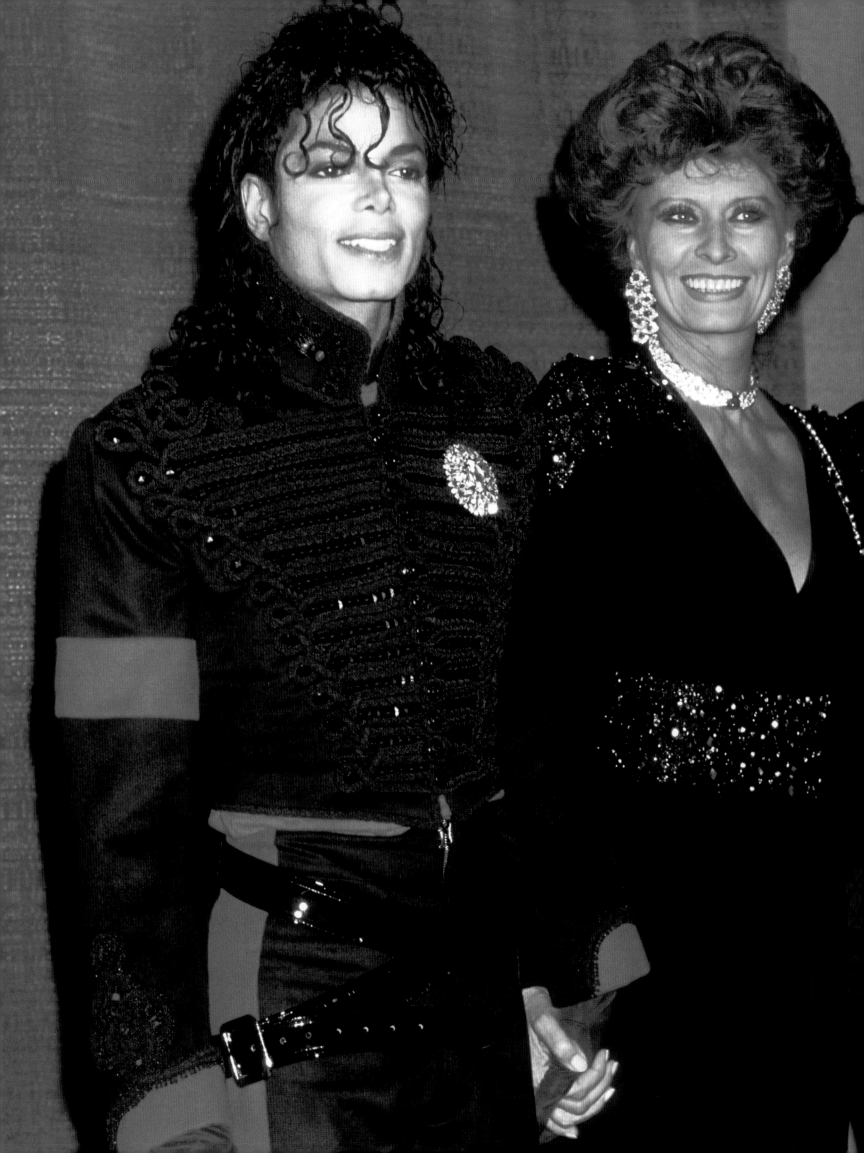

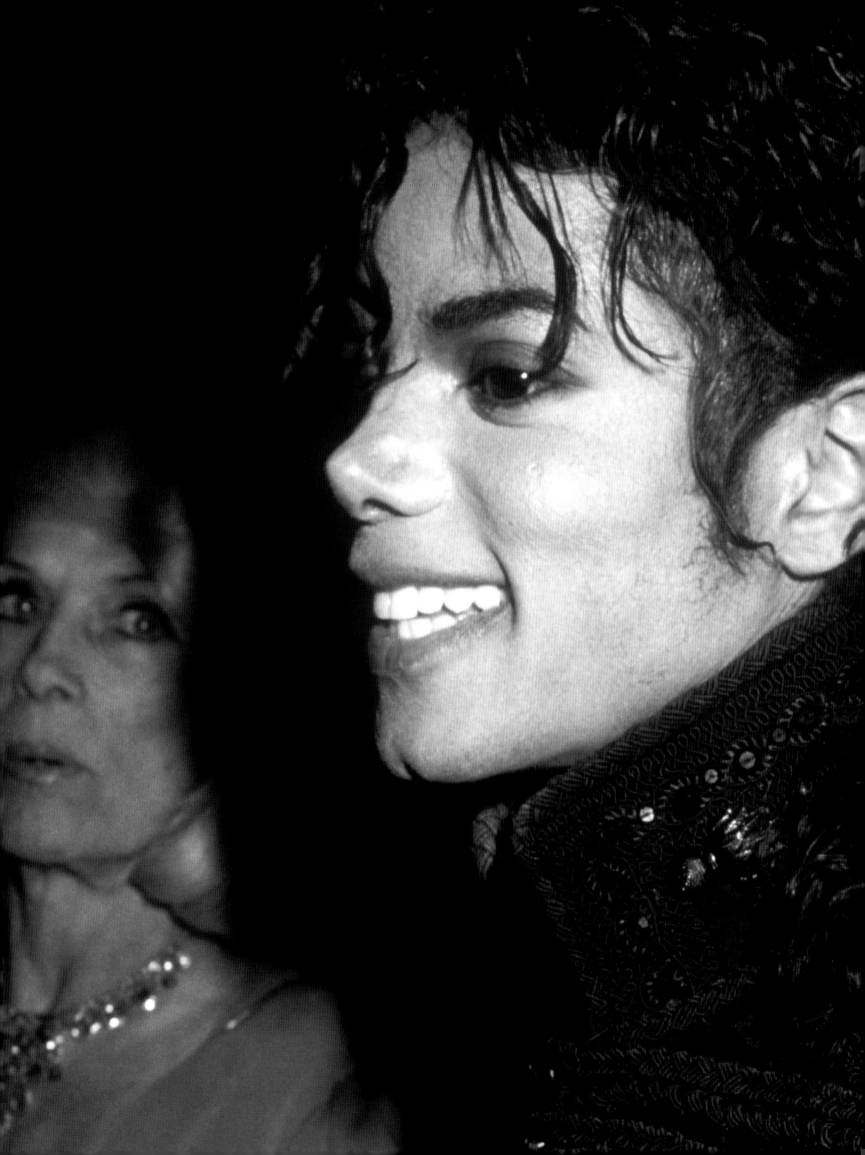

YOU HAVE TO HAVE THAT TRAGEDY, THAT PAIN TO PULL FROM. THAT'S WHAT MAKES A CLOWN GREAT. YOU CAN SEE HE'S HURTING BEHIND THE MASQUERADE. HE'S SOMETHING ELSE EXTERNALLY. CHAPLIN DID THAT SO BEAUTIFULLY, BETTER THAN ANYONE. I CAN PLAY OFF THOSE MOMENTS, TOO. I'VE BEEN THROUGH THE FIRE MANY TIMES.

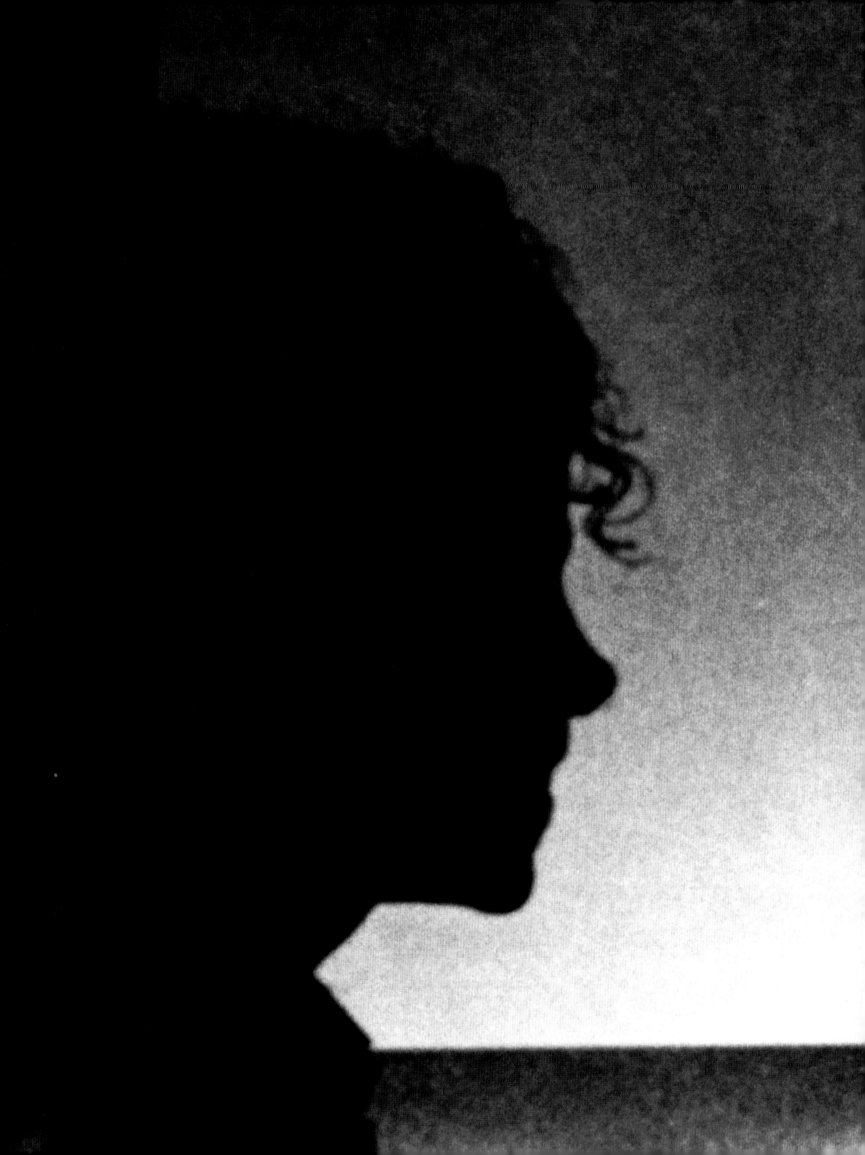

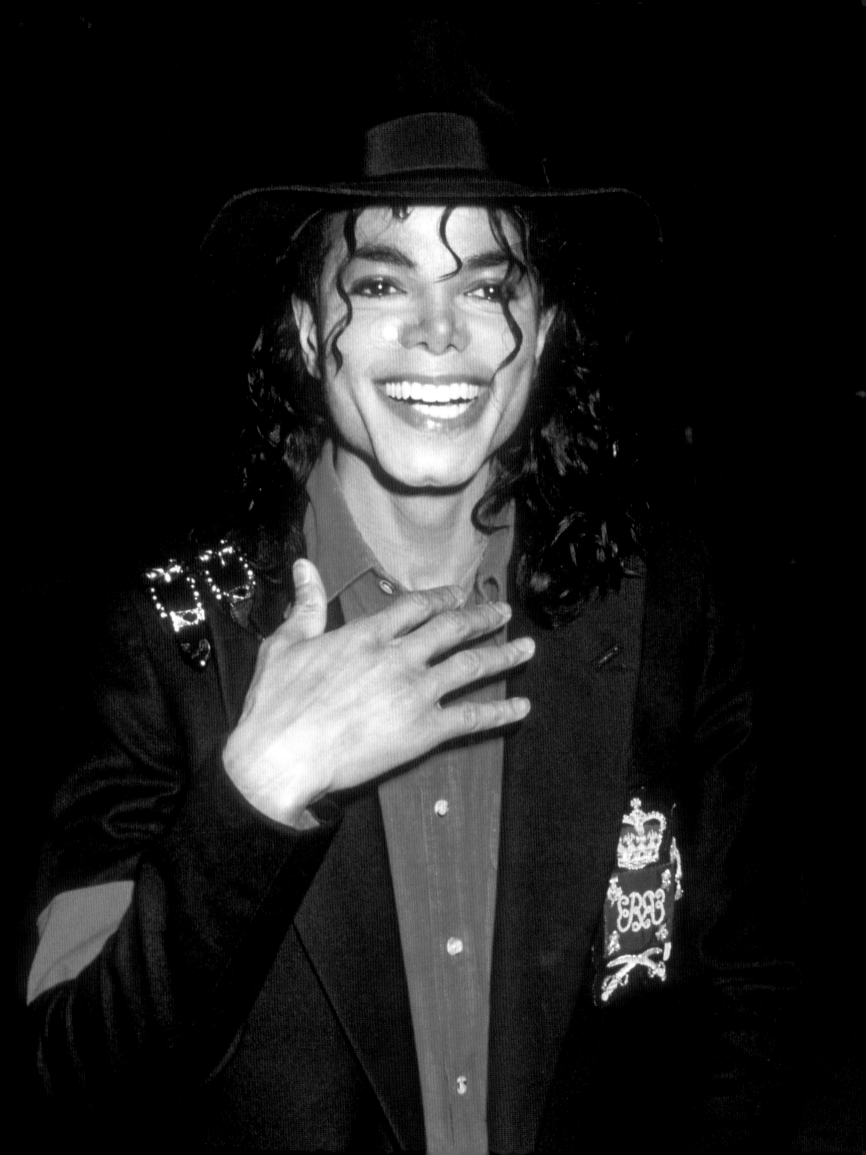

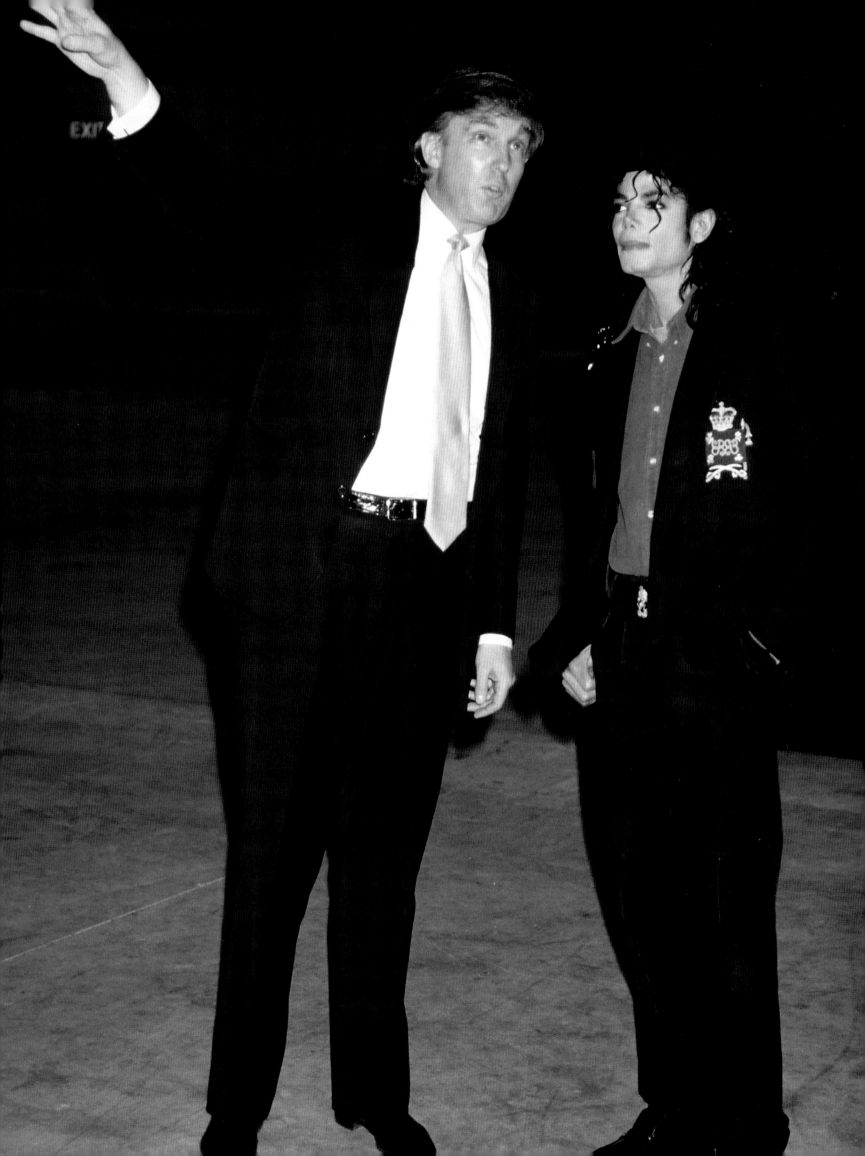

HE WAS THE GREATEST ENTERTAINER I'VE EVER KNOWN. HE HAD MAGIC. HE WAS A GENIUS. WE WERE AT THE TRUMP TAJ MAHAL IN ATLANTIC CITY. THERE WERE THOUSANDS OF PEOPLE LITERALLY CRUSHING US. WE HAD 20 BODYGUARDS, BUT IT WAS REALLY DANGEROUS. HE DROPPED TO HIS KNEES AND STARTED CRAWLING TO THE EXIT. HE DID IT SO ROUTINELY, I THOUGHT HE FELL. AND I SAID, "MICHAEL IS IT ALWAYS LIKE THIS?" HE GOES "YEAH, THIS IS NOTHING. JAPAN IS MUCH WORSE." HE HAD A LOT OF PROBLEMS, A LOT OF DIFFICULTIES. BUT MICHAEL IN HIS PRIME——THERE'S NEVER BEEN ANYBODY LIKE HIM.

Donald Trump

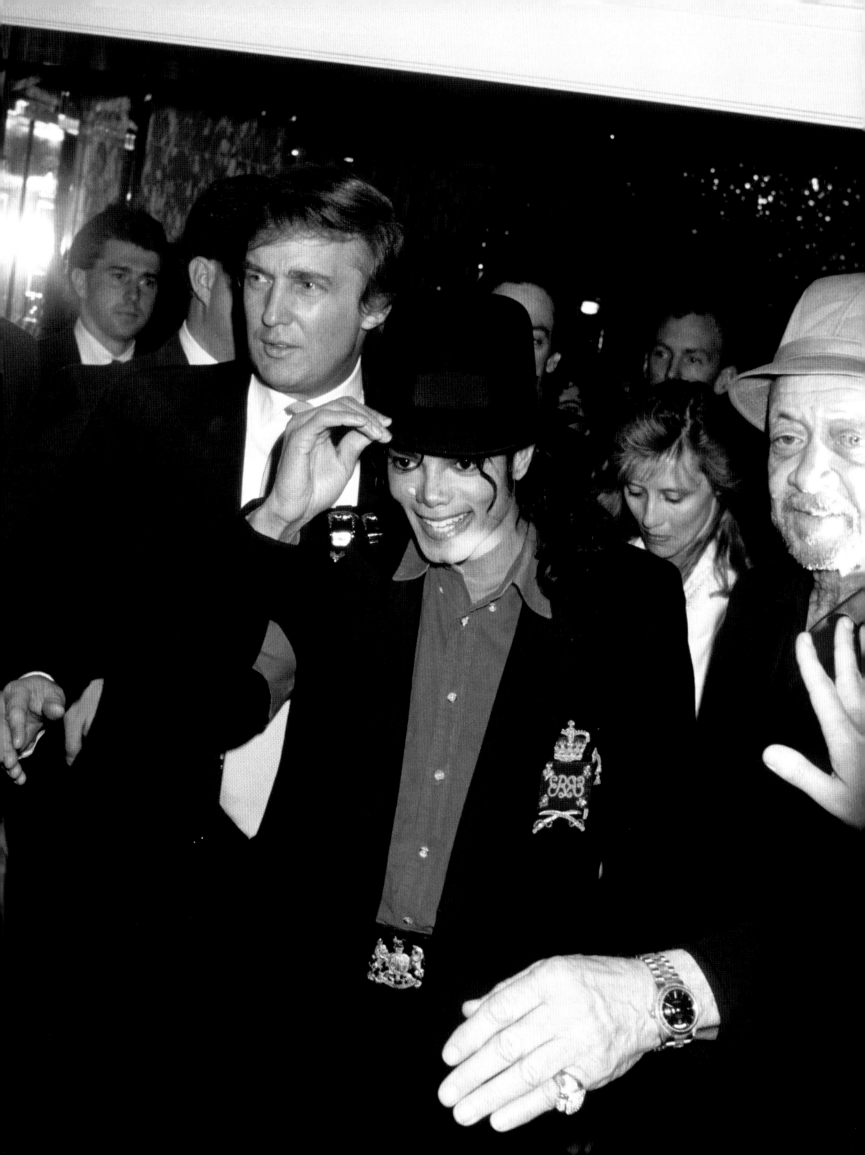

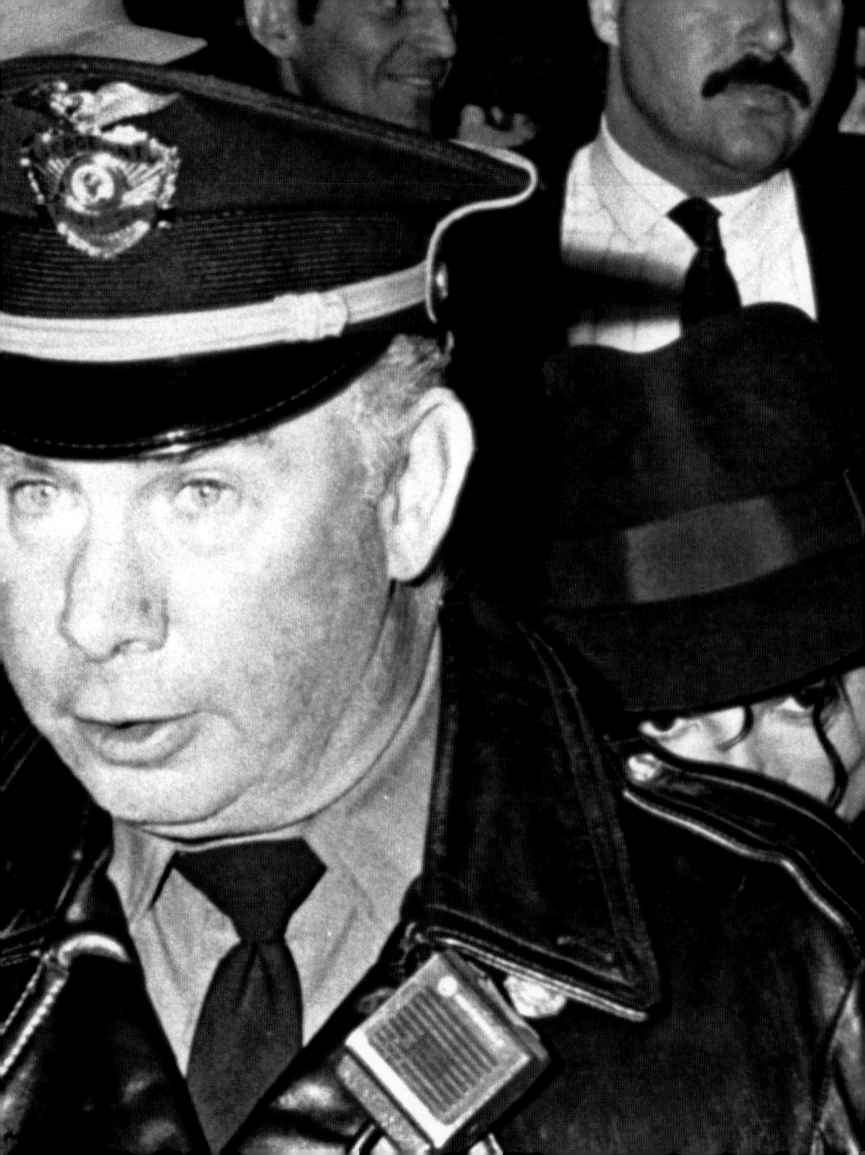

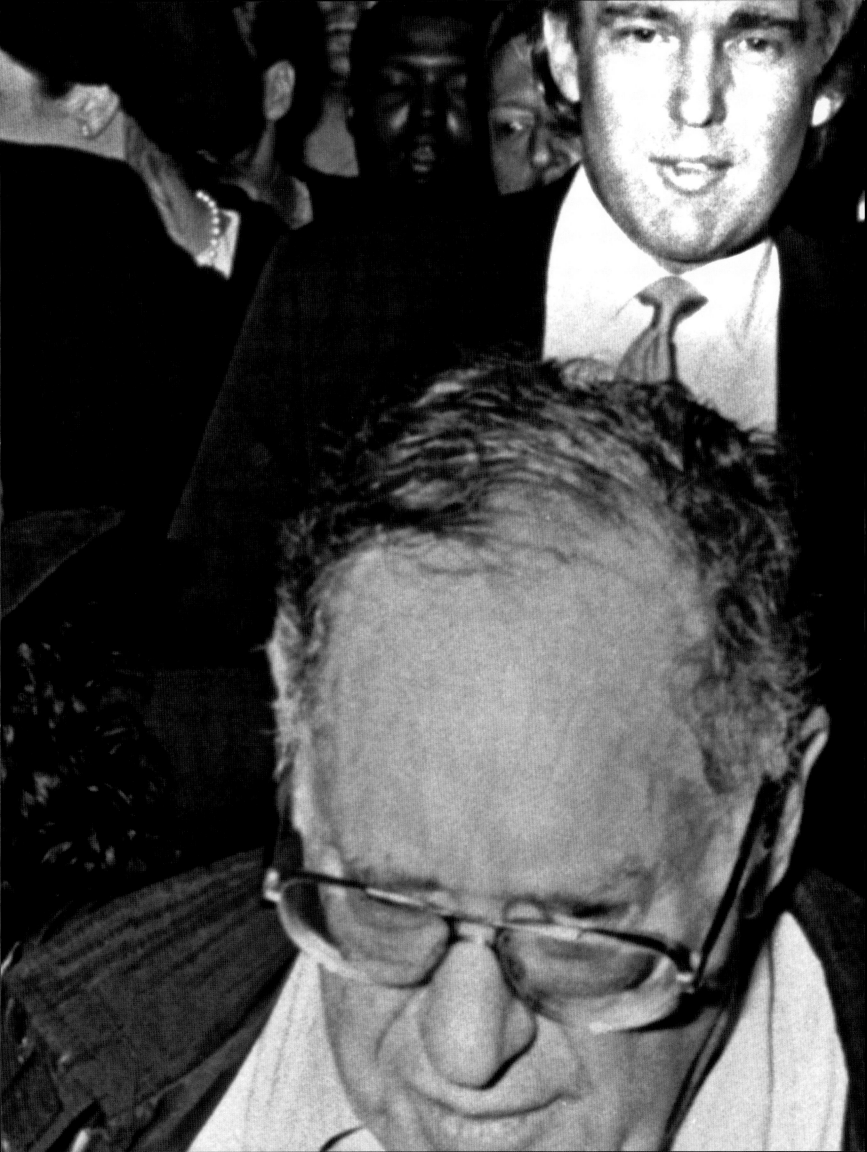

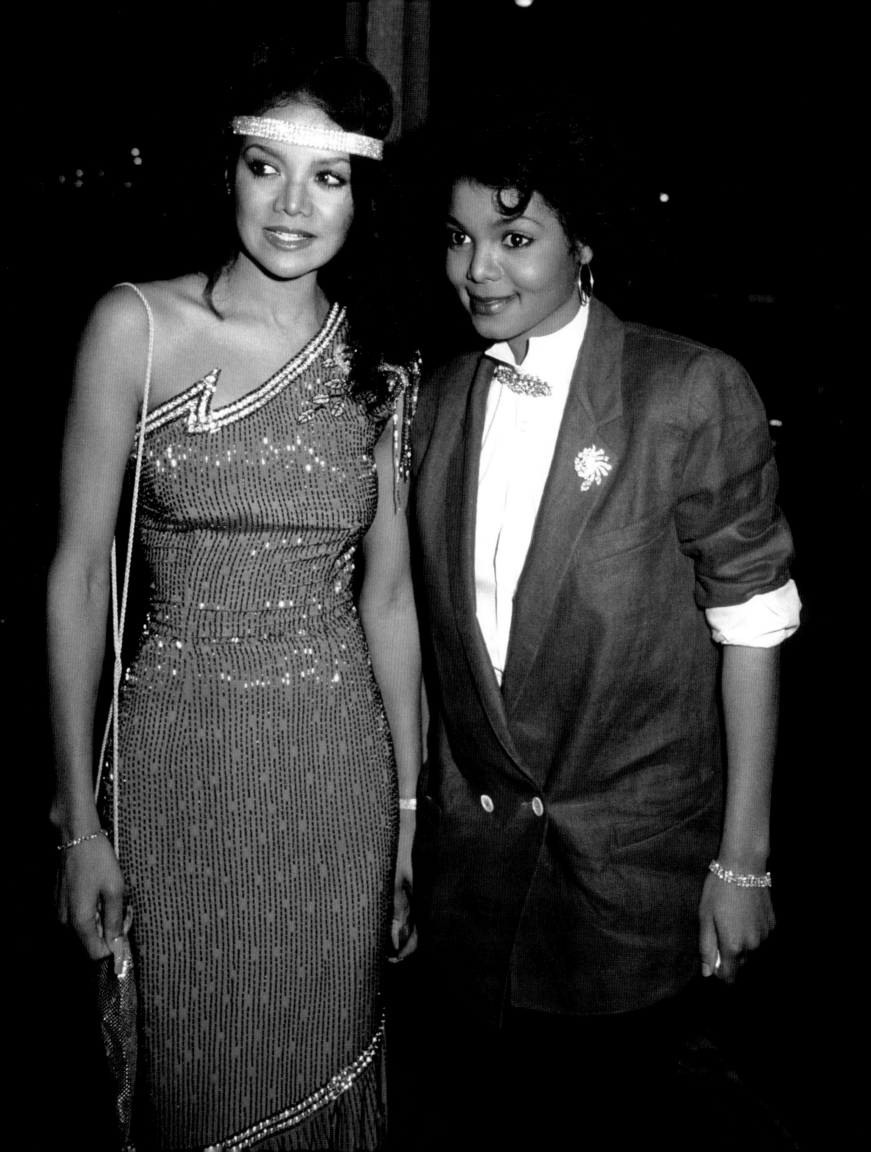

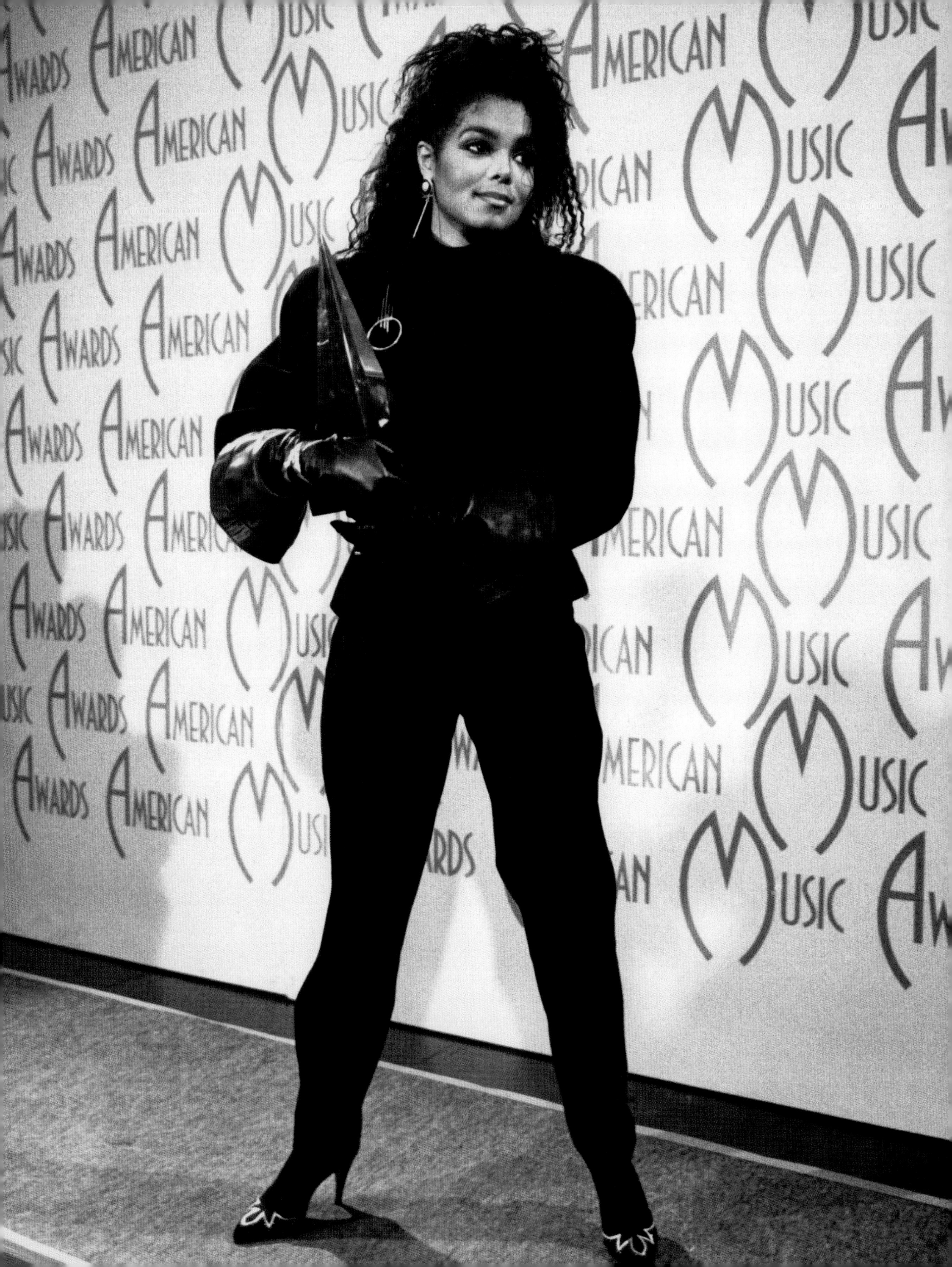
AMERICAN MUSIC AWARDS

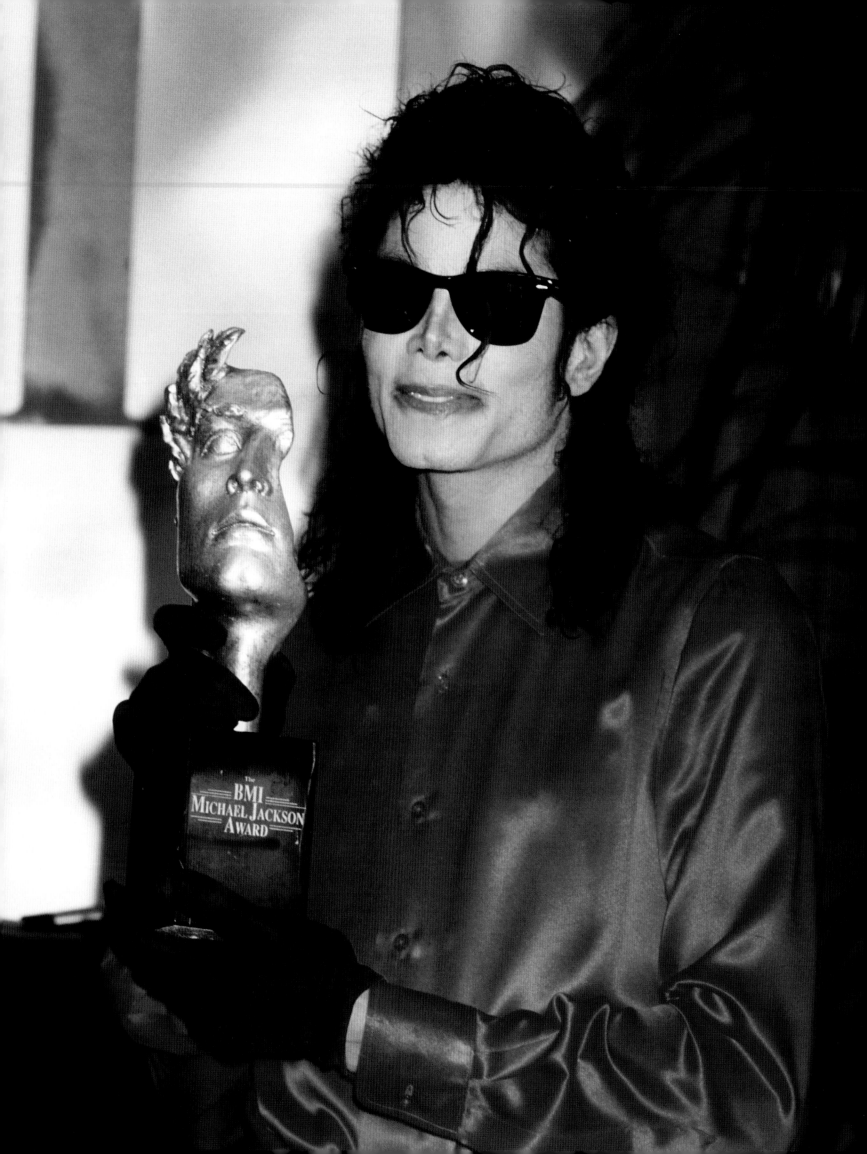

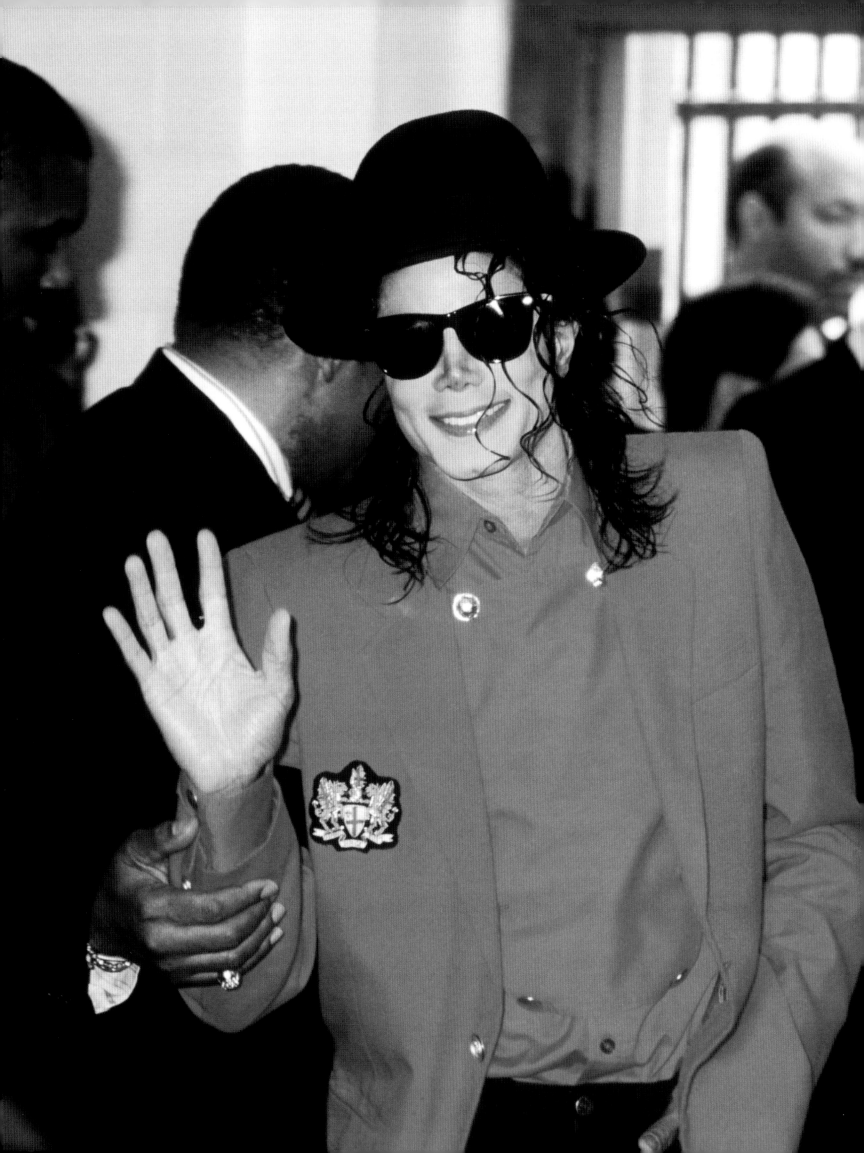

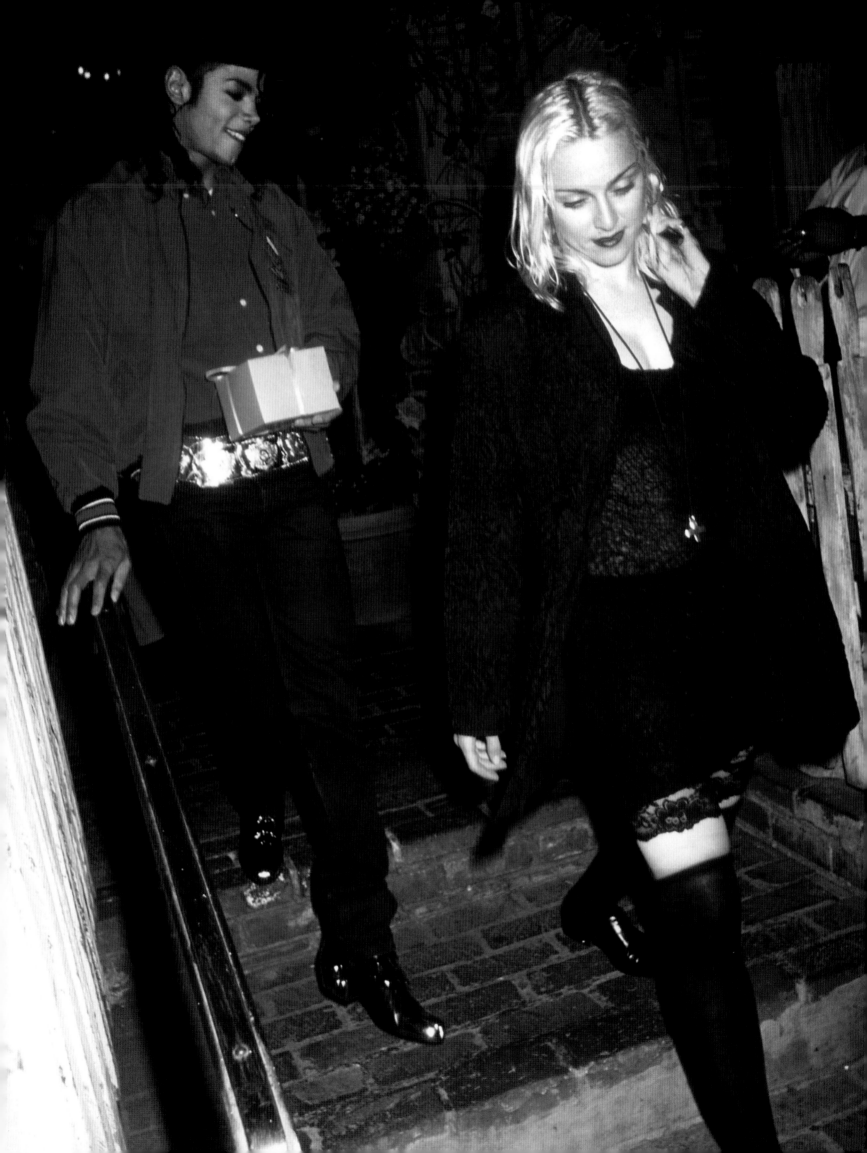

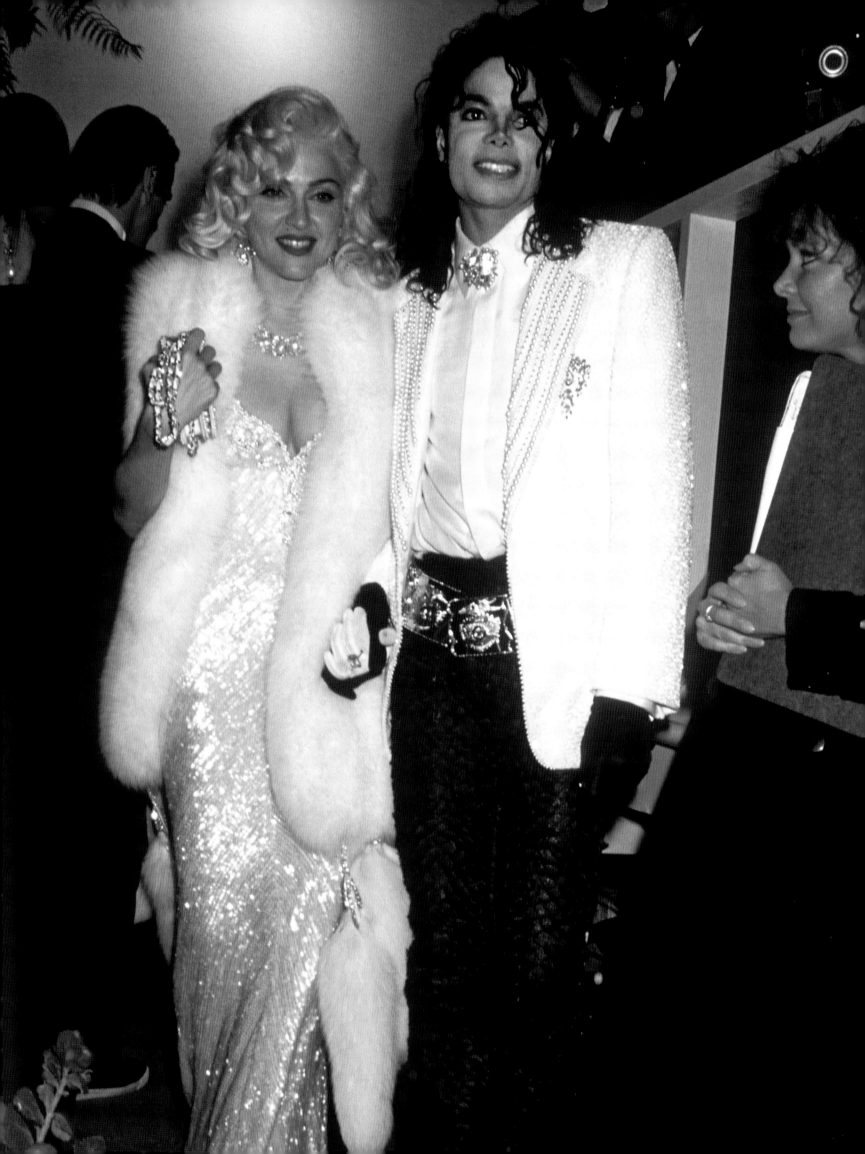

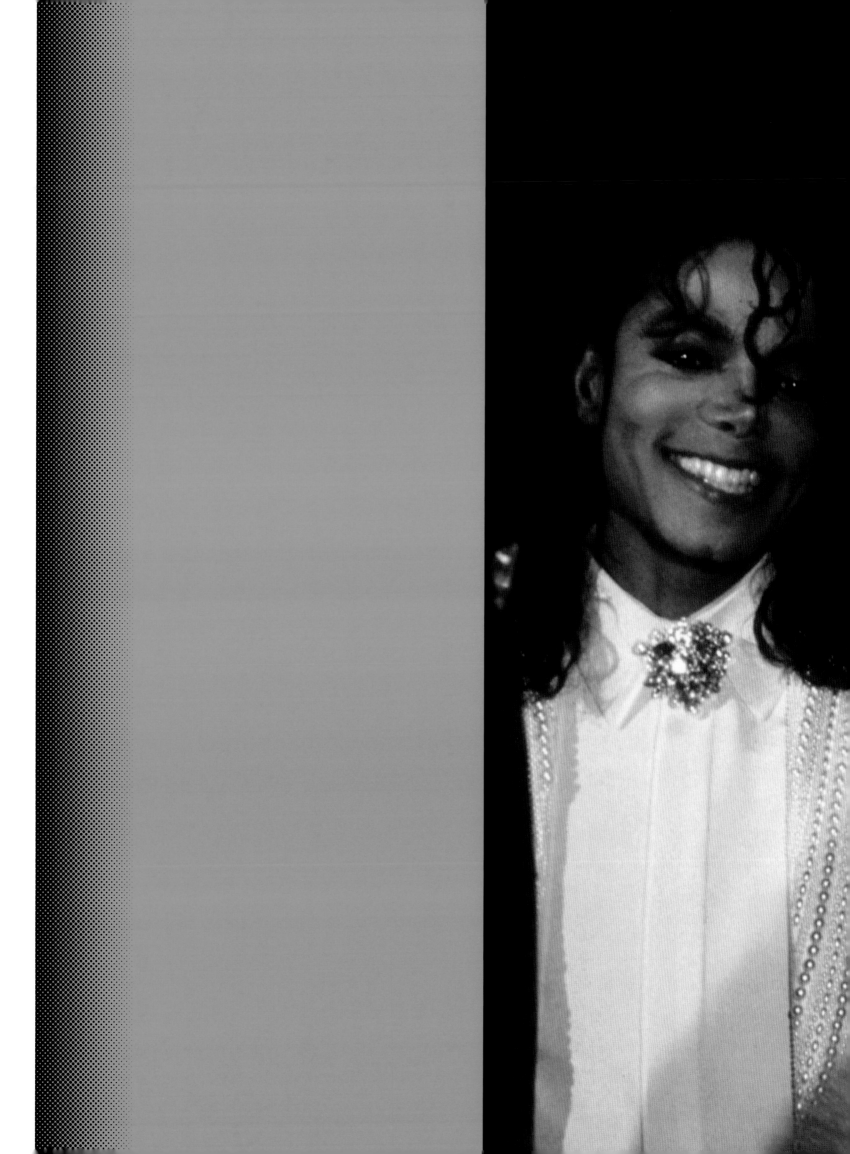

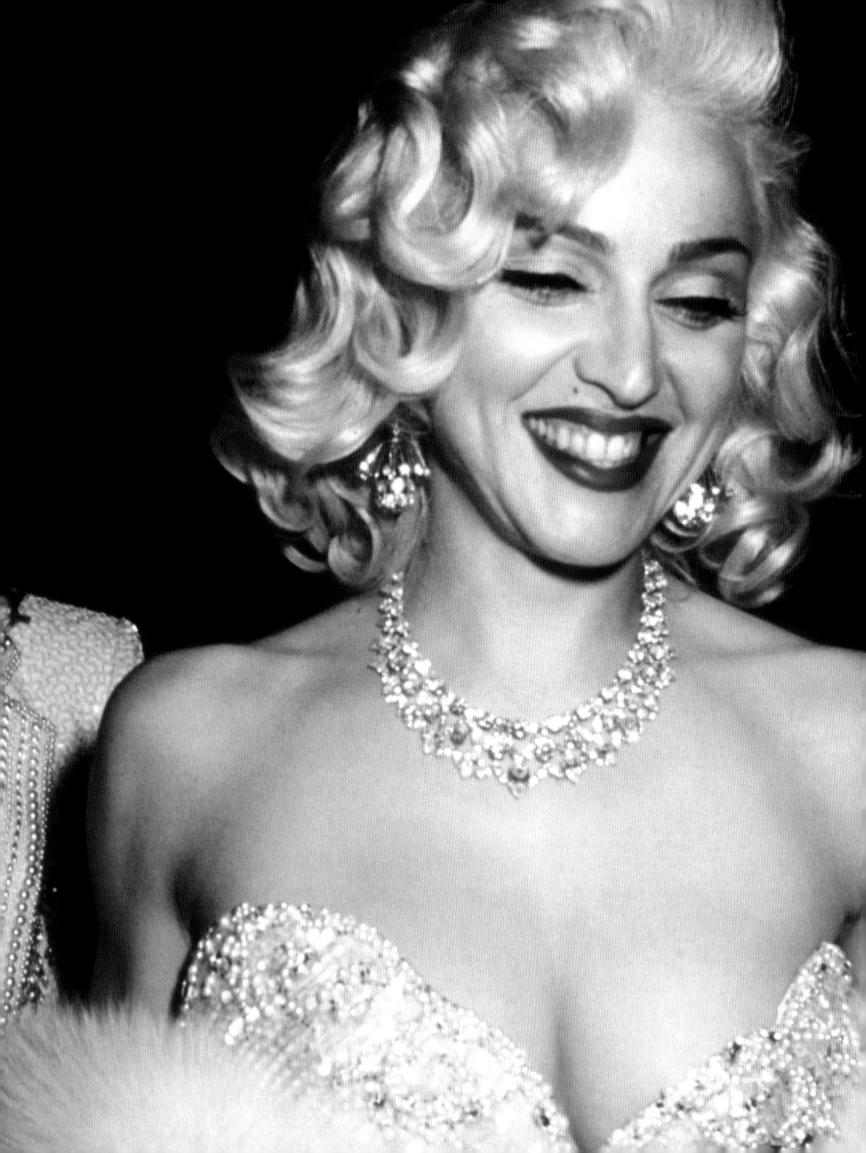

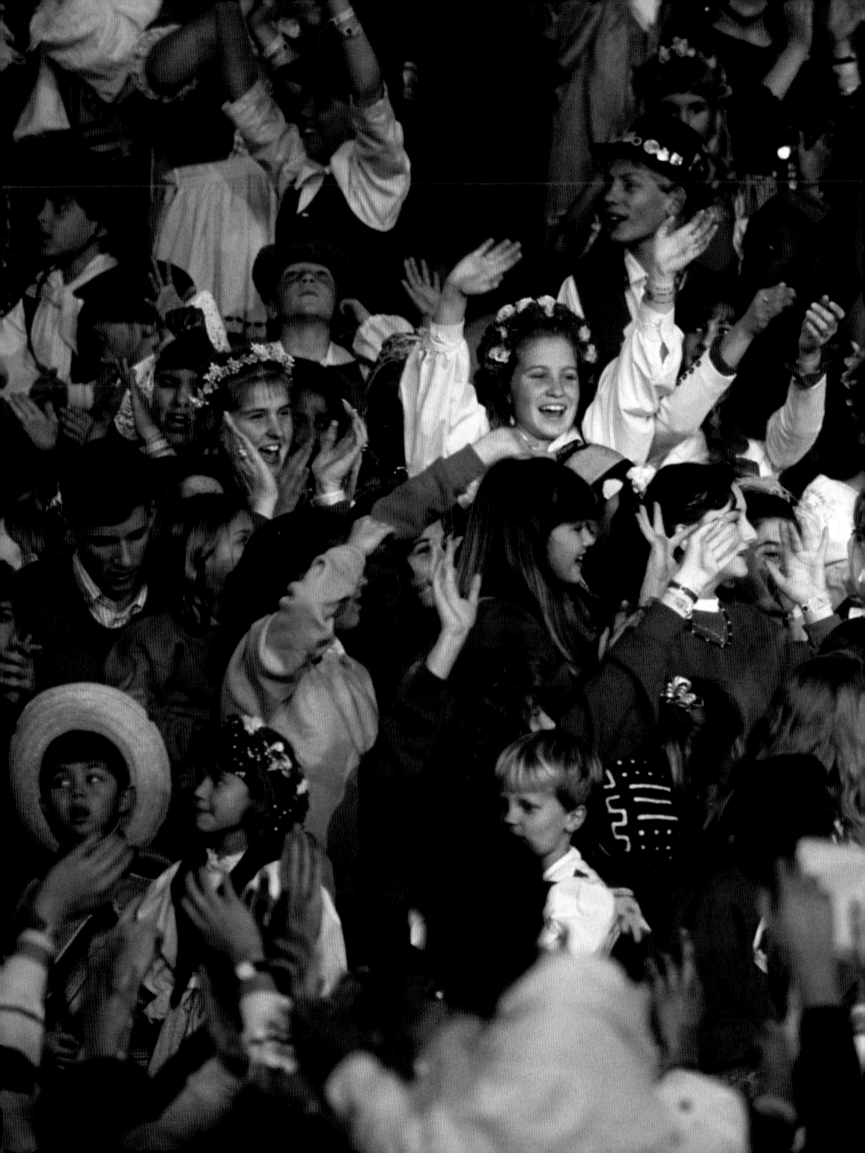

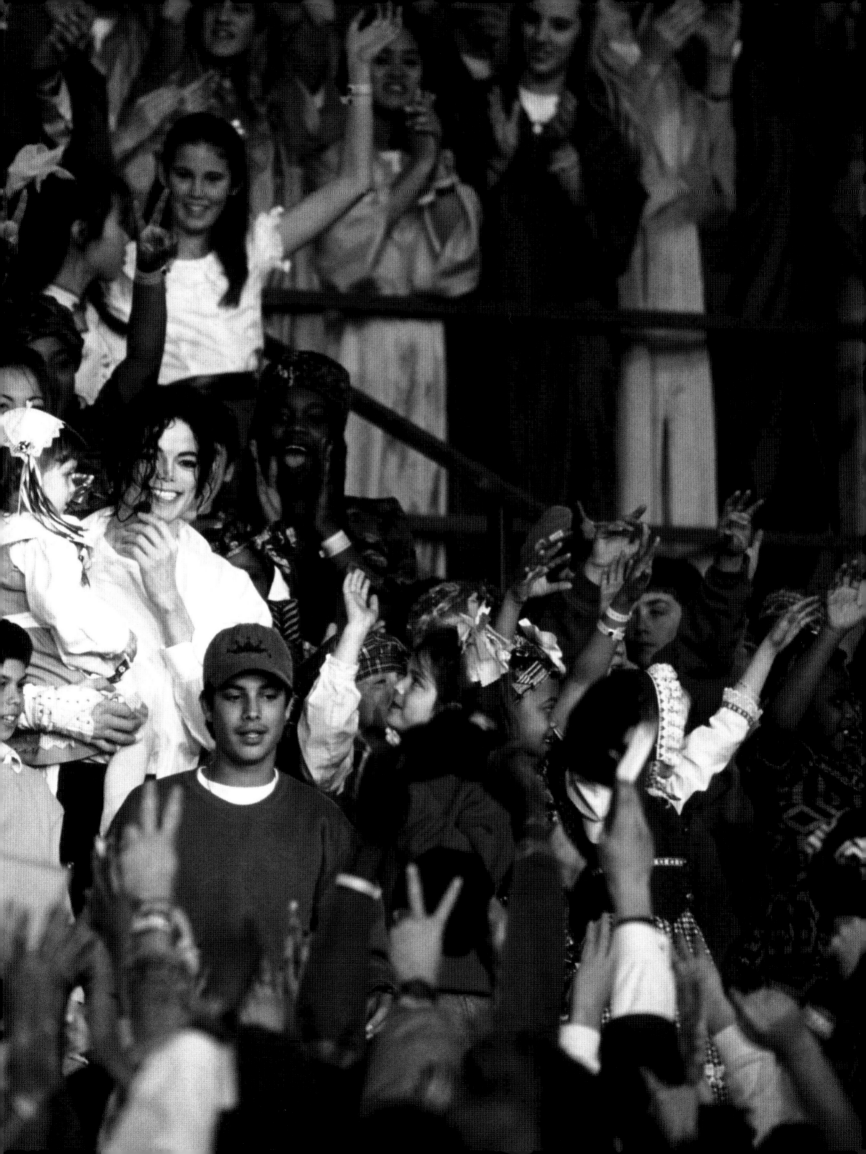

IT'S ALWAYS A GOOD FEELING. I NEVER TAKE IT FOR GRANTED. I'M NEVER PUFFED UP WITH PRIDE OR THINK I'M BETTER THAN THE NEXT-DOOR NEIGHBOR. TO BE LOVED IS A WONDERFUL THING. THAT IS THE MAIN REASON I DO THIS.

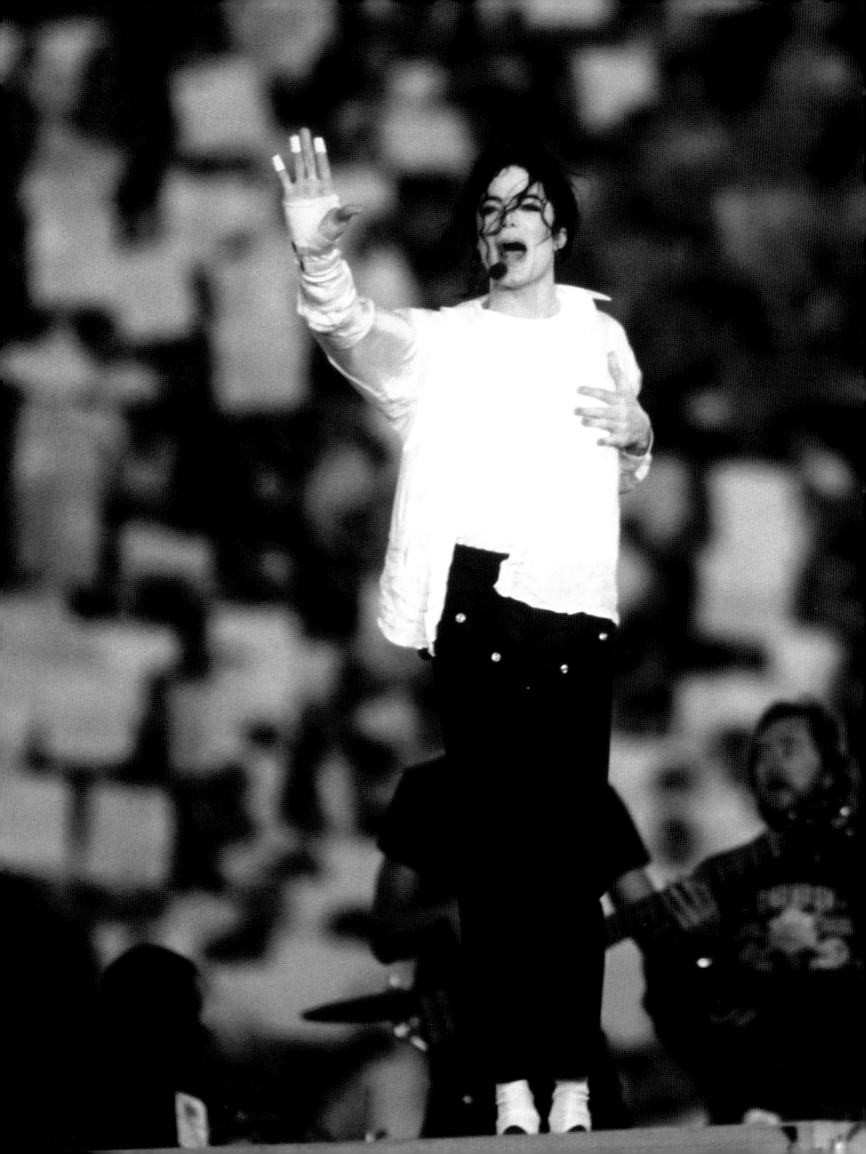

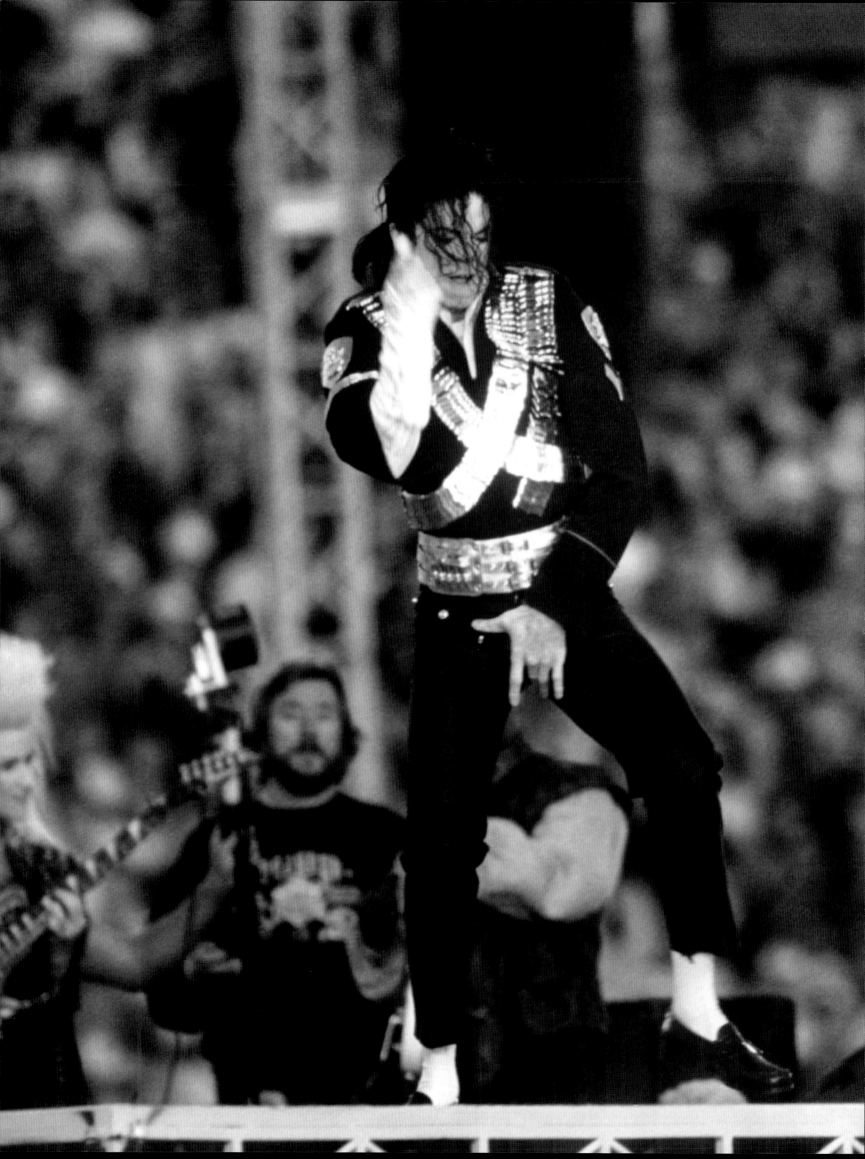

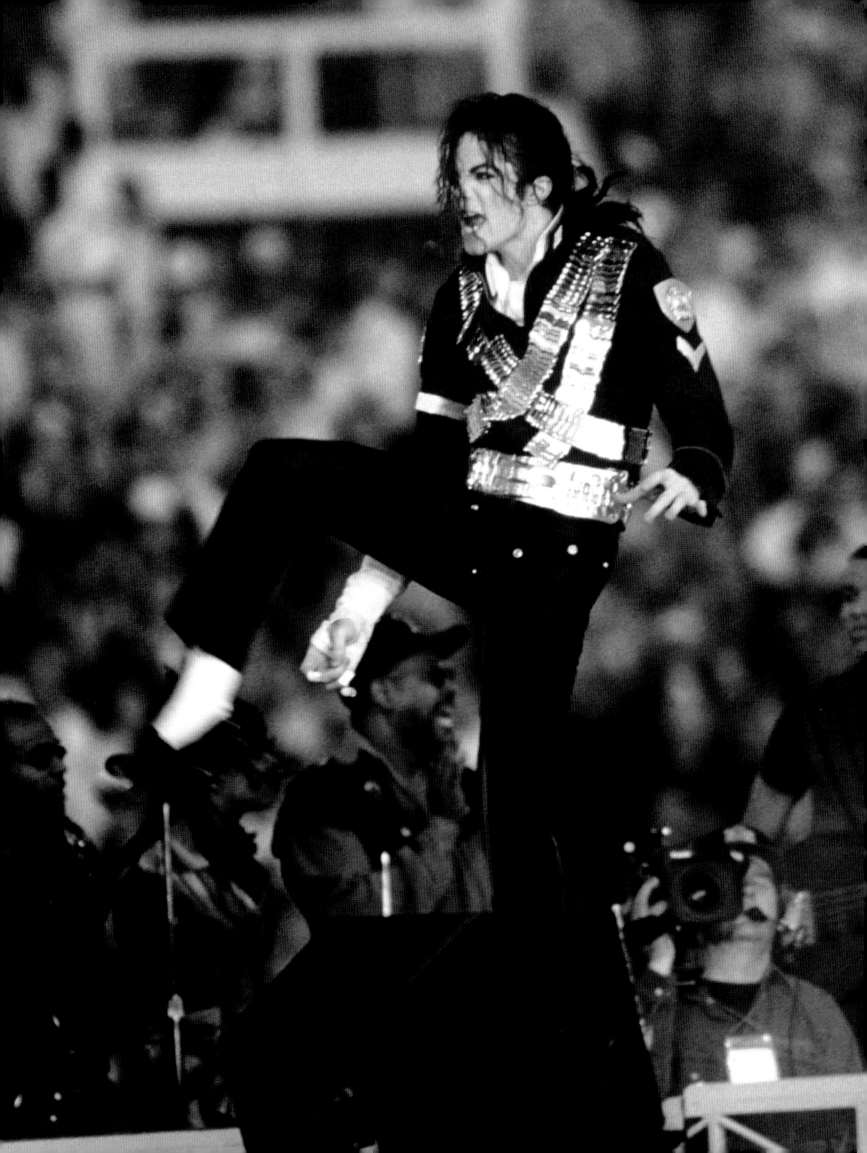

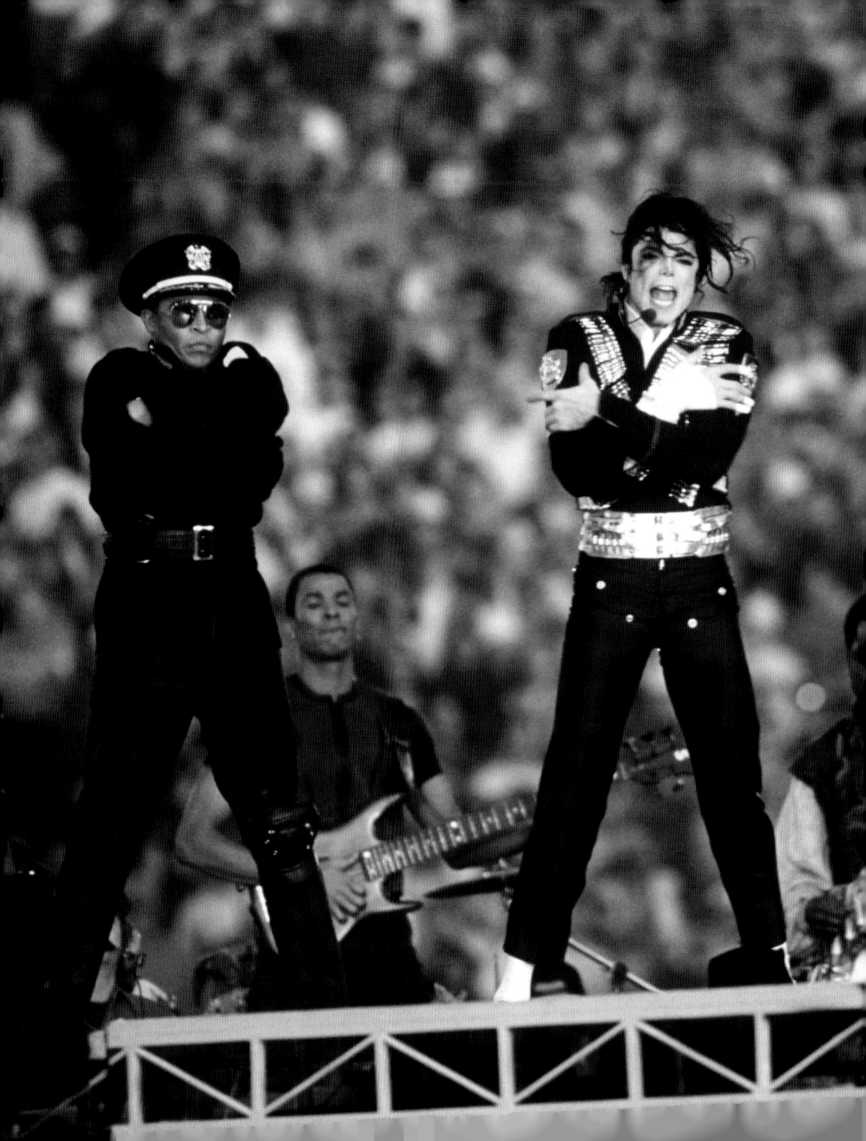

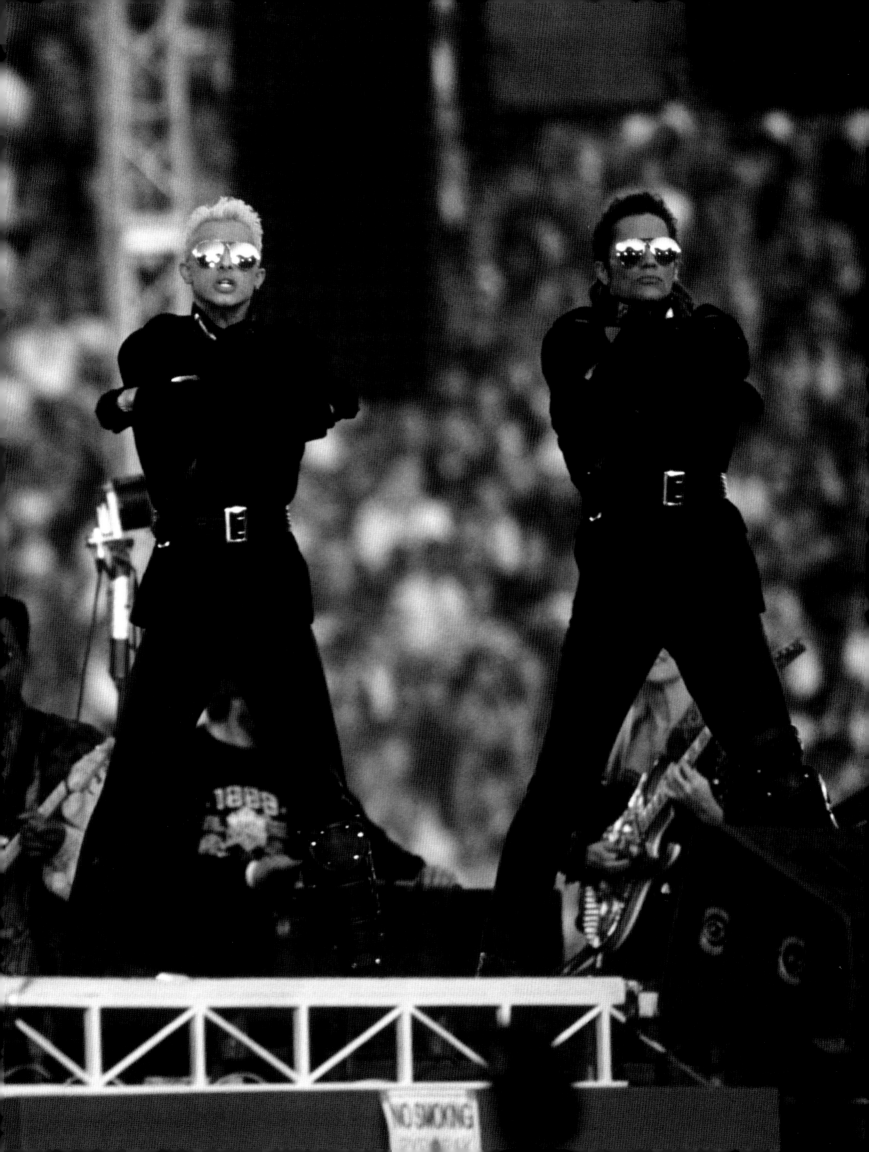

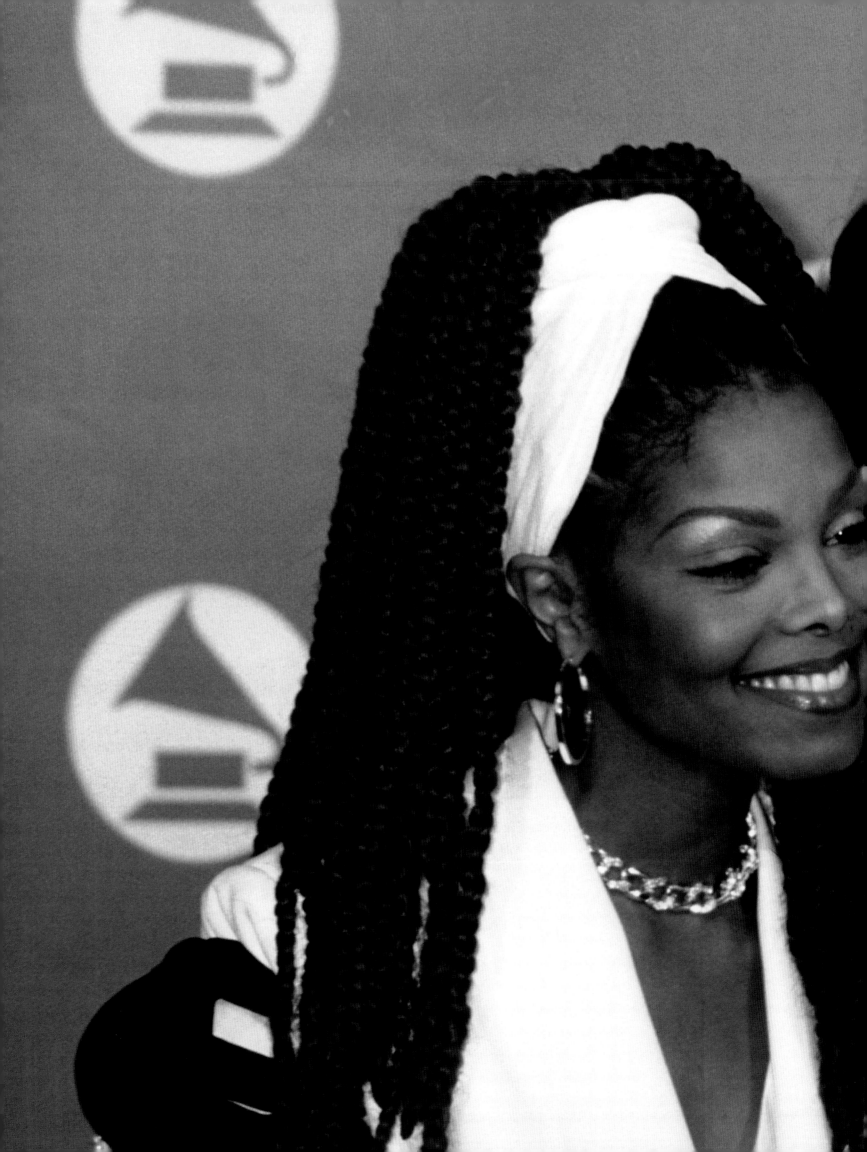

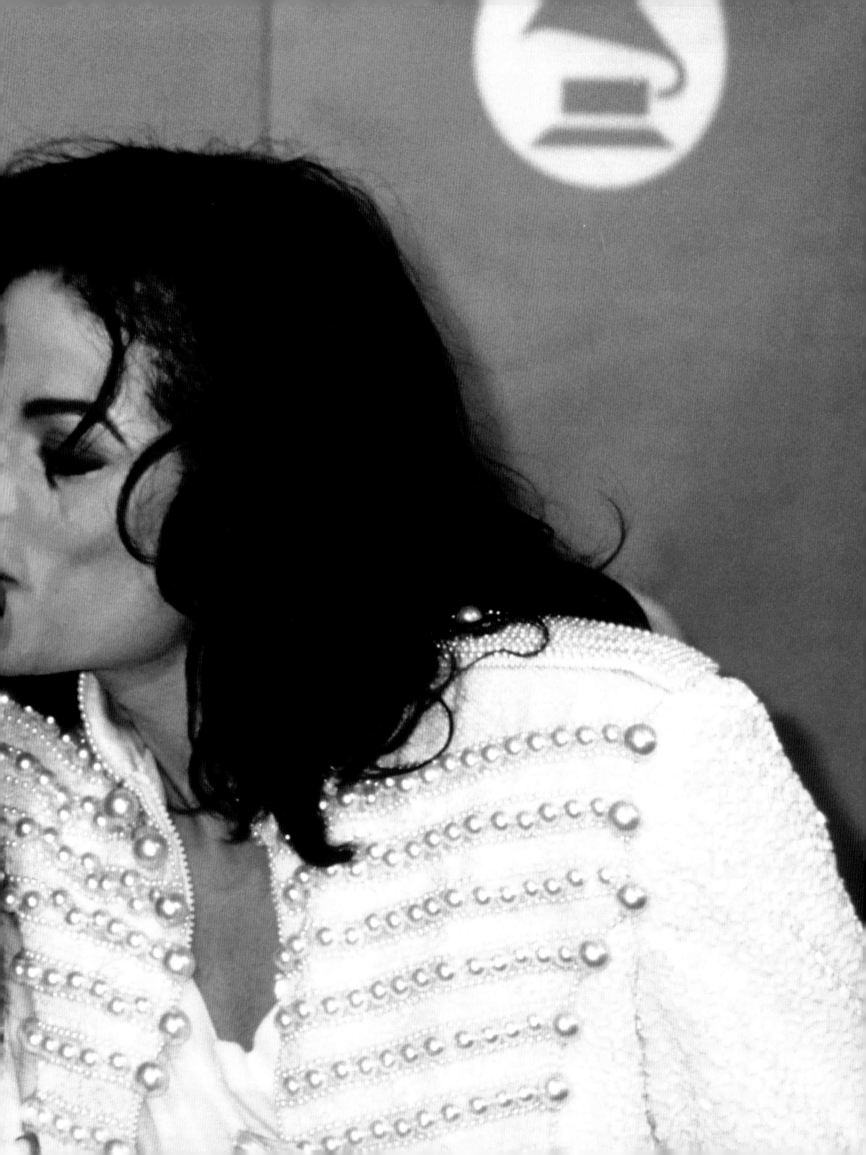

I HOPE THIS FINALLY PUTS TO REST ANOTHER RUMOR THAT HAS BEEN IN THE PRESS FOR TOO MANY YEARS. . .ME AND JANET REALLY ARE TWO DIFFERENT PEOPLE!

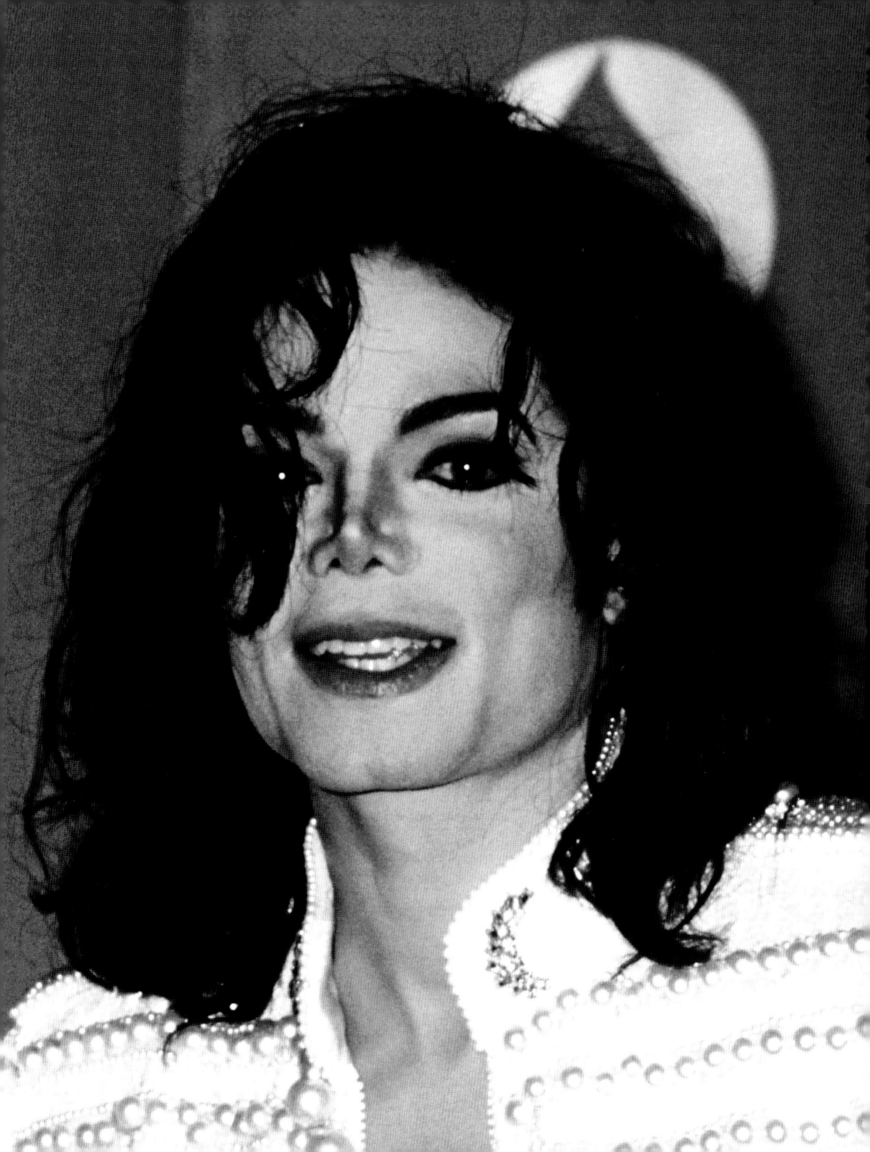

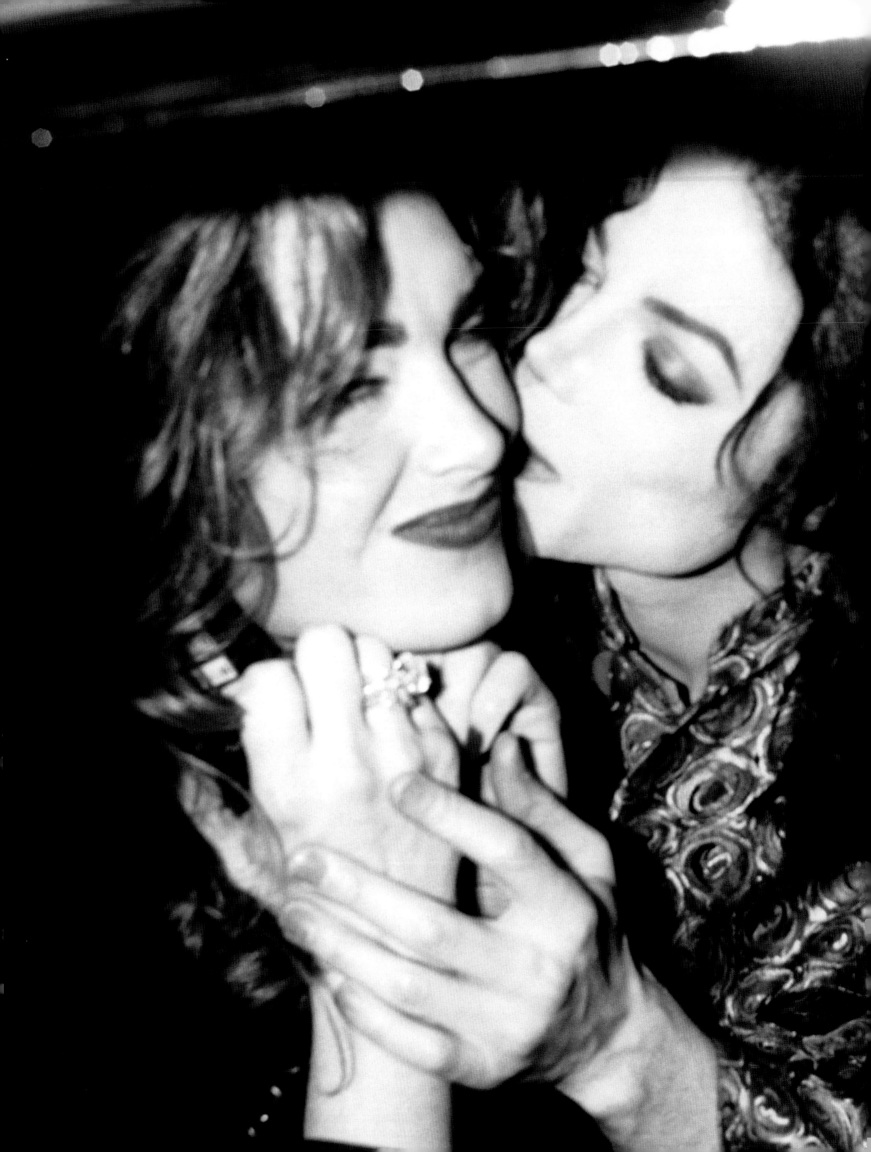

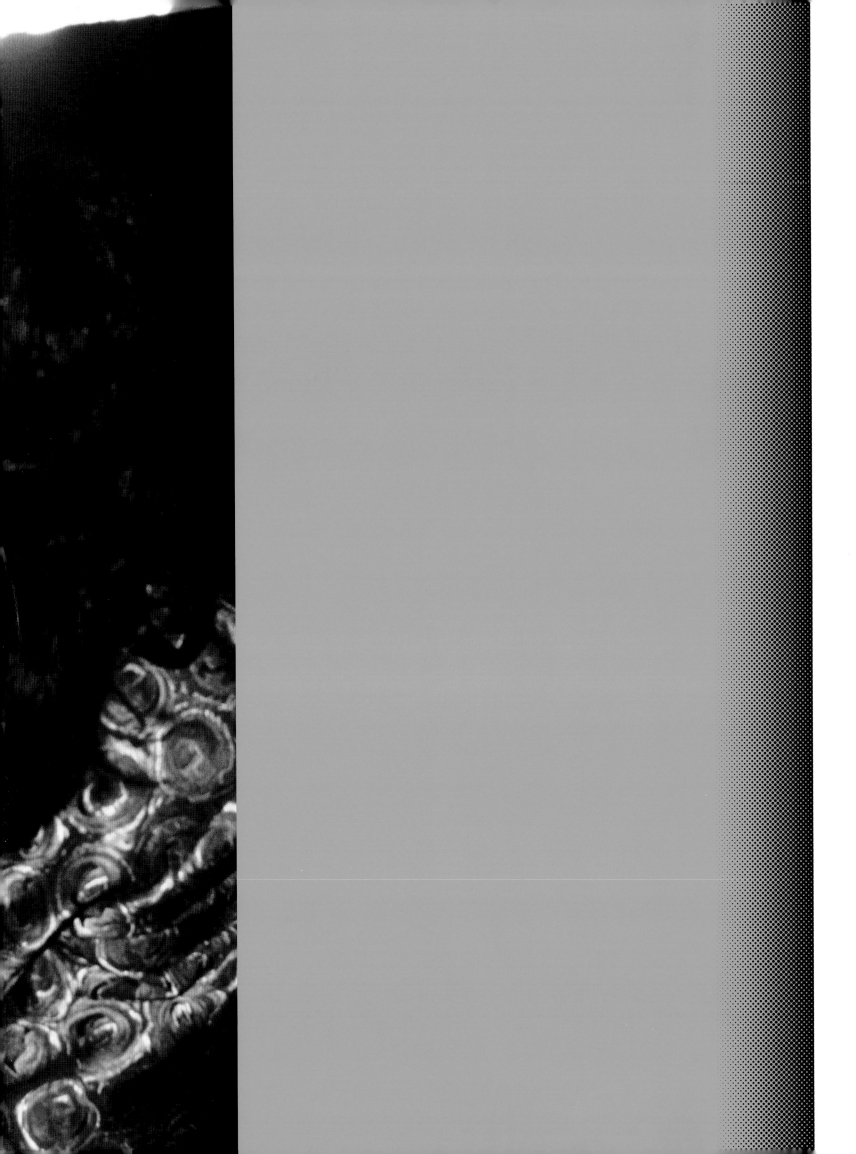

I'M SORRY ABOUT THIS. . . .VERY SORRY. I WAS DANCING AND WENT INTO A SPIN AND TWISTED MY ANKLE VERY BADLY. BUT I WANTED TO COME HERE TO THANK EVERYBODY.

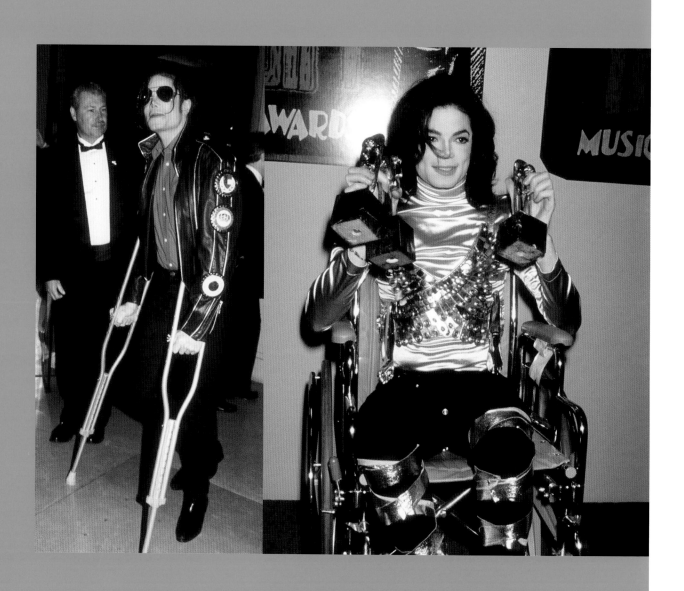

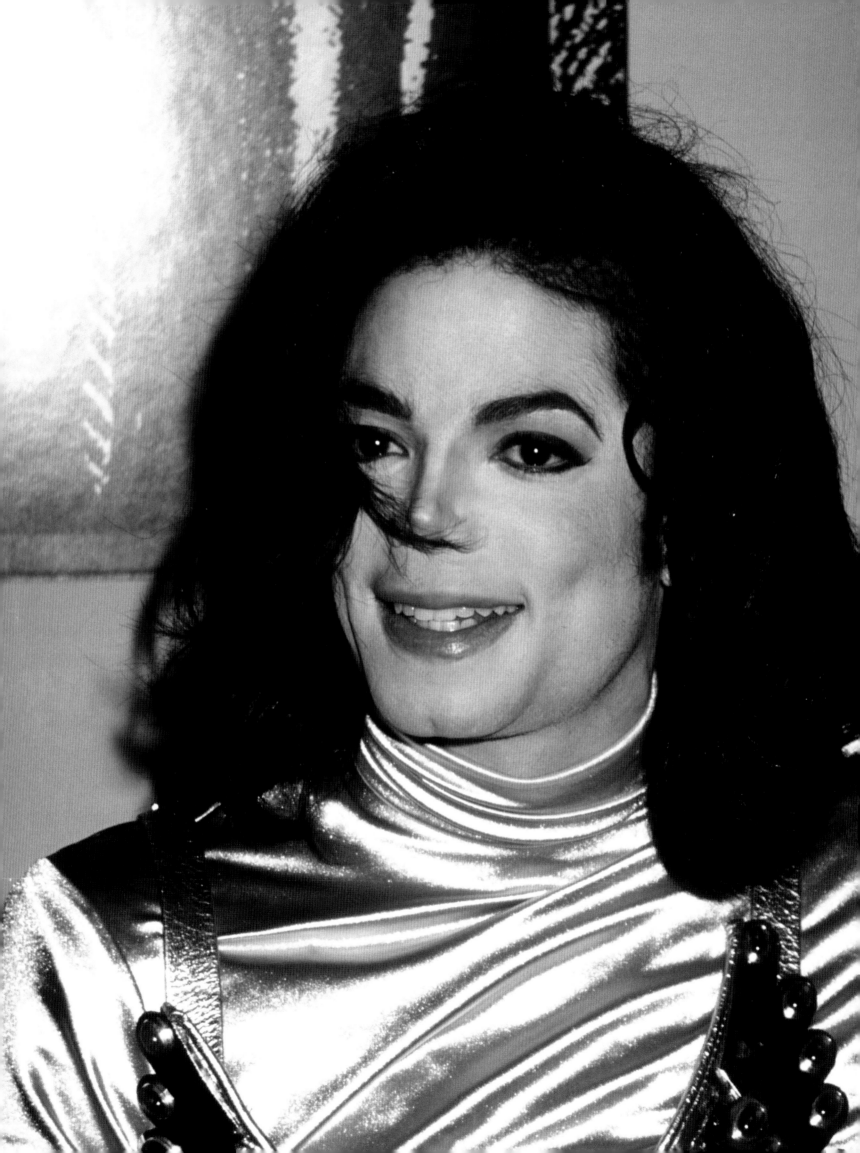

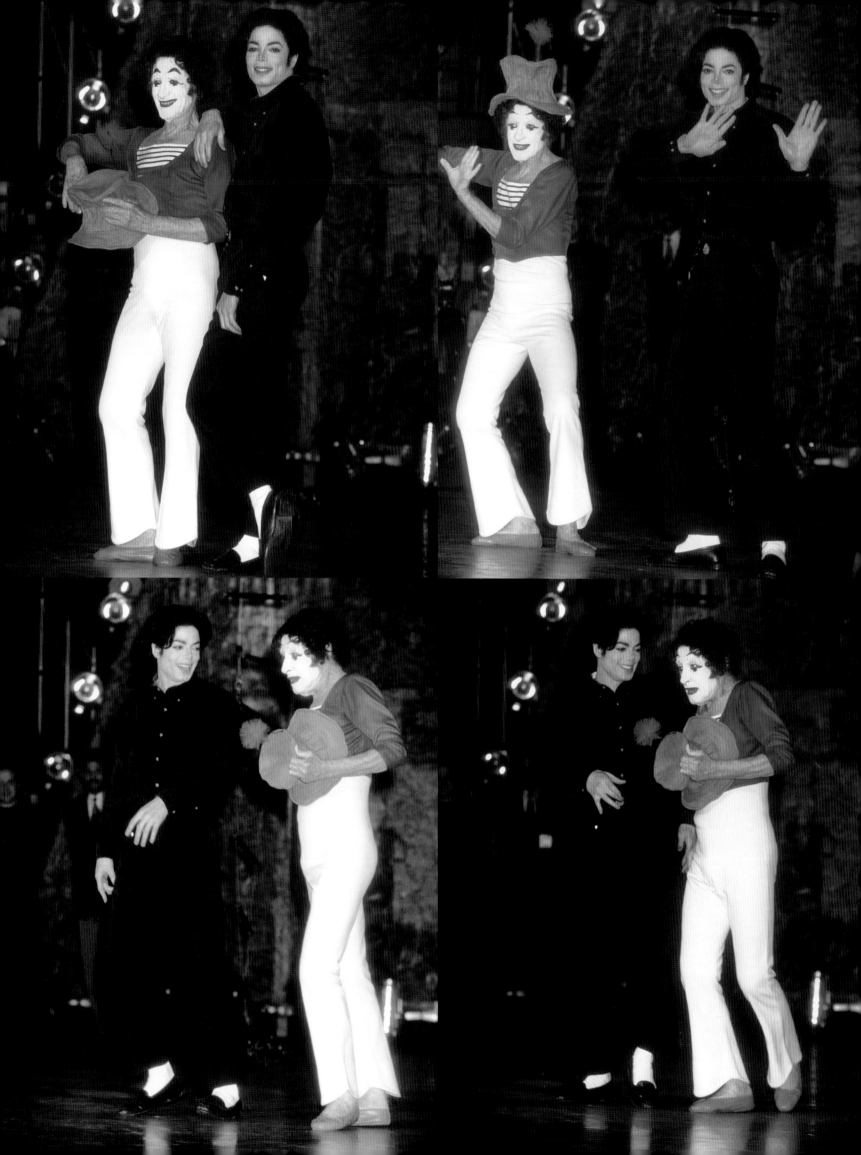

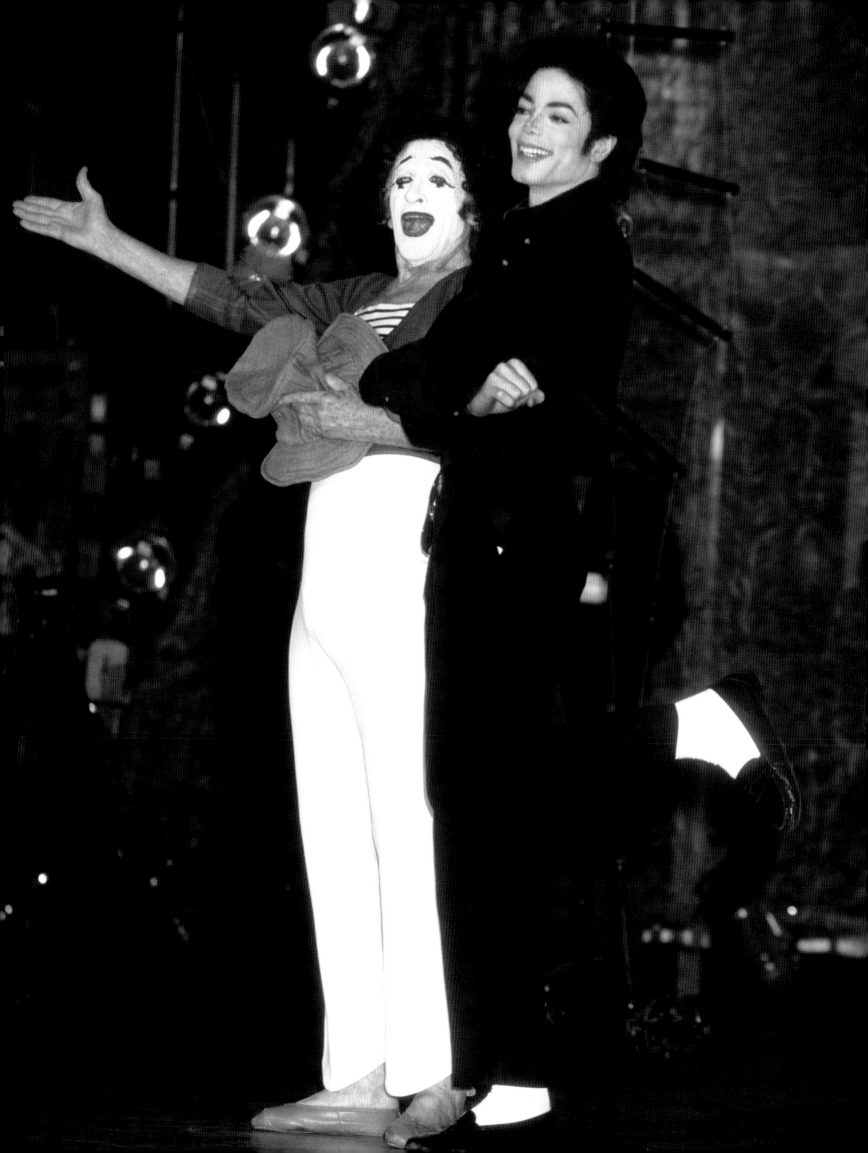

# I JUST LOVE WORKING HARD ON SOMETHING, PUTTING IT TOGETHER, SWEATING OVER IT AND THEN SHARING IT WITH PEOPLE.

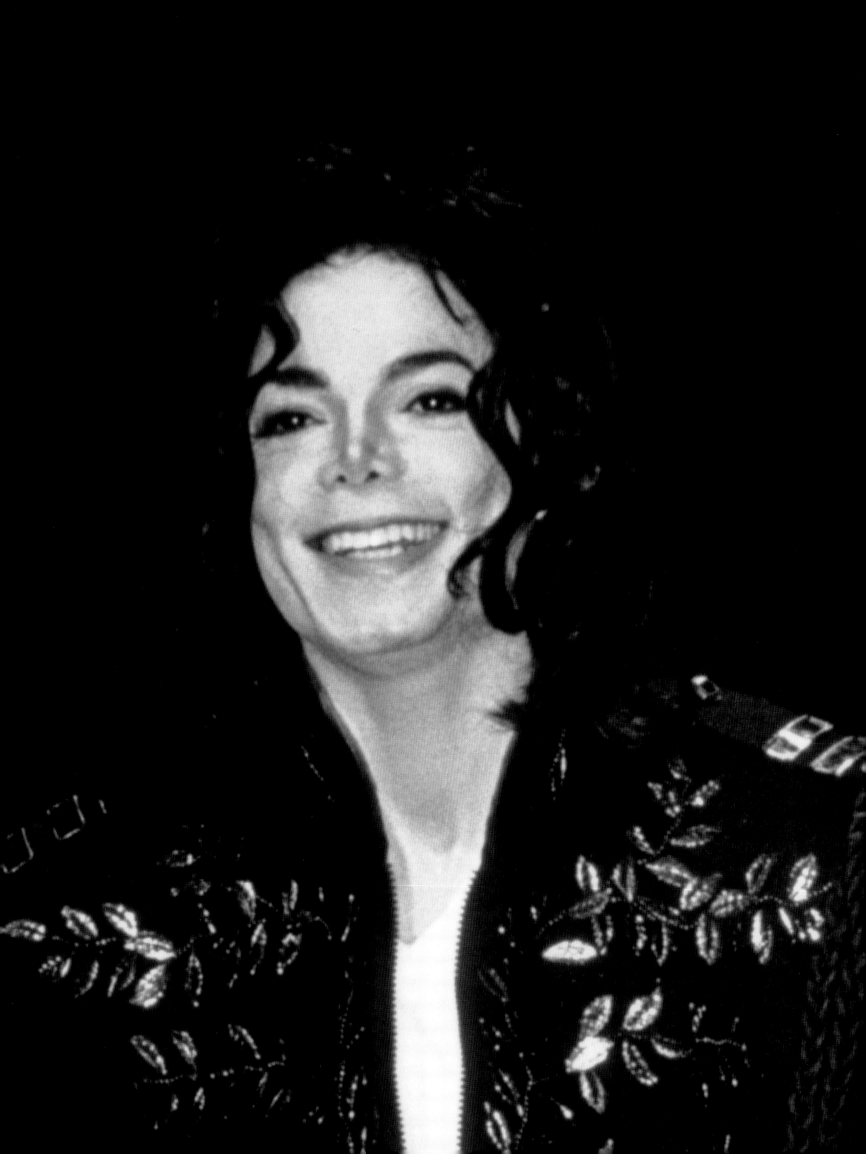

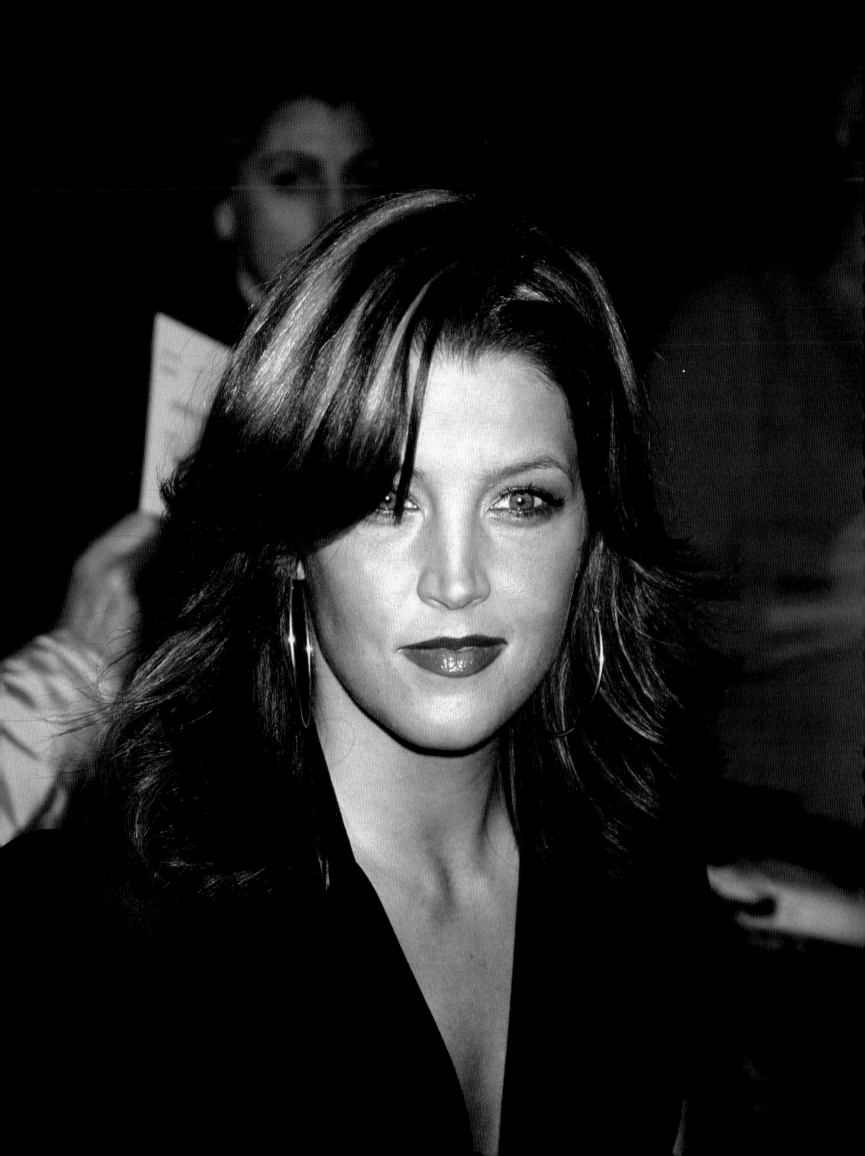

WHEN SHE WAS 18, I USED TO TELL MY LAWYER... "DO YOU KNOW LISA MARIE PRESLEY?" HE'D GO, "WELL I REPRESENT HER MOTHER," AND I'D GO "WELL CAN YOU GET IN TOUCH WITH HER, 'CAUSE I THINK SHE'S REALLY CUTE!"

OFTEN IN THE PAST, PERFORMERS HAVE BEEN TRAGIC FIGURES....IT'S SO SAD. YOU FEEL CHEATED AS A FAN THAT YOU DIDN'T GET TO WATCH THEM EVOLVE AS THEY GREW OLDER.

I ALWAYS WANTED TO HAVE A BIG FAMILY....I WAS ALWAYS TELLING MY FATHER I WOULD OUTDO HIM. HE HAD 10 CHILDREN. I WOULD LOVE TO HAVE LIKE 11 OR 12 MYSELF.

CHILDREN SHOW ME IN THEIR PLAYFUL SMILES THE DIVINE IN EVERYONE....THIS SIMPLE GOODNESS SHINES STRAIGHT FROM THEIR HEARTS.

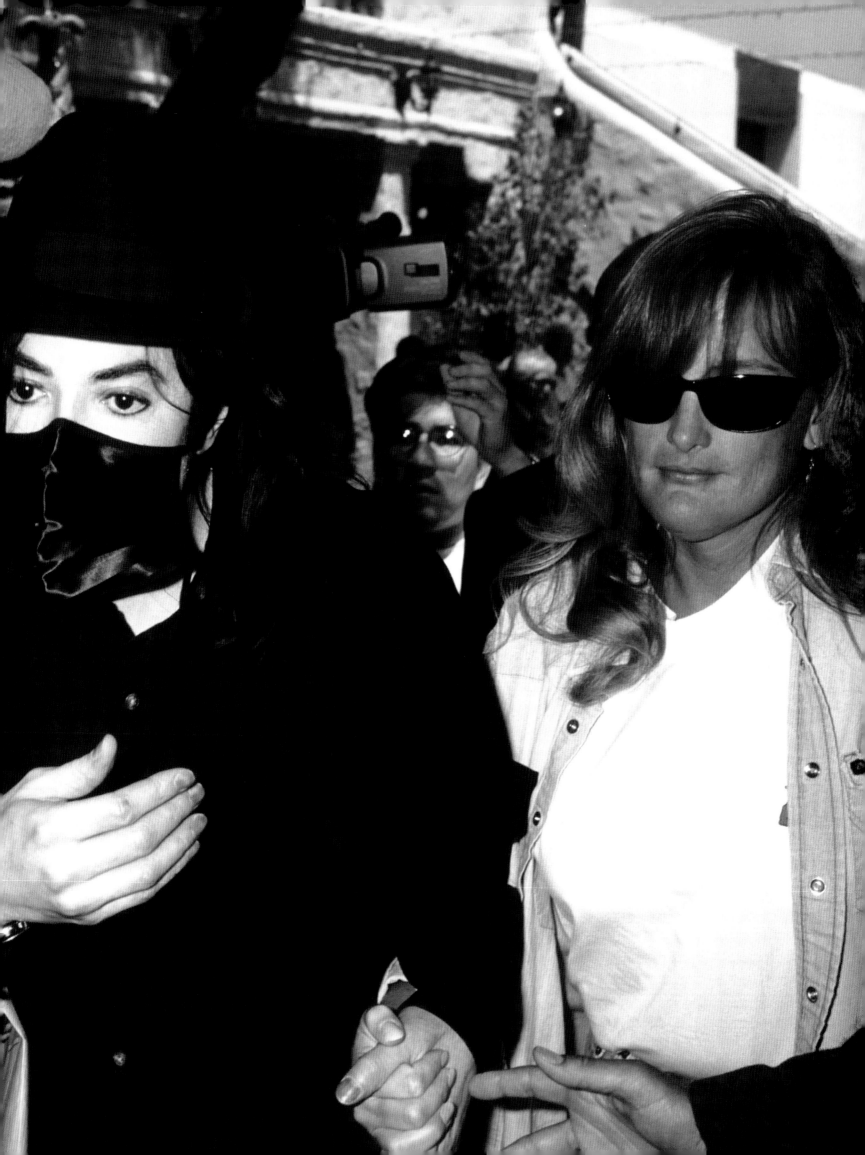

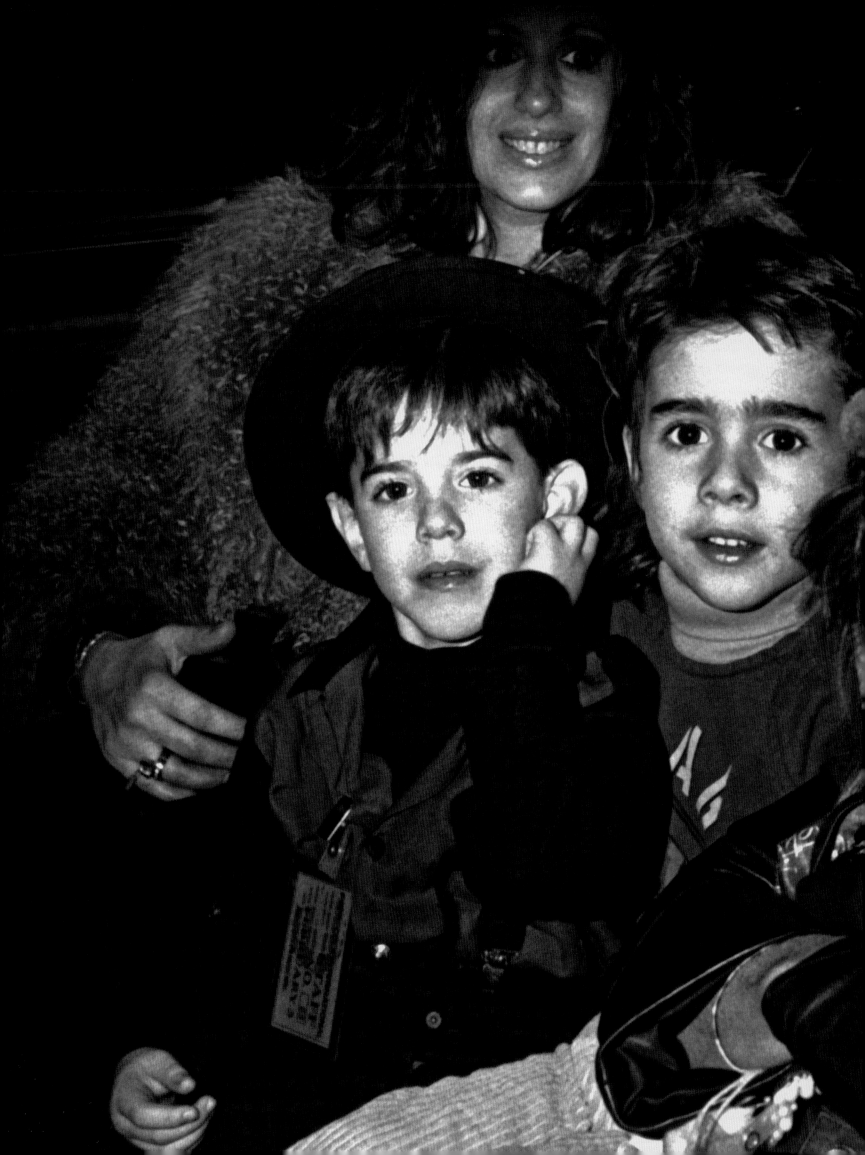

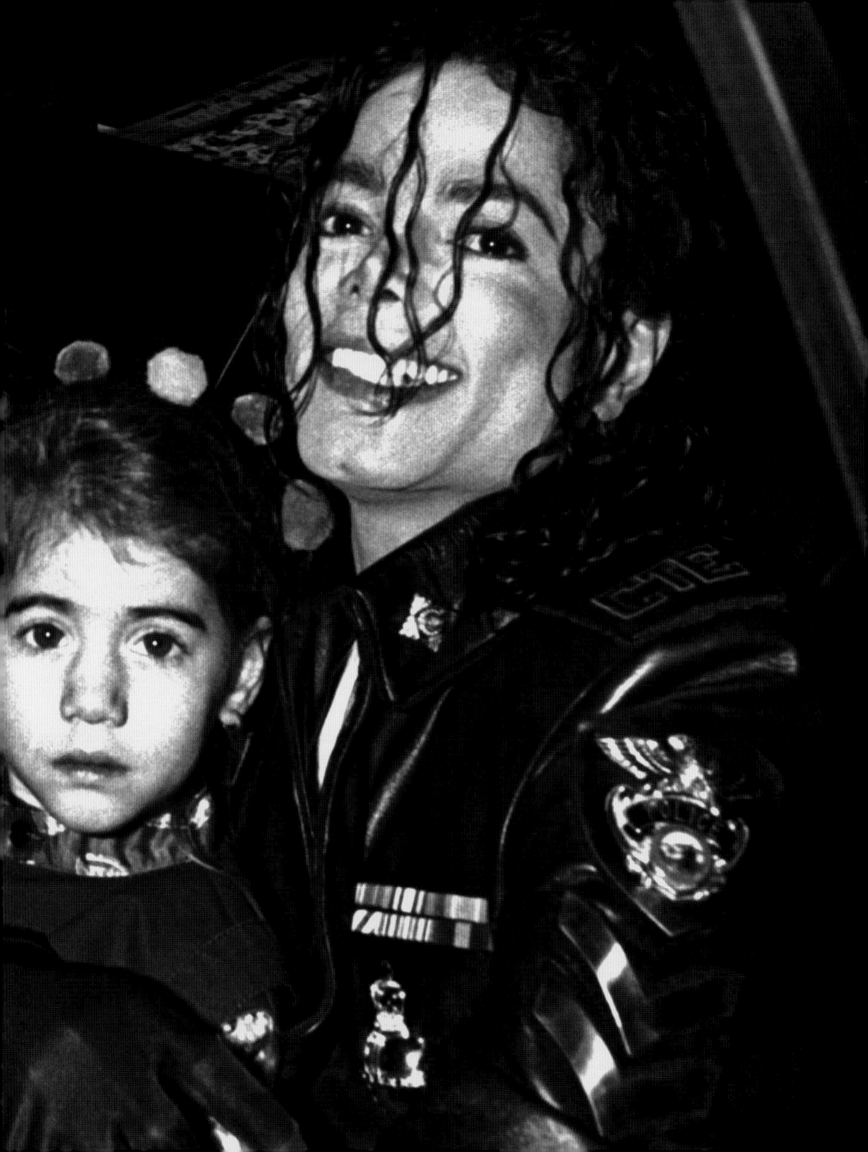

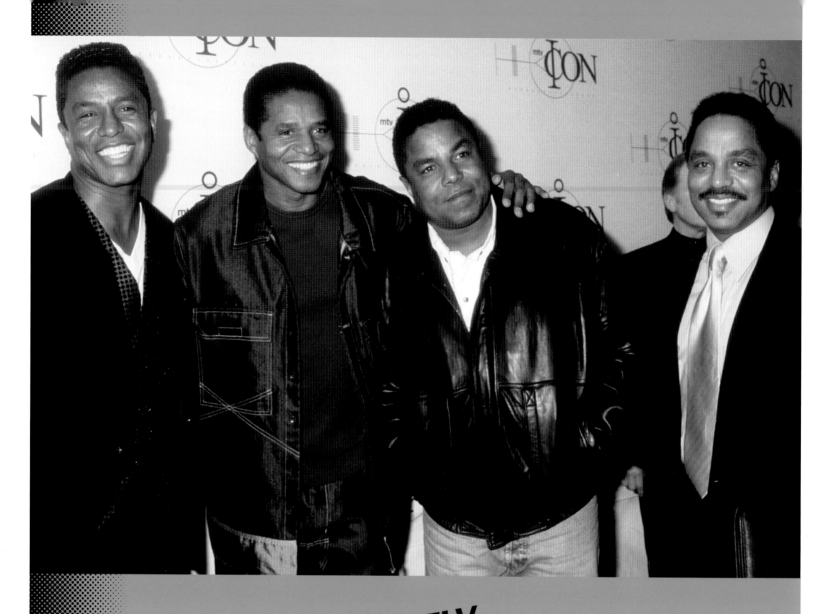

WE SANG CONSTANTLY IN THE HOUSE. WE SANG GROUP HARMONY WHILE WASHING DISHES. WE'D MAKE UP SONGS AS WE WORKED. THAT'S WHAT MAKES GREATNESS.

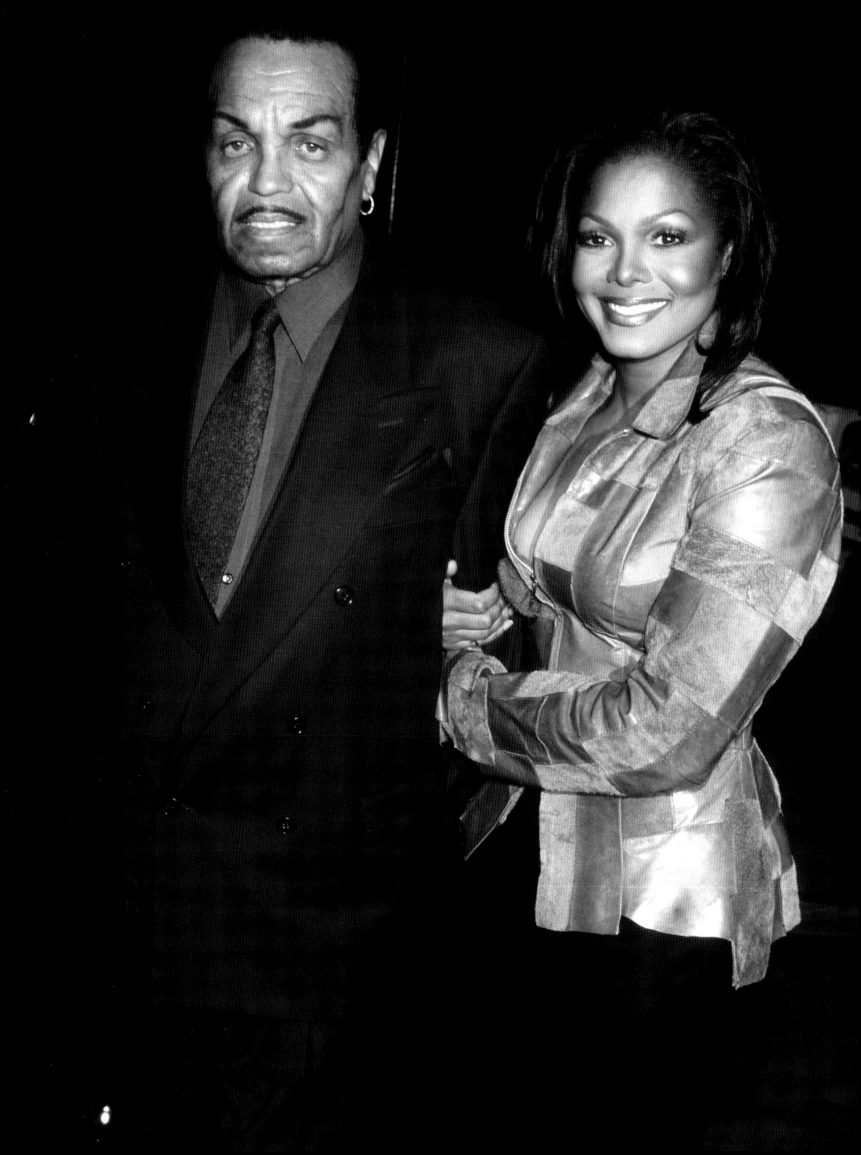

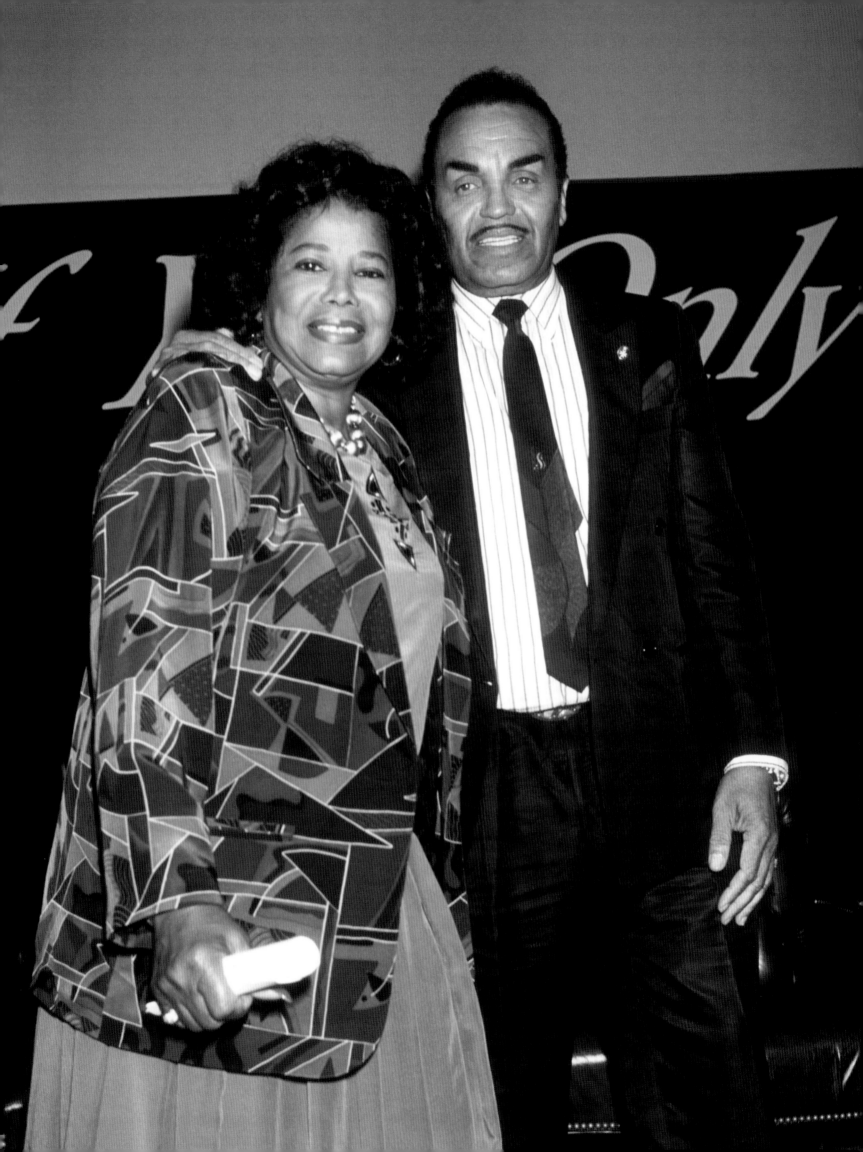

MY FATHER IS A MUCH NICER PERSON NOW. I THINK HE REALIZES HIS CHILDREN ARE EVERYTHING. WITHOUT YOUR FAMILY, YOU HAVE NOTHING. HE'S A NICE HUMAN BEING. AT ONE TIME, WE'D BE HORRIFIED IF HE JUST SHOWED UP. WE WERE SCARED TO DEATH. HE TURNED OUT REALLY WELL. I WISH IT WASN'T SO LATE.

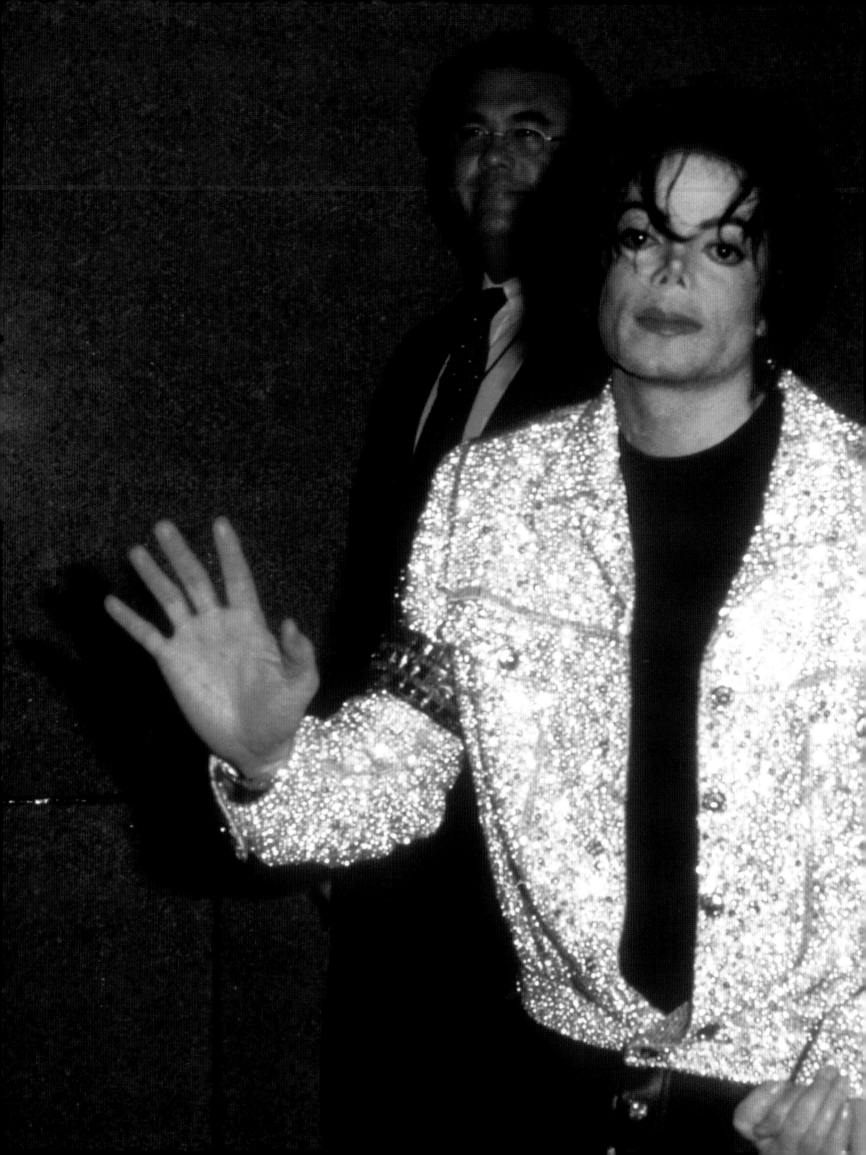

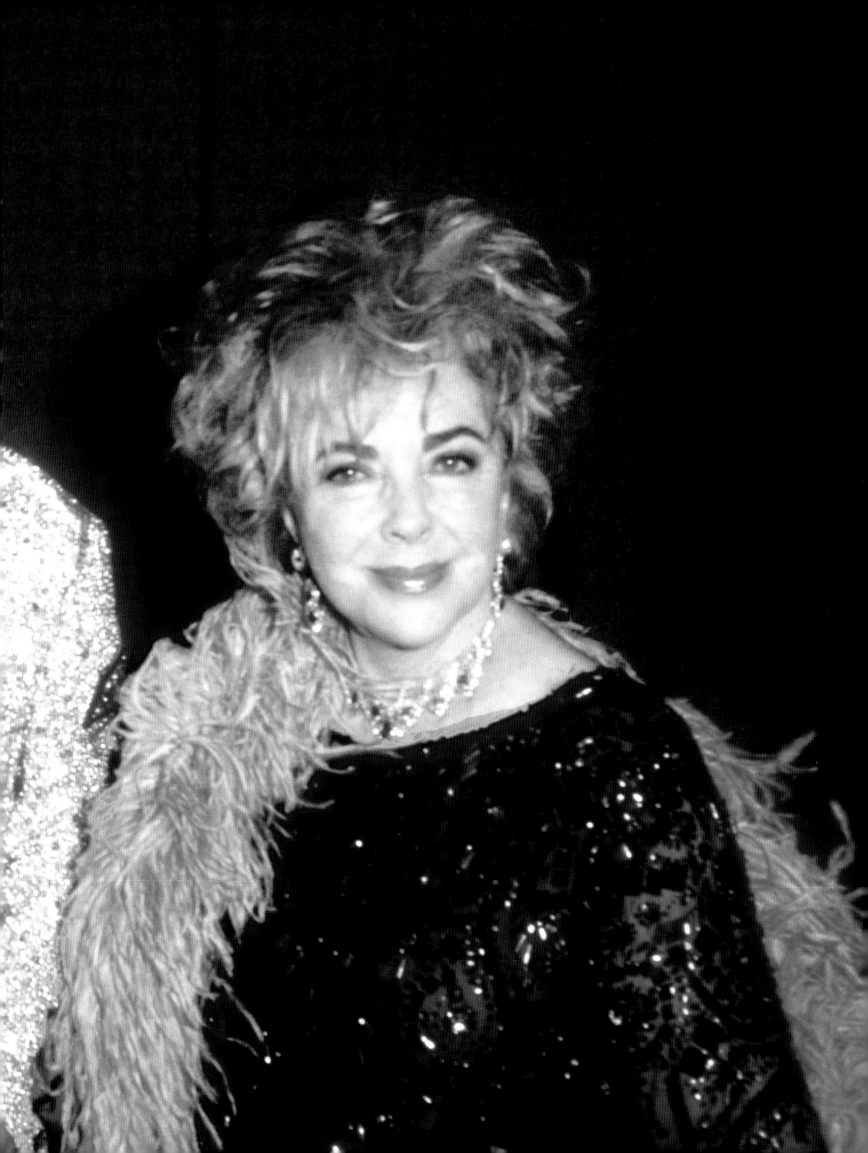

I WILL SAY AGAIN THAT I HAVE NEVER, AND I WOULD NEVER, HARM A CHILD. IT SICKENS ME THAT PEOPLE HAVE WRITTEN UNTRUE THINGS ABOUT ME.

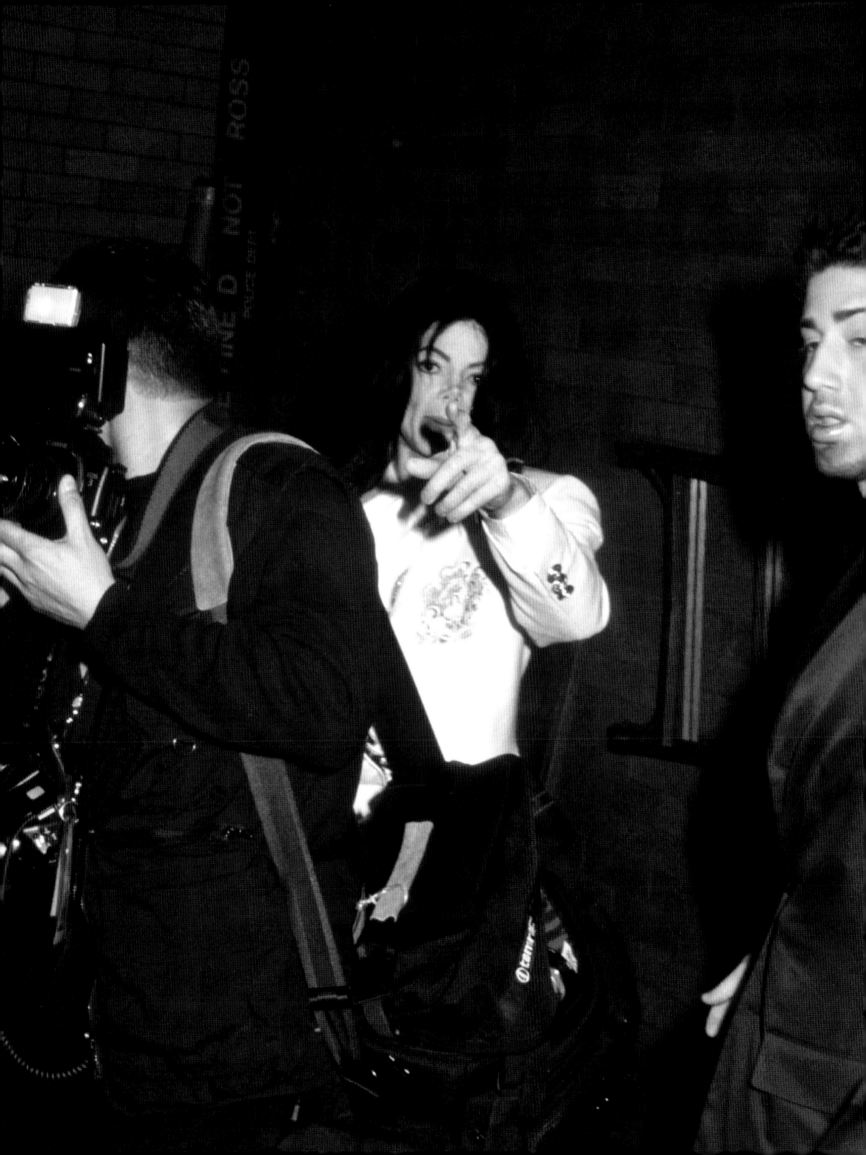

I'M VERY PROUD WE OPENED DOORS. WHEN YOU LOOK OUT OVER THE STAGE, AS FAR AS THE NAKED EYE COULD SEE, YOU SEE PEOPLE. IT'S A WONDERFUL FEELING BUT IT CAME WITH A LOT OF PAIN.

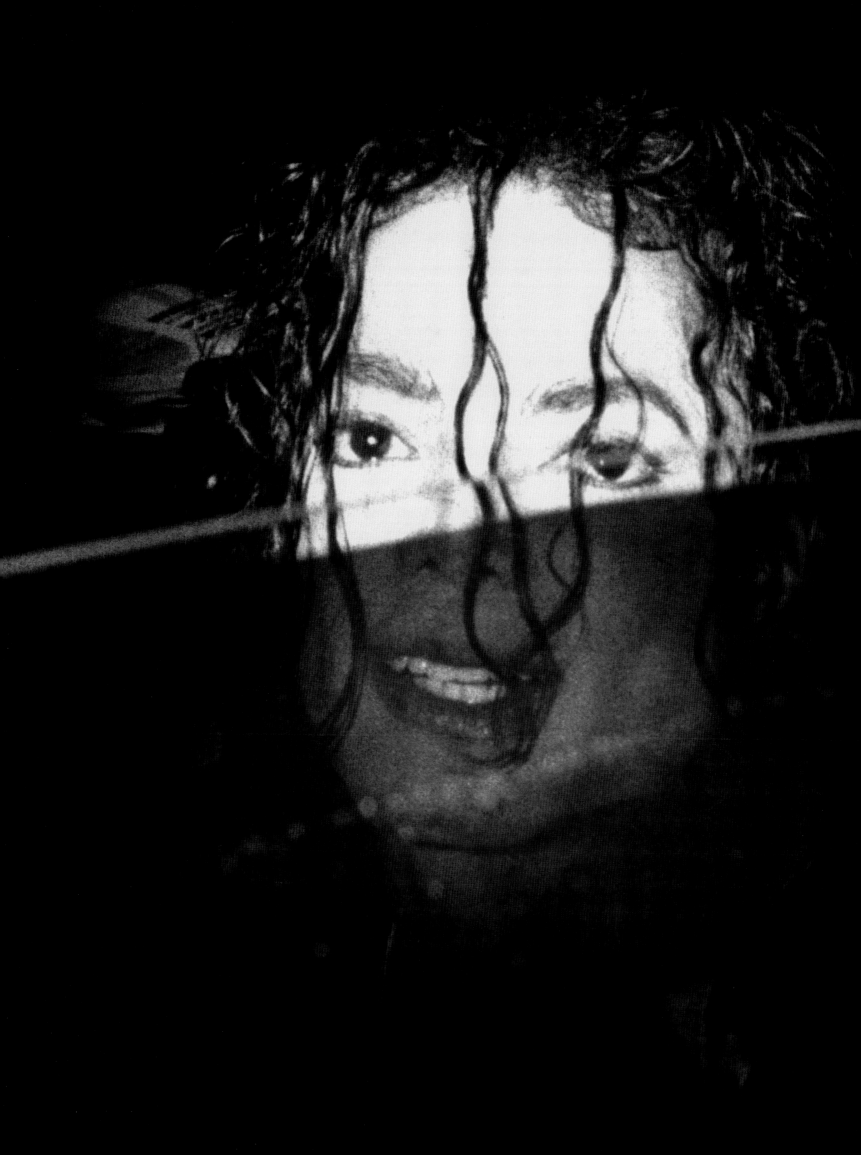

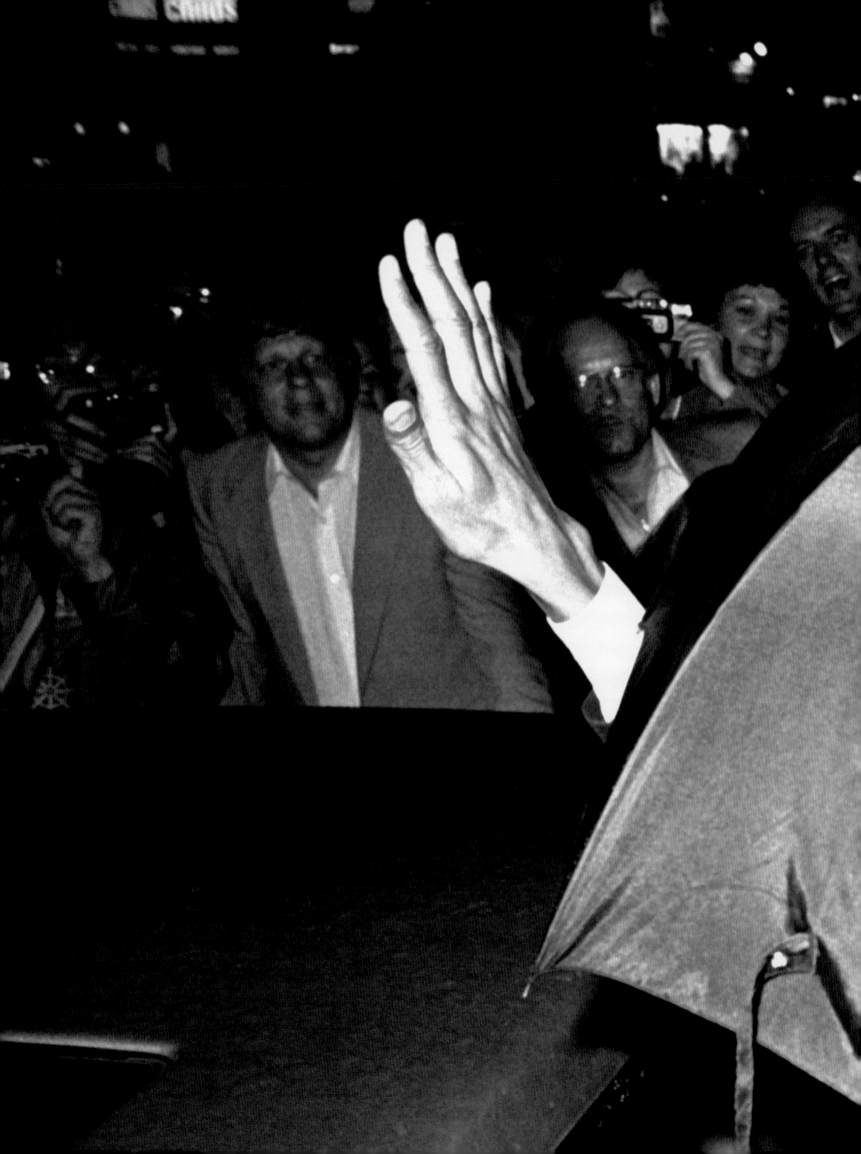

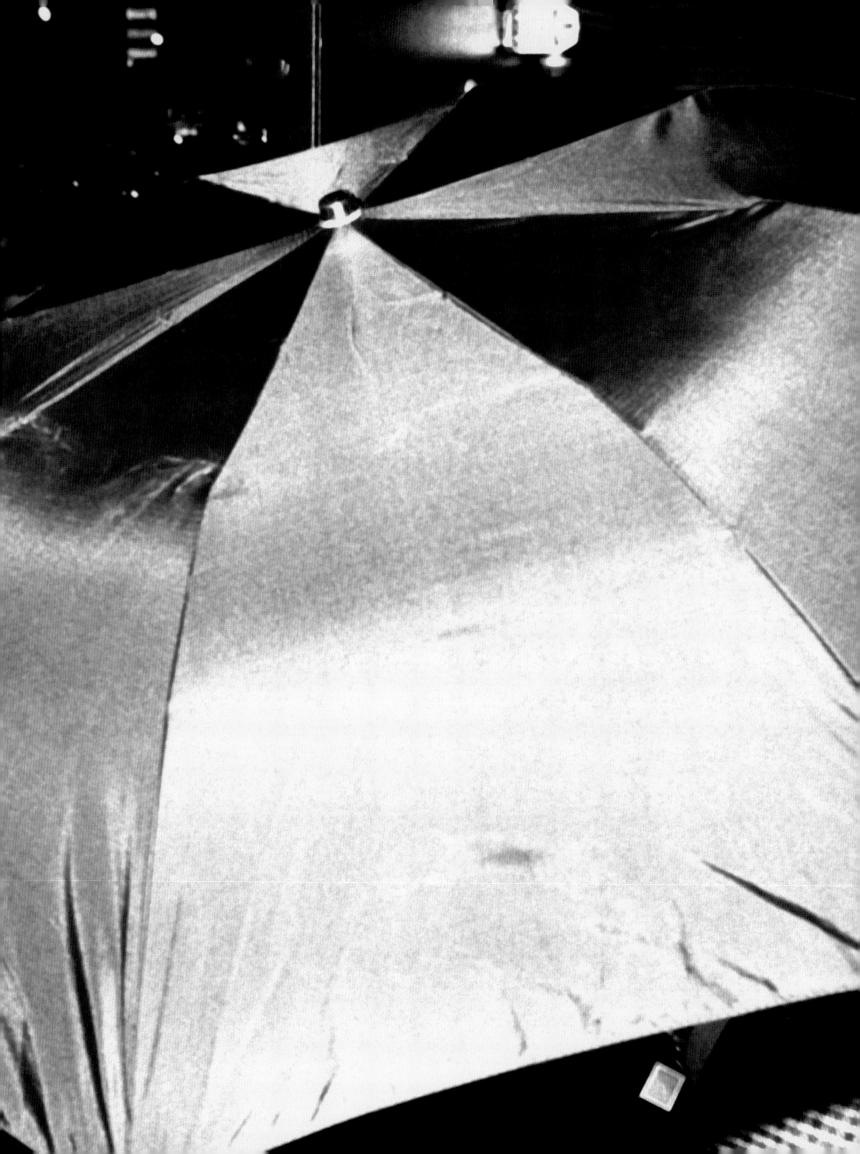

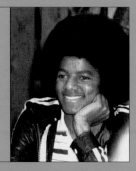 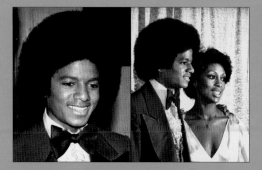 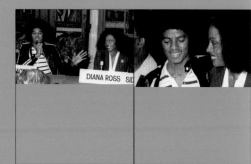

P.11 September 28, 1977: New York City
Twenty-year-old Michael Jackson attends a press conference for the movie The Wiz at a vacant studio. Fellow cast
members Diana Ross and Nipsey Russell were also on hand
to promote the film.

January 31, 1977: Santa Monica, California
Santa Monica Civic Auditorium
The 4th Annual American Music Awards

P.12 Michael Jackson.
P.13 Michael Jackson and Lola Falana.

P.14–15 September 28, 1977: New York City
Twenty-year-old Michael Jackson and Diana Ross attend
a press conference for the The Wiz. Jackson starred as the
Scarecrow and Ross as Dorothy.

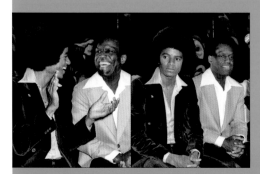 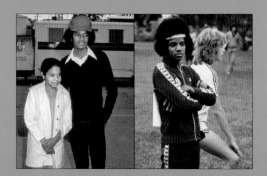 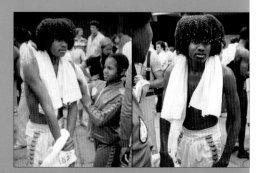

P.16–17 August 22, 1977: New York City
Copacabana Club
Michael Jackson and Nipsey Russel.

P.18 January 30, 1977: Santa Monica, California
Santa Monica Civic Auditorium
Michael Jackson takes his ten-year-old sister, Janet, to
The 4th Annual American Music Awards. After his death on
June 25, 2009, a grief-stricken Janet appeared to the BET
Awards audience and said, "To you, Michael is an icon, to
us he is family."

P.19 March 10, 1978: Irvine, California
University of California
First Annual Rock & Roll Sports Classic
Michael Jackson and Leif Garrett.

March 10, 1978: Irvine, California
University of California
First Annual Rock & Roll Sports Classic

P.20 Michael and Janet Jackson.
P.21 Michael dries off after competing in seven events.

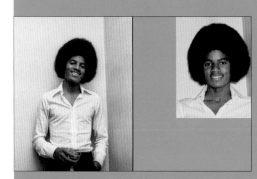 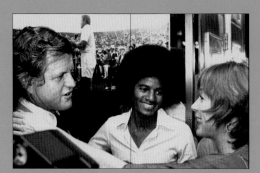 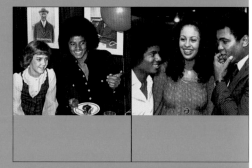

P.22–23 August 26, 1977: New York City
The Rainbow Room, Rockefeller Plaza
Sixth Annual Robert F. Kennedy Pro-Celebrity Tennis
Tournament Gala
Michael Jackson.

P.24–25 August 26, 1977: New York City
The Rainbow Room, Rockefeller Plaza
Sixth Annual Robert F. Kennedy Pro-Celebrity Tennis
Tournament Gala
Ted Kennedy, Michael Jackson, and Shirley MacLaine.

P.26 November 4, 1977: New York City
Gallagher's Steak House
Twenty-year-old Michael Jackson helps Broadway's "Little
Orphan Annie" Andrea McArdle celebrate her 14th birthday.

P.27 August 26, 1977: New York City
The Rainbow Room, Rockefeller Plaza
Sixth Annual Robert F. Kennedy Pro-Celebrity Tennis
Tournament Gala
Michael enjoys a conversation with boxing legend
Muhammad Ali and wife Veronica Porche. Ali commented
on the visible hair growth on Michael's cheeks.

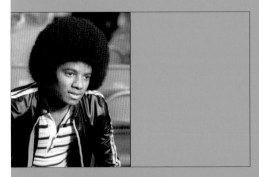

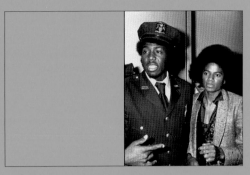

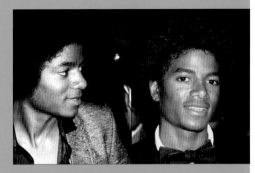

**P.28** September 28, 1977: New York City
Michael Jackson attends a press conference for *The Wiz*.

**P.31** October 24, 1978: New York City
Windows on the World
World Trade Center's North Tower
*The Wiz* premiere party.

**P. 32** October 24, 1978: New York City
Windows on the World
World Trade Center's North Tower
*The Wiz* premiere party.

**P. 33** January 27, 1980: Hollywood, California
Hollywood Palladium
The 12th NAACP Image Awards.

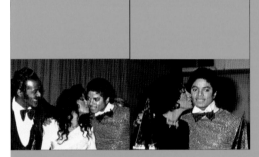

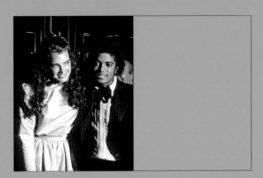

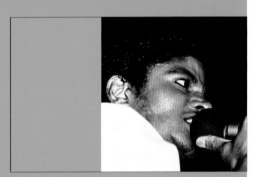

January 30, 1981: Los Angeles, California
Shrine Auditorium
The 8th Annual American Music Awards

**P.34** Michael Jackson and La Toya Jackson are on hand to help honor Chuck Berry, the man who all but invented Rock & Roll.
**P.35** Diana Ross warmly gives the 22-year-old Michael Jackson a congratulatory kiss. Jackson won Favorite Male Soul/R&B Artist and his *Off the Wall* album received the Favorite Soul/R&B Album, besting friend Diana Ross' *Diana* album. Ross, however, matched Jackson's two awards with the Favorite Female Soul/R&B Artist award and Favorite Soul/R&B Single award.

**P.36** March 31, 1981: Los Angeles, California
Dorothy Chandler Pavilion
53rd Academy Awards
Brooke Shields and Michael Jackson.

**P.38–39** August 19, 1981: New York City
Madison Square Garden
Billed the "Triumph Tour," Michael Jackson performs a solo hit during a concert with his brothers, The Jacksons.

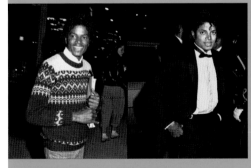

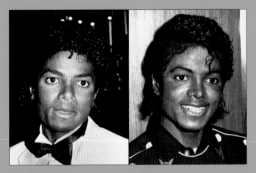

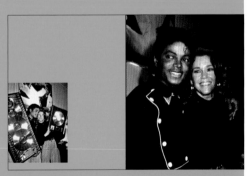

**P.40** April 16, 1982: West Hollywood, California
Twenty-three-year-old Michael Jackson leaves the Westlake Recording Studios. Jackson was working on his sixth studio album, *Thriller*, with legendary producer Quincy Jones. Seven of the nine songs on the album were released as singles and each would break into the Billboard Top 10 chart. In 2003, *Rolling Stone* magazine ranked *Thriller* number 20 on their list, "The RS 500 Greatest Albums of All Time."

**P.41** October 10, 1982: New York City
The Plaza Hotel
Michael Jackson was among a glittering array of celebrities and Hollywood royalty who attended the lavish wedding ceremony of Steve Ross and Courtney Sale. Following the nuptials at Ross' 37-room Park Avenue apartment, Jackson is snapped arriving at the hotel reception sporting a more traditional look—a tuxedo.

**P.42** July 17, 1982: Beverly Hills, California
The Beverly Hilton Hotel
Michael Jackson attends a gala tribute to honor Quincy Jones. Jones had co-produced Jackson's 1979 album, *Off the Wall*, and his 1982 album, *Thriller*.

**P.43** February 25, 1983: Century City, California
CBS Records
Michael Jackson is presented with the *Thriller* platinum record plaque.

**P.44–45** February 25, 1983: Century City, California
CBS Records
Jane Fonda is on hand to present Michael Jackson with the *Thriller* platinum record plaque. During the week of February 28, 1983, Jackson achieved the number one pop, dance, and R&B album, with *Thriller*, and the number one pop and R&B single, with "Billie Jean." Since its release on November 30, 1982, *Thriller* has reportedly sold over 110 million copies worldwide, making it the best selling album of all time.

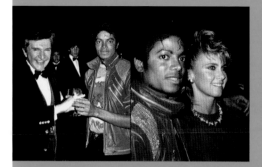
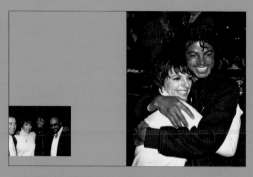
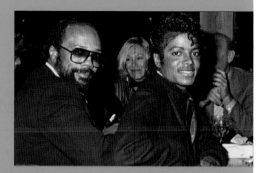

March 20, 1983: Hollywood, California
TVC Studios
*Dreamgirls* opening party

**P.46** Liberace and Michael Jackson. Jackson's signature style was a mix of military tailoring and Liberace glitz.
**P.47** Michael Jackson and Olivia Newton-John.

April 9, 1983: Universal City, California
Whomphopper's Restaurant

**P.48** David Geffen, Liza Minnelli, Michael Jackson, and Quincy Jones attend an after party for Liza Minnelli's concert performance at the Universal Amphitheater.
**P.49** Liza Minnelli and Michael Jackson share a warm embrace at a party for Ms. Minnelli. Earlier in the evening, Jackson came out to support Minnelli's sold-out concert series at the Universal Amphitheater.

**P.50–51** April 9, 1983: Universal City, California
Whomphopper's Restaurant
Friends and co-producers, Quincy Jones and Michael Jackson, at a party for Liza Minnelli.

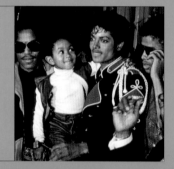
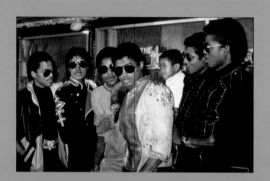
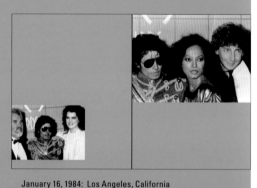

**P.52–53** November 30, 1983: New York City
Tavern on the Green
Marlon Jackson, Emmanuel Lewis, Michael Jackson, and Randy Jackson at the Jackson's press conference announcing their forthcoming "Victory Tour" for the summer of 1984.

**P.54–55** November 30, 1983: New York City
Tavern on the Green
Marlon Jackson, Michael Jackson, Tito Jackson, Randy Jackson, Emmanuel Lewis, Jermaine Jackson, and Jackie Jackson.

January 16, 1984: Los Angeles, California
Shrine Auditorium
The 11th Annual American Music Awards

**P.56** Kenny Rogers, Michael Jackson, and Brooke Shields.
**P.57** Michael Jackson, Diana Ross, and Barry Manilow.

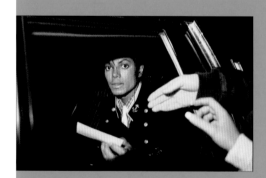
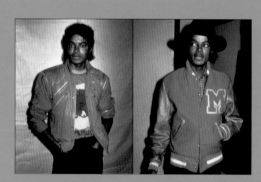
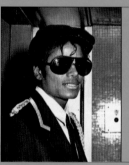

**P.58–59** February 8, 1984: New York City
Helmsley Palace Hotel
Michael Jackson, 25, leaving from the hotel's garage to see *The Tap Dance Kid* at the Broadhurst Theatre. He was accompanied by Sean Lennon.

**P.60** March 20, 1983: Hollywood, California
TVC Studios
*Dreamgirls* opening party
Michael was one of many stars to celebrate the musical's opening night. The show, starring Jennifer Holliday, is loosely based on the origin of The Supremes, and Diana Ross' split from the group and from Motown. Ms. Ross has expressed strong disapproval of the links between her career and the plot of the musical, however her friend, and former Motown artist, Michael Jackson decided to attend the show.

**P.61** February 9, 1984: New York City
Helmsley Palace Hotel
Michael Jackson.

**P.62** February 27, 1984: New York City
Michael Jackson sporting a unique outfit—the Helmsley Palace Hotel's doorman's uniform—arriving at JFK Airport ready to return to Los Angeles. He had been in New York for nearly a month, seeing Broadway shows and doing promotions for his new Pepsi commercial.

**P.63** February 28, 1984: Beverly Hills, California
L'Ermitage Hotel
After escorting Brooke Shields and her mother Teri Shields to the 26th Annual Grammy Awards after party, Michael Jackson and Emmanuel Lewis return to their limousine.

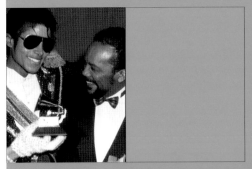

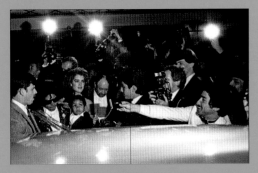

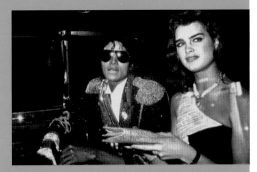

P.64 February 28, 1984: Los Angeles, California
Shrine Auditorium
26th Annual Grammy Awards
Michael Jackson and Quincy Jones share a good laugh
after sharing four Grammy wins.

P.66–67 February 28, 1984: Beverly Hills, California
L'Ermitage Hotel
Michael Jackson, Emmanuel Lewis, and Brooke Shields.

P.68–69 February 28, 1984: Beverly Hills, California
L'Ermitage Hotel
26th Annual Grammy Awards After Party
Michael Jackson and Brooke Shields spotted inside their
limousine.

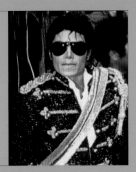

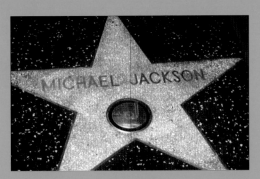

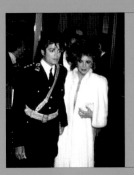

November 20, 1984: Hollywood, California
Michael Jackson's Hollywood Walk of Fame Star Unveiling
Ceremony, for his contribution to the recording industry.

P.70 Michael Jackson and Joe Jackson.
P.71 Michael Jackson.

P.72–73 November 20, 1984: Hollywood, California
6927 Hollywood Boulevard
Michael's star, in front of Grauman's Chinese Theatre.

P.74 January 27, 1986: West Hollywood, California
Le Dome Restaurant
Michael Jackson and Elizabeth Taylor departing the after
party for The 13th Annual American Music Awards.

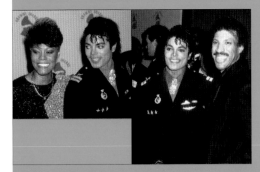

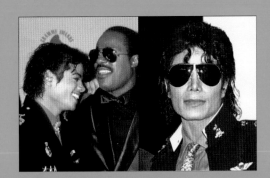

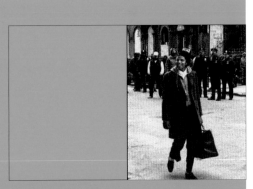

February 25, 1986: Los Angeles, California
Shrine Auditorium
28th Annual Grammy Awards

P.76 Dionne Warwick and Michael Jackson.
P.77 Michael Jackson and Lionel Richie are all smiles after
their collaborative project, "We Are the World," won Song
of the Year. It was written by Michael and Lionel, and co-
produced by Quincy Jones and Michael Omartian for the
1985 album of the same name.

P.78 February 25, 1986: Los Angeles, California
Shrine Auditorium
28th Annual Grammy Awards
Michael Jackson and Stevie Wonder congratulate each
other on their respective Grammy wins. Jackson won
the Song of the Year Award for "We Are the World," and
Wonder won Best Male R&B Vocal Performance for "In
Square Circle."

P.79 May 6, 1986: New York City
The Red Parrot
Michael Jackson, covered by his sunglasses, attends a
press conference to announce his new, $50 million contract
with Pepsi.

P.81 November 12, 1986: Harlem, New York
Michael Jackson took a break from filming his new music
video, "Bad," near 122nd Street.

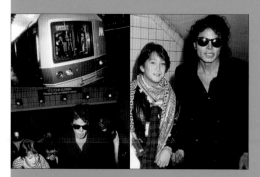 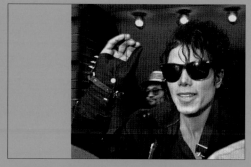 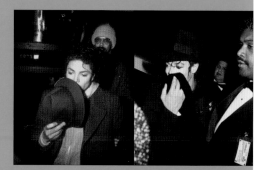

**P.82,** top  November 19, 1986: The Bronx, New York
Michael Jackson and video crew travel the subway in between the shooting for Jackson's new music video. His security team, including close friend and security chief Bill Bray, escorted Michael throughout the subway ride.

**P.82,** bottom & **P.83** November 28, 1986: Brooklyn, New York
Hoyt-Schermerhorn Subway Station
Michael Jackson allows Sean Lennon to visit him while filming the music video, "Bad." Sean, son of John Lennon and Yoko Ono, was featured in the cast of Michael Jackson's film, *Moonwalker*.

**P.84–85** November 25, 1986: Brooklyn, New York
Michael Jackson goes underground to film his latest music video, "Bad," at the Hoyt-Schermerhorn subway station. The album, *Bad*, went on to sell an estimated $32 million copies.

**P.86** November 19, 1986: The Bronx, New York
Grand Central Terminal
While traveling in the subway during the filming of "Bad," Michael begins a new trend of covering his face from photographers.

**P.87** March 2, 1988: New York City
Radio City Music Hall
30th Annual Grammy Awards
Michael Jackson, trailed by his friend Miko Brando, is covered by heavy security as they enter Michael's limousine.

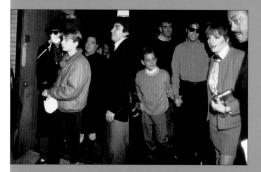 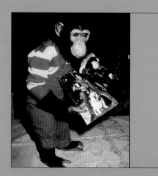 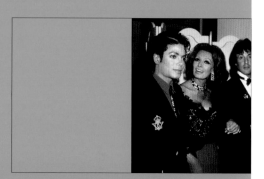

**P.88** December 19, 1986: New York City
Beekman Theater
*Little Shop of Horrors* premiere
Michael Jackson, covered by a surgical mask, leaves the screening with manager Frank DiLeo following behind him.

**P.89** March 9, 1988: New York City
Majestic Theatre
Michael Jackson, accompanied by Jimmy Safechuck and Liza Minnelli, at *The Phantom of the Opera*. Safechuck appeared in a Pepsi commercial with Jackson in 1987.

**P.90** October 13, 1987: Beverly Hills, California
Beverly Hilton Hotel
3rd Annual Amanda Foundation Celebrity Fashion Show
Michael Jackson's pet chimp, Bubbles. In 1985, Jackson rescued Bubbles from a lab animal breeder in Texas. He traveled with Jackson on tour and lived at Jackson's Neverland Ranch.

**P.93** January 9, 1987: Beverly Hills, California
Beverly Wilshire Hotel
4th Annual American Cinema Awards
Michael Jackson, Sophia Loren, and Sylvester Stallone at the event saluting Sophia Loren and Kirk Douglas. Michael Jackson attend this event specifically to see Sophia Loren receive her Lifetime Achievement award.

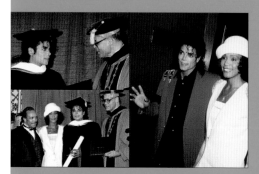 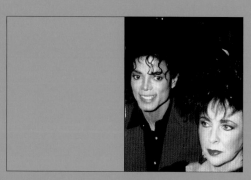 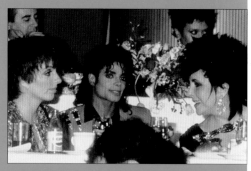

March 10, 1988: New York City
United Negro College Fund's 44th Anniversary Dinner

**P.94,** top  The United Negro College Fund honors Michael with the Frederick D. Patterson Award named for the organization's founder.
**P.94,** bottom  Quincy Jones, Whitney Houston, and Michael Jackson.
**P.95** Michael Jackson and Whitney Houston.

**P.97** March 10, 1988: New York City
United Negro College Fund's 44th Anniversary Dinner
Michael Jackson and Elizabeth Taylor.

**P.98–99** March 10, 1988: New York City
United Negro College Fund's 44th Anniversary Dinner
Liza Minnelli, Michael Jackson, and Elizabeth Taylor.

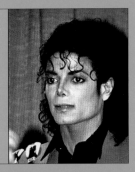
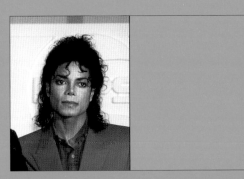
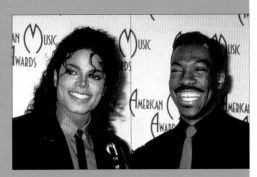

**P.101** March 10, 1988: New York City
United Negro College Fund's 44th Anniversary Dinner
Michael Jackson.

**P.102** March 1, 1988: New York City
Club 1018
Michael Jackson and Pepsi-Cola CEO Roger Enrico hosted a press conference to present Jackson with a $600,000 check for the United Negro College Fund.

**P.104–105** January 30, 1989: Los Angeles, California
Shrine Auditorium
The 16th Annual American Music Awards
Michael Jackson and Eddie Murphy.
Jackson lost out to George Michael in the Favorite Male categories—Pop/Rock and Soul/R&B. However, Jackson did receive the American Music Awards' special Award of Achievement honor.

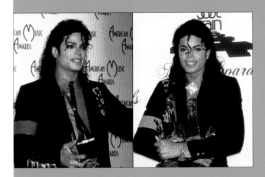
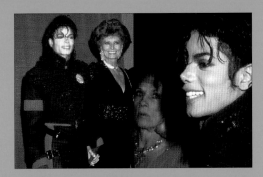
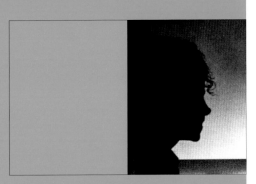

**P.106** January 30, 1989: Los Angeles, California
Shrine Auditorium
The 16th Annual American Music Awards
Michael Jackson.

**P.107** April 12, 1989: Los Angeles, California
Shrine Auditorium
The 3rd Annual Soul Train Music Awards
Michael Jackson poses with his plethora of awards. He won Best Male R&B/Soul Artist of the Year for "Man in the Mirror." He was also presented with the Heritage Award and the Sammy Davis, Jr. Entertainer of the Year Award.

**P.108** January 27, 1990: Beverly Hills, California
Beverly Hilton Hotel
7th Annual American Cinema Awards
Michael Jackson and Sophia Loren.
Loren was a friend and neighbor of Jackson's.

**P.109** January 1990: Beverly Hills, California
Beverly Hilton Hotel
Michael Jackson at a Disney press conference announcing the release of *Captain Eo*, a 17-minute film written by George Lucas, directed by Francis Ford Coppola, and starring Michael, to be shown only at Disney theme parks.

**P.111** March 1, 1988: New York City
Club 1018
Michael Jackson.

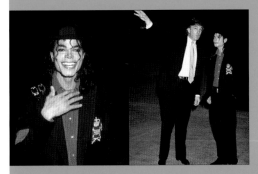
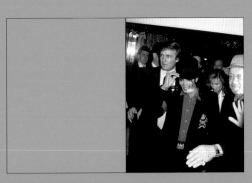
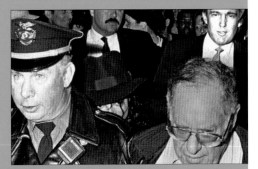

April 6, 1990: Atlantic City, NJ
Trump Taj Mahal Casino Resort Grand Opening Celebration

**P.112** Michael Jackson.
**P.113** Donald Trump and Michael Jackson.

**P.115** April 6, 1990: Atlantic City, NJ
Trump Taj Mahal Casino Resort Grand Opening Celebration
Donald Trump, Michael Jackson, and Bill Bray.

**P.116–117** April 6, 1990: Atlantic City, NJ
Trump Taj Mahal Casino Resort Grand Opening Celebration
Michael Jackson, Donald Trump, and Lee Solters.

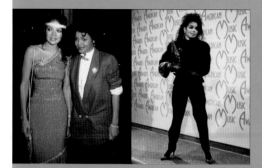

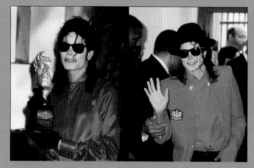

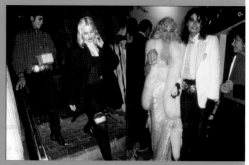

P.118 February 28, 1984: Los Angeles, California
Shrine Auditorium
Janet and La Toya Jackson attend the 26th Annual Grammy
Awards.

P.119 January 26, 1987: Los Angeles, California
Shrine Auditorium
Janet Jackson holds her AMA for Favorite Soul/R&B
Female Video Artist. She is following so closely in the foot-
steps of her superstar brother, she even looks like him.

P.120 May 8, 1990: Beverly Hills, California
Regent Beverly Wilshire Hotel
38th Annual BMI Pop Music Awards
Michael Jackson, 31, holds the BMI Michael Jackson
Award. Broadcast Music Incorporated (BMI) inaugurated
the award that year and Jackson was its first recipient.

P.121 July 26, 1991: Los Angeles, California
Michael Jackson visiting the Community Youth Sports
& Arts Foundation Center. Donating his time and money,
Jackson took the advice of fellow musician Kenny Rogers to
be more visible to the public, rather than being as reclusive
as he had been.

P.122 April 9, 1991: West Hollywood, California
Ivy
During this time, Michael Jackson and Madonna were plan-
ning a duet for Michael's upcoming album Dangerous.

P.123 March 25, 1991: Beverly Hills, California
Spago Beverly Hills
63rd Academy Awards after party
At the party hosted by Irving "Swifty" Lazar, Madonna
and Michael created quite a media frenzy as they entered
the star-studded event hand in hand. Madonna's Marilyn
Monroe-inspired dress was a creation of Bob Mackie.
Jackson wore a sparkly, white, sequined jacket to match
Madonna's glistening dress.

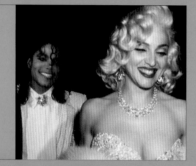

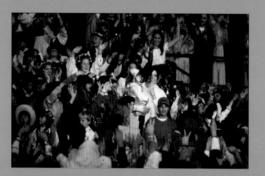

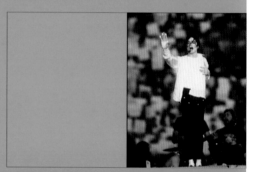

P.124–125 March 25, 1991: Beverly Hills, California
Spago Beverly Hills
63rd Academy Awards after party
Madonna and Michael leave the bash after partying with
some of Hollywood's elite. Madonna and Jackson clutched
each other's hands as they braved the many lenses of the
paparazzi.

P.126–127 January 30, 1993: Pasadena, California
Super Bowl XXVII, Buffalo Bills vs. Dallas Cowboys
Michael performs during the game's halftime. As the only
performer during the halftime event, Jackson wooed the
crowd with his hits "Jam," "Billie Jean," and "Black or
White," and ended the show with an uplifting performance
of "Heal the World," backed up by a Los Angeles children's
choir.

P.129 January 30, 1993: Pasadena, California
Super Bowl XXVII, Buffalo Bills vs. Dallas Cowboys
Michael Jackson.

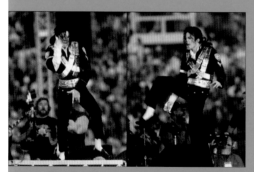

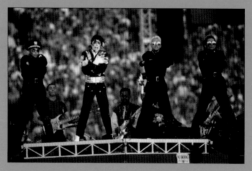

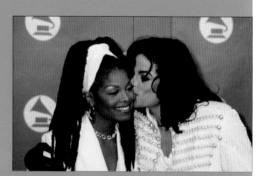

P.130–131 January 30, 1993: Pasadena, California
Super Bowl XXVII, Buffalo Bills vs. Dallas Cowboys
Michael Jackson.

P.132–133 January 30, 1993: Pasadena, California
Super Bowl XXVII, Buffalo Bills vs. Dallas Cowboys
Michael Jackson with backup dancers.

P.134–135 February 24, 1993: Los Angeles, California
Shrine Auditorium
35th Annual Grammy Awards
Janet Jackson and Michael Jackson. Michael received the
Grammy Legends award.

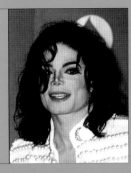 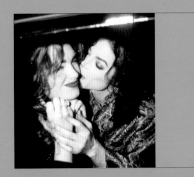 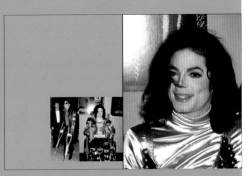

P.137 February 24, 1993: Los Angeles, California
Shrine Auditorium
35th Annual Grammy Awards
Michael Jackson.

P.138–139 February 24, 1993: Beverly Hills, California
Jimmy's Restaurant
35th Annual Grammy Awards after party
Michael is caught pecking Brooke Shields, his date, on the cheek. The two made the post-Grammy party circuit together. Jackson was supposed to perform at the awards show, but instead gave a nine-minute acceptance speech for his Grammy Legends award.

P.140–141 March 9, 1993: Los Angeles, California
Shrine Auditorium
The 7th Annual Soul Train Music Awards
Michael Jackson, bound to a wheelchair or crutches after suffering a sprained ankle during rehearsals, managed to perform, be a presenter, and accept three awards.

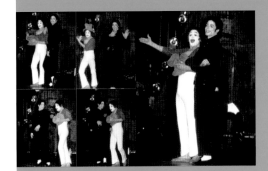 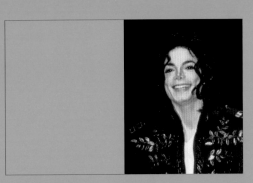 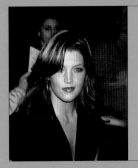

P.142–143 December 4, 1995: New York City
Beacon Theatre
Michael Jackson and French pantomimist Marcel Marceau rehearse for Jackson's upcoming HBO concert special, "Michael Jackson: One Night Only." There is some speculation that Marceau influenced Michael's creation of his trademark "moonwalk" dance move. However, Michael never verified these claims.

P.145 April 28, 1994: New York City
New York City Center
Michael Jackson receives the Caring for Kids Award.

P.146 October 24, 2000: Hollywood, California
Paramount Studios
Lisa Marie Presley at the *Lucky Numbers* premiere. In 1994, Lisa Marie Presley, Elvis' only child, married Michael Jackson. They divorced in 1996.

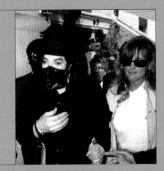 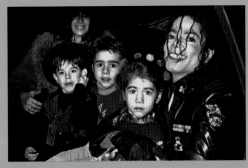 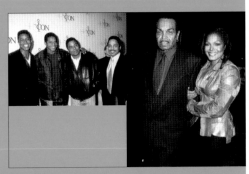

P.148–149 April 28, 1996: Pasadena, California
Michael Jackson, continuing to go out in public wearing various types of surgical masks, stepped out with his partner, Debbie Rowe, for the closing-night performance of *Sisterella*. Jackson was one of the executive producers of the musical.

P.150–151 February 3, 1992: New York City
Radio City Music Hall

P.152 March 10, 2001: Culver City, California
Sony Pictures Studios
*MTV Icon: Janet Jackson* premier
Jermaine Jackson, Jackie Jackson, Tito Jackson, and Marlon Jackson.

P.153 July 24, 2000: Universal City, California
Universal Amphitheater
*Nutty Professor II: The Klumps* premiere
Joe Jackson escorts his daughter Janet Jackson to the premiere. Her brothers Jermaine and Tito also came out to lend their support to Janet, who had a starring role in the film.

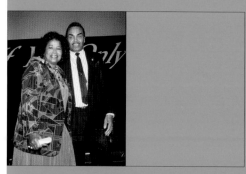

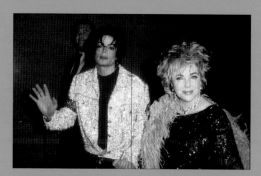

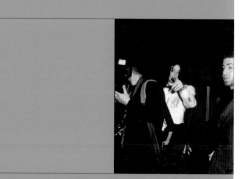

**P.154** August 30, 1993: North Hollywood, California
Goldstone Theatre, Academy Plaza
Katherine and Joe Jackson help the Jackson family give a press conference to announce their upcoming NBC television special "The Jackson Family Honors." The special included music, comedy, and lifetime achievement awards for Elizabeth Taylor and Berry Gordy, all in the name of charity.

**P.156–157** September 7, 2001: New York City
Madison Square Garden
Michael Jackson is escorted by his longtime friend Elizabeth Taylor to the television special "Michael Jackson: 30th Anniversary Celebration." The two-night event featured performances from musical artists of all genres paying tribute to Michael Jackson's 30-year career as a solo performer. Liza Minnelli, Usher, Dionne Warwick, Gladys Knight, Whitney Houston, Marc Anthony, Destiny's Child, *NSYNC, and Britney Spears were some of the many who honored Jackson. Michael Jackson roused the crowed with favorites like "Billie Jean," "Beat It," "The Way You Make Me Feel," and "Black or White." Michael also reunited with his brothers for a special medley of Jackson 5 hits. Both evenings ended with the charity-themed song "We Are the World," with all the performers joining Michael Jackson on stage.

**P.159** March 19, 2001: New York City
Four Seasons Hotel Parking Garage
Michael Jackson departs the Four Seasons after the 16th Annual Rock and Roll Hall of Fame Induction Ceremony.

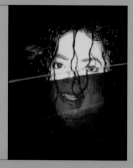

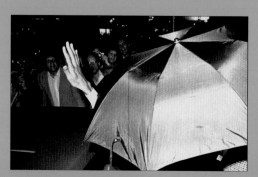

**P.161 and BACK COVER** February 3, 1992: New York City
Radio City Music Hall
Michael attends a press conference to announce his third sponsorship deal with Pepsi-Cola to underwrite his 18-month, international tour.

**P.162–163** May 8, 1984: New York City
Winter Garden Theatre
Michael Jackson, hidden by an umbrella, waves to his many fans after seeing *Cats* on Broadway.

# CREDITS

Michael Jackson

P.10—*People*, 1973  (*People*, "The King of Pop 1958–2009," July 13, 2009.)

P.14—Associated Press, 2007

P.23—*The Oprah Winfrey Show*, 1993

P.29—*Moonwalk* (Doubleday, 1988)

P.30—*People*, 1980, response to the question: What is the hardest part of growing up?
(*People*, "The King of Pop 1958–2009," July 13, 2009.)

P.38—*People*  (*People*, "The King of Pop 1958–2009," July 13, 2009.)

P.38—*Ebony*, 2007  (Bryan Monroe, "Q&A: Michael Jackson in His Own Words," *Ebony*, December 2007.)

P.70—*The Oprah Winfrey Show*, 1993

P.75—*USA Today*, 2001  (Edna Gundersen, "Michael in the Mirror," *USA Today*, December 14, 2001.)

P.80—*Keep Hope Alive* (Jesse Jackson's radio show), 2005

P.84—*USA Today*, 2001  (Edna Gundersen, "Michael in the Mirror," *USA Today*, December 14, 2001.)

P.91—*Moonwalker*, (Doubleday, 1988)

P.96—*USA Today*, 2001  (Edna Gundersen, "Michael in the Mirror," *USA Today*, December 14, 2001.)

P.100—*People*, 1984  (*People*, "The King of Pop 1958–2009," July 13, 2009.)

P.103—*Living with Michael Jackson*, 2003

P.110—*USA Today*, 2001  (Edna Gundersen, "Michael in the Mirror," *USA Today*, December 14, 2001.)

P.128—*USA Today*, 2001  (Edna Gundersen, "Michael in the Mirror," *USA Today*, December 14, 2001.)

P.136—Grammy acceptance speech, 1993

P.140—Soul Train Awards acceptance speech, 1993

P.144—Super Bowl XXVII press conference, 1993

P.147—*Primetime*, 1995

P.147—*Moonwalker*, (Doubleday, 1988)

P.148—*USA Today*, 2001  (Edna Gundersen, "Michael in the Mirror," *USA Today*, December 14, 2001.)

P.148—"Heal the World," 1991

P.152—*USA Today*, 2001  (Edna Gundersen, "Michael in the Mirror," *USA Today*, December 14, 2001.)

P.155—*USA Today*, 2001  (Edna Gundersen, "Michael in the Mirror," *USA Today*, December 14, 2001.)

P.158—MJJ Productions press release, 2003

P.160—*Ebony*, 2007  (Bryan Monroe, "Q&A: Michael Jackson in His Own Words," *Ebony*, December 2007.)


P.15—Diana Ross, *Newsweek*, 1970
(Jim Miller and Janet Huck, "Michael Jackson: The Peter Pan of Pop," *Newsweek*, January 10, 1983.)

P.35—Diana Ross, *Rolling Stone*, 1983
(Gerri Hirshey, "Michael Jackson: Life in the Magic Kingdom," *Rolling Stone*, February 17, 1983.)

P.37—Brooke Shields, public statement, June 25, 2009

P.44—Jane Fonda, Twitter, June 25, 2009

P.48—Liza Minnelli, *Entertainment Tonight*, June 25, 2009

P.52—Emmanuel Lewis, *People*, 1984
(Jane Hall, "Emmanuel Lewis Got a Boost From Michael Jackson, but as Webster He Stands on His Own," *People*, April 09, 1984.)

P.56—Diana Ross, *Rolling Stone*, 1983
(Gerri Hirshey, "Michael Jackson: Life in the Magic Kingdom," *Rolling Stone*, February 17, 1983.)

P.57—Barry Manilow, *Entertainment Tonight*, June 26, 2009

P.65—Quincy Jones, *Newsweek*, 1983
(Jim Miller and Janet Huck, "Michael Jackson: The Peter Pan of Pop," *Newsweek*, January 10, 1983.)

P.76—Dionne Warwick, *Larry King Live*, 2009

P.92—Sophia Loren, Associated Press, June 25, 2009

P.114—Donald Trump, *Time*, 2009  (*Time*, "Remembering Michael," July 7, 2009.)

# ACKNOWLEDGEMENTS

I would like to thank the following people for their generous contributions:

Michael Jackson and the Jackson family for always being cooperative with the press and me.

Brooke Shields, for her amazing and heartfelt introduction.
Susan Bond, for her impressive essay.

Daniel Power, Craig Cohen, Mine Suda, and everyone at powerHouse Books for making this book possible.

My loving wife, Betty, for her photographs and research.

A.J. Miller
Nicholas Stepowyj
Jeffrey Leone
Ellen Ford
Kathy Lener

Wouter van Leeuwen, Staley-Wise Gallery, Acte2Galerie, and the Hollywood Roosevelt Hotel for exhibiting my work.

My cousin and fellow patron of the arts, Ottavio Galella, for orchestrating my exhibits in Montreal, Québec; and in Muro Lucano and Policoro, Italy.

# Man in the Mirror
# MICHAEL JACKSON
## by Ron Galella

Compilation & editing © 2009 powerHouse Cultural Entertainment, Inc.
Photographs & text © 2009 Ron Galella
Introduction © 2009 Brooke Shields
Essay © 2009 Susan Bond

Published in the United States by powerHouse Books,
a division of powerHouse Cultural Entertainment, Inc.
37 Main Street, Brooklyn, NY 11201-1021
telephone: 212 604 9074, fax: 212 366 5247
e-mail: maninthemirror@powerhousebooks.com
website: www.powerhousebooks.com

First edition, 2009

Library of Congress Control Number: 2009937686

Hardcover ISBN 978-1-57687-535-3

Printing by Pimlico Book International, Hong Kong

Book design by Mine Suda

A complete catalog of powerHouse Books and Limited Editions is available upon request;
please call, write, or visit our website.

10 9 8 7 6 5 4 3 2 1

Printed and bound in China